THE STORY OF REASON IN ISLAM

Cultural Memory
in
the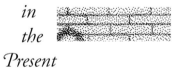
Present

Hent de Vries, Editor

THE STORY OF REASON IN ISLAM

Sari Nusseibeh

STANFORD UNIVERSITY PRESS

STANFORD, CALIFORNIA

Stanford University Press
Stanford, California

Printed on acid-free, archival-quality paper

Printed and bound in Great Britain by
Marston Book Services Ltd, Oxfordshire

Library of Congress Cataloging-in-Publication Data

Names: Nusseibeh, Sari, author.
Title: The story of reason in Islam / Sari Nusseibeh.
Description: Stanford, California : Stanford University Press, 2016. |
    Series: Cultural memory in the present | Includes bibliographical
    references and index. | Description based on print version record and CIP
    data provided by publisher; resource not viewed.
Identifiers: LCCN 2016021294 (print) | LCCN 2016020140 (ebook) |
    ISBN 9781503600584 (electronic) |
    ISBN 9780804794619 (cloth :alk. paper) |
    ISBN 9781503600577 (pbk. :alk. paper)
Subjects: LCSH: Faith and reason—Islam—History. | Islamic
    philosophy—History.
Classification: LCC BP190.5.R4 (print) | LCC BP190.5.R4 N87 2016 (ebook) |
    DDC 297.209—dc23
LC record available at https://lccn.loc.gov/2016021294

Typeset by Bruce Lundquist in 11/13.5 Adobe Garamond

Contents

A Note on Transliteration

Diacritics have been kept to a minimum in the text. We have retained the marks that distinguish between glottal and guttural sounds within terms but have eliminated the intial ayin from proper names. Arabic speakers should have no difficulty recognizing the phonetic value of the English letters, and it is hoped that the omission of the extra marks will make the Arabic terms more reader-friendly for those unfamiliar with the language.

Introduction

Three quick observations may prove helpful in setting out, two of which concern the title of the book, and the third its content.

First, the average Western reader might find the use of the word *reason* in association with Islam somewhat incongruous, especially given the horrors that various groups around the world are committing in the name of this religion today. The work at hand does not mean to dismiss the phenomenon, nor does it propose to study it. Rather, its aim is to take a historical look at the rise and use of reason in early Islam. Since the term has many different, but wholly legitimate, meanings across cultures—and within Islam itself—it is advisable to specify how it is understood here. In this context, it simply refers to a methodical and systematic approach to analyzing problems: the "philosophical" ways that ideas were entertained and discussed, regardless of the "discipline" to which they belonged (e.g., philosophy, linguistics, jurisprudence, or any of the other, traditional or science fields). Islamic history has many aspects, of course; while broaching adjacent terrain, this book focuses on the evolution of reason in the manner described.

In turn, *story* underscores the fact that this work is not meant as a specialized study. Indeed, it could hardly fulfill such an ambition, given the different subjects and periods it covers. Rather, it is meant as a personal interpretation or "take" on the history of ideas as they came to be expressed in classical Arabic, which first served as a medium for the rise of reason in the eighth century, and then, by the eighteenth, for its decline (if not extinction). In this sense, the book may hold interest for anyone who wishes to learn more about the history of ideas, irrespective of the form or setting in which they found expression. The theme of the story is the integral relationship between thought and language. The acts are played out in classical Arabic. Its scenes just happen to be set in Islam.

Finally, it should be observed that, inasmuch as what follows is a story, the reader familiar with Islamic intellectual history and philosophy will not find the customary signposts in chapter titles (for instance major names, disciplines, periods, or schools of thought). Rather, the story extends forward and backward in time, here and there, highlighting the themes I consider key for understanding a developmental flow of ideas and events over a long period of Islamic history, when brilliance shone in many lights. Consequently, the treatment given to some of the material does not conform to standard views. Occasionally, it may strike those who know something about it already as controversial. In the end, this story is meant both to challenge and be enjoyed by the reader. This is no easy task by any measure. On the one hand, a proper appreciation of some of the ideas discussed requires a fair amount of in-depth explication; on the other hand, a readable "story theme" that can maintain the interest of the general reader should prevail. I hope that—given the way the ideas and the historical narratives are interspersed in the text—I have managed to achieve this dual objective. That said, the general reader must be forewarned that some of the material may seem somewhat detailed and ponderous; however, inasmuch as the major themes are revisited in different forms in the various chapters, some of the arguments can be glossed over quickly by anyone wishing to avoid too much detail.

One issue, in particular, poses difficulties in a work of this kind. The sheer multitude of unfamiliar Arabic names may distract the reader from being able to follow the arguments and ideas presented. Unfortunately, this obstacle cannot be eliminated entirely, as names naturally provide points of reference throughout the chapters' many twists and turns. That said, the figures featured on these pages certainly merit attention; familiarizing oneself with them should provide instruction, if not amusement!

Finally, where needed, I have included references in footnotes to more specialized articles or books associated with the matters discussed and the arguments made. The general reader, on the other hand, may consult a short bibliography, at the end, of further readings on the various subjects dealt with in the text. More extensive and specialized bibliographies can be found in some of these works. Some of the main primary sources in Arabic that I draw on have been translated into English; whenever possible, this information is included.

.   .   .

My gratitude for writing this work extends to innumerable people from whom I have learned over the years—teachers, colleagues, and students. Needless to say, none of them bears responsibility for any shortcomings the book may contain. Most immediately, I owe thanks to my son Buraq, who once asked me why I couldn't write something "readable" on the history of ideas in Islamic thought; then to Hent De Vries, whose gentle prodding turned an idea into a project; and finally to Stanford's editor Emily-Jane Cohen who picked up the manuscript and steered it through its various stages in the press. Along the way, I benefited from the assistance of Henry Erik Butler, whose magical editorial wand smoothed out the style, and from the learned comments and criticisms provided by readers chosen by the publisher; I have tried—perhaps not always successfully—to address the problems and issues they raised. I also relied (perhaps unfairly) on Jamil Rajeb as I was trying to make sense of what was special about Islamic astronomy from a layman's point of view. I would like to recognize his kind and friendly guidance while making clear that any deficiencies in this area are my own.

Finally, as always, I am greatly indebted to my wife, Lucy, for ever-present moral and intellectual support. In many more ways than I can even begin to articulate, this book is authored as much by her as by the person whose name appears on the jacket.

THE STORY OF REASON IN ISLAM

1

The Arabian Desert

By any measure, the changes that gripped Arabia and its surroundings in the seventh century CE are extraordinary. The major players of the day—the Roman, Byzantine, and Sassanid Empires—set the course of history on a broad scale. Yet within a few decades an Arab world, previously regarded as a culturally insignificant backwater, catapulted to center stage. Besides constituting a major political power in its own right, the Arab world emerged as an intellectual powerhouse that energized a new phase in the history of civilization. A desert people—hardly in possession of a script for their language (much less adequate material for making use of such writing)—brought forth, as if by magic, scholars and intellectual giants who made invaluable contributions to intellectual history. A marginal language spoken by a marginal people transformed into a *language of power*—a medium bearing the most advanced scientific thought. How did this transformation occur? What sparked this intellectual revolution, the birth of reason, which ultimately produced some of the greatest minds in the history of thought and science?

The Arabian Desert had always provided a natural setting for those who sought meaning in the glory of nature and the infinitude of space. Prophets, poets, monks, hermits, pagan sects, and simple mystics roamed the vast expanse, seeking refuge from the chatter of their communities. It seems that here, in silence and emptiness, they could hear the heartbeat of the world, feel the majesty of the stars. They came to the desert in order to reflect; worshippers sought seclusion and refuge in the caves dotting the cliffs of rugged mountains; lonesome travelers devised their first poetic rhymes following the soft, rhythmic beats of camels treading along the undulating sands; from this soil, the finest lyric of Arabic literary tradition would grow.

One knows, even in today's crowded world, how spellbinding pristine nature is. Still today, the vastness and silence of empty deserts impress nature's majesty on those who live or journey there. One must try to picture how much more acutely this was felt by the wayfarer in times past, how the contrast between unity and difference, spatial and temporal, must have faded before his or her mind's eye. Such collapsing of borders and categories—between earth and sky, present and past, and beholder and beheld—marks much early philosophical speculation. Under modern conditions of life, where space and time fall into smaller and shorter units—where, by any account, distances and differences seem to melt into each other more and more—this underlying coherence of the surrounding world often assumes discrete and fractured contours. But for the desert wanderer, the poet, the solitary traveler in times past, pondering the surrounding vastness, a totally different spectacle must have appeared. How much, if at all, does what one sees by day or night, scattered in time and space, possess a single essence? How much, if at all, is one human being part of the boundless expanse? Indeed, how may an individual, contemplating the stars or trudging through the scorching sands, relate her fragile existence to the sovereign majesty that governs or envelops all that surrounds her?

That said, the deserts did not stand in complete isolation; their magical and bewildering beauty was not known only to native inhabitants and the rare parties who wandered among them. In a broader view, the inner desert regions along the Mediterranean coast, the Red Sea, and the Persian Gulf bordered lands rich in cultures and belief systems stretching back to antiquity. Joined on all sides by one ancient civilization after another, with trade routes linking coastal and inland regions across three continents, the deserts straddling Africa and Asia bustled with echoes from outside—the reverberations of Pharaonic, Assyrian, Nabatean, Phoenician, Hittite, Greek, Roman, and Persian cultures. Later echoes included the turbulence surrounding the earliest Christian schism: the feud, associated with the Alexandrian Arius (d. 336), about whether God and Christ were one. Closer to the sixth century, the deserts heard tell, from itinerant merchants and monks, about the lives and thinking of luminaries such as St. Augustine (d. 430), the Roman-Algerian bishop and Trinitarian theologian, and Hypatia (d. 415), the Greco-Egyptian mathematician who died at the hands of an angry Christian mob.[1]

One must imagine the stories and ideas that passed over routes inland and at sea, both from the surrounding Mediterranean civilizations and their colonial settlements at the periphery of the Arab world, as well as from India and Persia and farther east. Arteries of trade and communication stretched from the deserts of North African to those of Asia Minor. They reached from wondrous Ionian cities—and spiritual capitals—all the way to Mesopotamia, where churches and temples for worshipping the sun and the stars dotted what is now the Turkish-Syrian border. The paths also led south, into the "heartland" itself, the Arabian Peninsula. Onward still, they plunged into the fertile lands once ruled by the legendary Queen of Sheba. A day's journey across the Red Sea would bring the traveler to the Horn of Africa, the seat of one of the ancient world's most venerable kingdoms, Ethiopia. From this site, it is now believed, *homo sapiens* first emerged, later crossing over to Arabia and Asia Minor; at any rate, the first great empire that officially embraced Christianity—and later welcomed Muslims—flourished here.

The Arabian Peninsula stood surrounded by historical riches told and untold. This is where the biblical prophets once roamed—where Jewish, Christian, and other religious communities had long found a home. And here, in Mecca, the main center of commerce for the Arabian heartland—not far from the Red Sea and close to the desert mountains where he would receive his first revelations—was born the Muslim Prophet Muhammad (570–632). The unique and divine visions he beheld and the message he imparted sparked extraordinary events that would shape world history.

In retrospect, it should not have seemed so extraordinary that Muhammad appeared in this part of the world. People with their ears to the ground—those of the Jewish faith and others, too—knew the trading posts in the desert were teeming with rumors about the imminent arrival of the Messiah. Similar rumors had flourished in this part of the world for centuries, including the years surrounding the advent of Jesus. Around the time that Muhammad declared his mission, at least two or three other individuals also claimed to have received the prophetic gift. In addition to these men—and to say nothing of the many hermits, mystics, and monks who belonged to different Christian orders, or members of Jewish communities living across Arabia—the desert abounded in sects and communities representing more ancient religions and civilizations; they hailed from places as far away as Persia and the Indian subcontinent; they included Zoroastrians, moon worshippers, sun worshippers, Brahmins, and Manicheans.

Situated between contending empires, the Byzantine and the Sassanid, the major northern and southern Arab tribes made alliances with these two sides, respectively. Inner Arabia, then, represented a middle ground where cultures, ideas, religions, and ethnic groups encountered one another. Indeed, the northern outreaches of Arabia lay firmly within the two empires' spheres of influence. The Sassanid Empire not only propagated Zoroastrianism, but also welcomed Nestorian Christian fathers when their seat of learning, the ancient city of Edessa (Urfa), was ordered closed by the Byzantine emperor Zeno in the late fifth century. This occurred just after the emperor in Rome acquiesced to the demand of Cyril, archbishop of Alexandria, that Nestorius, archbishop of Constantinople, be deposed.

Approximately two hundred years earlier, following an even earlier Christian tradition going back to Jesus himself, Arius had proposed that God and Christ were not one. Subsequently, Alexandria and Antioch became synonymous with different schools of Christian thought. Alexandria took an increasingly strict view of Christianity and assumed a hostile stance toward other sects and cultures (including Jewish and pagan communities). Remnants of more glorious days still existed—perhaps embodied most fully by the learned, beautiful, and tragic Hypatia (350–415), whose end drew the curtain on the storied Greek tradition of scholarship. But in general neither the "pagan" sciences nor free thought were tolerated by the city's bishops. Thus, inquisitive or otherwise restless religious scholars began to migrate; many of them went to different parts of Arabia and the northern provinces. Nestorius advanced the view, associated with church leaders at Antioch, that Mary was but a mortal woman, and her son, though an instantiation of the divine Word, not God himself. At a council held in Ephesus (431), Cyril mobilized his supporters from Egypt and other reaches of the Empire, and Nestorian doctrines were declared heretical.[2]

Cyril's challenge to Nestorius represented more than a theological squabble about whether Christ is God or a human being. Many of those involved in the dispute would have felt the matter to concern the extent to which human beings may follow reason on their own (albeit with divine guidance). Nestorius's loss in the doctrinal battle may be read as the point where an ideological period ended. When Edessa was closed, in Byzantium, dissident scholars and churchmen wandered eastward and sought refuge in Sassanid-ruled territory. They founded a new center in a small settlement called Nusaybin (Nisibis) on the plains where Syria now borders Iraq. The intellectual traditions of both pagan and early-Christian Alexandria moved there, too—away from the West, into Sassanid-held territory. In closer geographical and political proximity to Persia, what came to be known as the Eastern Church was augmented and invigorated by the intellectual dynamism of the famous Gundeshapur Academy—undoubtedly the foremost seat of secular and medical learning in its day.[3]

In time—and in turn—Alexandria, Antioch, Edessa, Nisibis, and Gundeshapur played pivotal roles in the transmission of ancient Greek and Syriac science to the intellectual movement inspired by the Muslim prophet's message. In the tenth century, the renowned philosopher Alfarabi (d. 950) reportedly told of how ancient Greek philosophy had reached him in Baghdad—a day's ride, by mule, from Nisibis. Generations of scholars past and present put him in contact with one Youhanna bin Haylan, a Nestorian cleric under whom he studied the works of Aristotle (including the *Posterior Analytics*).[4]

But all that would come only later. First, conditions had to prove favorable for the rich intellectual heritage to penetrate the heartland of the Arabian Peninsula.

Long a major regional trade center on routes linking Asia, Africa, and the Mediterranean, Mecca emerged as a center of political, cultural, and religious life for tribes and communities throughout the region. The indigenous pagan religion focused on three goddesses said to inhabit Mecca, Medina, and Ta'if. Special places stood reserved for them within the square, black building called al-Ka'ba. Over the ages, this ancient structure, built where a meteor was said to have fallen from the sky, had become a hallowed place of worship for the Arab tribes. Once a year, it hosted a fair to which people flocked to exchange goods, renew old friendships, make new ones, and celebrate. The fair featured a competition to select the best poems of the year. Legend holds that winning odes were inscribed in gold on sheets of Coptic cotton, then draped on the outer walls of the al-Ka'ba for all to see. So greatly did the desert Arabs revere poetry! Over time, this tradition yielded the seven (by other accounts, ten) main pre-Islamic and early Islamic odes in the literary pantheon; their glory has not faded, even today.

A modern reader might ask where the beauty lies in the most famous ode that has been attributed to the poet-prince Imru'al-Qays. The first line simply names habitations that have ceased to exist, followed by an account of the author weeping as he calls them to mind. With a little effort, one can appreciate the depth and impact of these words by picturing how the poet felt as he passed the desert camp where his beloved had lived, the one who was the orbit of his soul and innermost being; now, he sees nothing but sifting sands—his heart's desire has moved elsewhere, in search of better pastures. The stark contrast between presence and absence, being and nothingness, meaningfulness and emptiness, and life and death fires the passion of the verses: names that promised sense and orientation now float over the vacuous and indeterminate desert plains. Such words share, in a magical combination of elements, how past and present, seeing and imagining, and joy and sorrow are woven together.

It may seem surprising to find mention of poetry right at the beginning of a story about reason. Yet poetry is key. Affirming the priority of poetry in social and intellectual evolution is not a new idea, as we will see when discussing the Muslim philosopher, Alfarabi, who followed Aristotelian tradition on this point. But poetry is far more than just a footstep on the ladder of intellect. As the natural and immediate medium of creativity and imagination, poetry is a progenitor of reason. Breaking free from elementary locutionary forms, it evokes a world invisible to the untrained eye yet immanent to the event or object described. Such transcendence through imagination—breaking loose from the confines of immediacy and concrete reality—is nothing if not an act of freedom. Approaching these newly revealed horizons of sense, reason grows bold, makes exploratory steps, and begins to search for order as yet undiscerned. Beginning to stir, over time, it comes to make fuller and better sense of what poetry has described. But even as it does so, consciously or otherwise, imagination remains its creative spark. One can easily see how, in this light, poetry and reason form a natural pair. Without the one, the life of the other cannot be sustained.

.   .   .

The eleventh-century philosopher Avicenna (d. 1037) identified imagination as the medium of reason. As we will see, he was not alone in giving credit—and then free reign—to the imaginative faculty both as a source and then as a "trans-rational" medium for the cognition of reality. An entire tradition of mysticism and imaginative discourse—often expressed in poetic and allegorical form—pre-existed him and flourished after his death. Just as importantly, as we will see, imagination was the power source for advances on various intellectual and scientific fronts—including philosophy, law, the sciences, mathematics, and astronomy.

There is, however, another side to the matter. After having been sparked and then flourishing, reason may ossify—and even turn against its (unacknowledged) sire. Adherents may come to view it as both self-generating and self-sufficient—indeed, as the antithesis of the imagination. Imagination, however self-consciously expressed, whether in poetry or in new and unconventional ideas, then comes to count as the enemy of the rational establishment and the authoritative system of thought. It comes to represent potential danger and a threat to order and stability. The poet—the receiver of visions, the freethinker, the Promethean emissary of light—now qualifies as an outsider, an outcast; he grows estranged from his own community and is forced to roam alone. He is feared and despised; sometimes, he is demonized to the point of suffering incarceration and crucifixion. How often, in the story that follows, will we encounter such victims: begetters of an order that turns against its creator! One wonders whether this—the sparks thrown by imagination and their subsequent extinction—underlies the (mis)adventures of reason in Islam: on the one hand, boundless expansion, and, on the other, restrictive authoritarianism.

To this day, Muhammad's sacred text exercises power because it counts as a "once-in-a-lifetime" miracle of Arabic poetic prose. In a world where the word was the privileged medium of imagination, its effect could in no way be overestimated. All the same, the foundations already existed in desert culture—the minds of freely roaming people attuned to beautiful language and the sentiments roused by poetry. Poets were the masters of sense. They expressed passions and articulated perceptions otherwise felt only vaguely. With paradoxical precision, they evoked the bewilderment the desert traveler experienced, the deep emotion and passion of the lover, the sorrow of the mourner, and the wounded pride of the affronted.

In the desert, the poet became the voice of his people. He magnified its virtues to other tribes, and he influenced its decisions more than any elder or merchant in the community ever could. Such was the power of words! Free-spirited poets were regarded with such awe and respect in those days that they were celebrated publicly. Such quasi-instinctive reverence, when combined with other factors, could yield still more, too. Thus, when a commanding, blue-eyed poet—who also happened to be a woman— sang of the wrongs she (or, more precisely, her camel) had experienced, one of the longest conflicts in pre-Islamic Arabia erupted. The Basous War, which derives its name from the lady in question, lasted forty years. Tellingly, when her indignant nephew spoke up to declare his readiness to fight on her behalf, the first phrase with which he addressed her was: "Ye free woman." These honorific words reflected his respect for her as a poet and a woman of dignity. (Should we be surprised, then, to learn that records mention more than forty female poets during the pre-Islamic period—in a desert environment where girls were often buried alive at birth?)

Pre-Islamic Arabia—and even for a few years after the advent of Islam—knew, besides the famous poets identified with their tribes, the singular phenomenon of lyrical vagabonds. The *Sa'alik* were outlaws one may liken, in an English context, to Robin Hood and his gang: a proud and self-possessed group of ostracized and dispossessed rebels who raided the caravans of the rich and shared the spoils with the poor. They were known equally for their daring and for their poetry, which celebrated anarchic social movement.

The two types are complementary: on the one hand, the authors of *mu'allaqat* (odes), whose individualistic and romantic spirit pondered the unfathomable space linking the stars above and the earthly human passions of the desert-dweller; on the other, the social rebels whose verse challenged hierarchy and authority and indicted the inequality of human fortunes. Together, they represent the unique personality of the desert poet: simultaneously an integral component of the social order and one who stands in opposition to it. The desert poet dwells at the border and inhabits two worlds, a hybrid entity belonging both to his closely-knit tribe and to the vast and limitless space outside this group. A gifted master of his people's everyday tongue, he also acts as the medium through which language magically transforms into an artistic tapestry of words, summoning meanings that seem to come both from under the sands and from the distant skies above.

The evocative power of poetry in desert culture and the free-spiritedness it reflects are key to understanding the cultural climate of the age when Muhammad announced the divine message. Language unquestionably represented the privileged form of expression, and poets were un-questionably the premier practitioners of the art. Both for its spellbinding imagery and because of its physically and mentally moving effects, poetry had no equal. But for all that—in spite of the power of poetic imagina-tion, which attuned the desert mind to the power of the word, created the framework for human thought and action, and prepared the cultural grounds for what would follow—nothing could compare with the up-heaval that occurred in the wake of Islam's message as expressed in the Qur'an. The holy message reverberated for years, decades, and centuries to come. It manifested a linguistically commanding form hitherto un-seen and unheard. Its sacred words and concepts seemed to come from realms unknown until now. The Qur'an elevated the spirit to unparalleled heights: reason in Islam was born. If earlier lyric had been the mistress of the body and soul, it paled in comparison to the transcendent and vibrant poem of the universe Muhammad had delivered.

Over time, the spiritual revolution caused by the message, which suf-fused the intellect with new life, would draw on other resources. Greek, Persian, and Indian science flowed into the Islamic world as its political power grew. They found a place because the spark of reason—the intellec-tual journey for order through the analysis of phenomena and texts—had been set aglow, and welcomed them.

At the dawn of Islam, it seemed for a moment as if the gates had been flung open for a movement of intellectual freedom to emerge. Above all, this possibility existed within the realm of the new religion; its sparks fired scholars to consider its full implications. At the same time, it was rooted in desert culture—the culture of the free-roaming poet embody-ing creativity, pride, independence of thought, and individual self-worth. However—and right from the beginning—the reason propelled by reli-gion proved intolerant to individual liberty, too. Over time, religion would grow rigid and grant less and less space for the free flow of creative think-ing. Eventually, the latter would be expelled from the religious realm alto-gether; henceforth, it would become the stock in trade of a philosophical movement at the edges of society, incapable of exerting any influence on the social center.

2

The Daunting Idea of God

Scholars debate whether Imru'al-Qays—prince of the northern Arab tribe of Kindah—was Christian, a Mazdakean like his grandfather, or a pagan of one kind or another. A famous legend tells how a royal messenger, when he brought urgent news that his father had been killed by a man of an enemy tribe, found the poet-prince drinking wine with like-minded companions. Imru'al-Qays is said to have greeted the messenger with a rhyming couplet: "Today we drink, and tomorrow we shall see how to handle the matter." The following day, he appealed to the Byzantines for help in avenging his father's murder. The move was logical. His tribe's affiliation was with the Byzantine Empire. (When Imru'al-Qays finally died, he was buried in Antalya [Turkey], which lay in Byzantine territory, too.)

The poet's free-roaming habits and the Byzantine space he moved in—where hermits and monks roamed or dwelled in scattered monasteries throughout the desert—must have offered him countless opportunities to learn something of the Christian faith. There is no doubt he was acquainted with Judaism, for Jewish tribes belonged to Arabia as much as his own pagan tribe did. The word for God in his ode, *Allah*—one hundred years before the advent of the Arab prophet—might therefore indicate a more general awareness, however vague or ambivalent, of the God of the Bible.

Indeed, as we saw in the last chapter, Arabia was bubbling with religious fervor, partly inspired by ideas from Egypt, Persia, and the Indian subcontinent, partly from its own wandering poets and hermits, but most of all, perhaps, from the stories told by the wandering monks and clergy of the major Christian sects; they disagreed about the nature of the relationship between God and Christ and were associated with rival schools at Alexandria and Antioch. Interestingly for our story—as we will see later—splinter groups even claimed that Christ had not been crucified at all; they asked whether he was the Son of God, begotten of Him, yet miraculously born of a woman.[1]

The Roman emperor Constantine I convened the First Council of Nicaea (modern-day Turkey) in the fourth century CE to settle these and other matters. The Council passed a decree banishing the early Alexandrian school of Arianism, which denied the divinity of Christ. But even this could not check the ongoing process of dissension among Christians—nor could the various synods and councils that followed. As monks traversed the deserts of Arabia, either seeking refuge because of their unorthodox beliefs or carrying messages from one bishop to the next, it is only reasonable to expect that these very different ideas about God spread quickly by word of mouth, from one person to the other, and from place to place—as news traveled in those days.

Other accounts about God and His relationship to the world fermented over the years. They came from monks, hermits, and clerics who related the controversies at various synods concerning which "testaments" were to be accepted, and which were not, as well as from indigenous, Arabian-Jewish rabbis' views on the transcendental and unitary nature of God, His act of creation, His awesome power and sovereign authority over all creatures, His prophets, and His ordered plan for the life of the world. Still more, pagan religions, both native and those adopted from proximate nations and cultures, offered other visions. By the middle of the seventh century, then, Arabia was ripe for a divine message of its own. Eventually, this message cast off the yoke of Byzantine and Sassanid rule, turned the tables on prevailing beliefs, and replaced them with something—in the form of God's Qur'an—that the desert Arabs welcomed as far more solid, comprehensive, and, above all, indigenous and suited for life as they knew it.

.   .   .

It lies beyond the scope of this work to describe (much less explain) the precise itinerary that the message of Islam followed as it spread among the divided and splintered desert Arabs in those early days; nor can we discuss, in detail, the impact it made or the hold it came to exercise. However, one may safely assume that a mentality existed—for one or more of the historical and psychological reasons mentioned above—that gave them a "meta-phenomenal" appreciation of objects and events in the world around them. In this context, two aspects of the message must have exercised undeniable force: the fact that its prophet was an indigenous Arab, and not of different ethnic stock, and the fact that it came in Arabic, a familiar language now given striking form. The first point may bear more weight in explaining the political dimension of the message's spread and the radical geo-political upheaval it caused. The second proves more important for explaining its subsequent, ever-growing *intellectual* impact—the revolution with which our story is concerned.

In language that continues to grip readers to this day, the sacred text directly captured the transcendental elements that had inspired wonder in poets and pagans alike. Invoking the all-powerful Deity already announced by the Hebrew Bible and New Testament, it presented a definitive framework for understanding God's relationship to the world as His *final word*. Unlike earlier scriptures, which, it was felt, could be translated from one language to another without losing their meaning, the distinctness of the sacred text seemed attached to the language it came in. At the time, as still today, it was held that the content of other (religious) texts could be readily transferred into tongues other than the ones in which they were written. In contrast, the Qur'an was and is believed to be so uniquely crafted that no one may fully appreciate it without learning the language and understanding it directly, whether by hearing or recitation. Its content and meanings were—and are—so inextricably linked to the language *as to be one with it*!

Now, the Arabs—whose sense of wonder may have been stoked by what they knew of Hebrew and Christian beliefs, which prompted them to engage in discussions of their own—no longer heard about God and the world of ancient prophets by way of languages they did not speak or texts they could not read (e.g., Aramaic, Syriac, Pahlavi, or Greek). Though an offshoot of the more ancient Aramaic, Arabic was their own tongue. Now they possessed divine discourse recounting the stories of earlier prophets and addressing existential questions in their own language; now they could pursue theological speculation unimpeded by a sense of distance or foreignness.

It made a difference that Muhammad had not come from a faraway, foreign land to proclaim the message. His indigenousness, the fact that he was of pure Arab stock, stood beyond question. To be sure, skeptics expressed doubt about his authority and contended that the verses and stories in the Qur'an had been fed to him by an itinerant monk during his journeys to Greater Syria. (Muhammad had worked for many years for the woman who later became his wife, guiding trading caravans across Arabia.) Others alleged that his brother-in-law—said to have been Jewish—introduced him to the Abrahamic faith. The Qur'an itself mentions, and refutes, these and other claims (including the charge that the Prophet was mad).

Murmurs of doubt notwithstanding, the verses Muhammad shared about the nature of God could now be thought about and discussed in earnest among his companions and followers. The divine poetry fueled imaginations already fired by the mystery of the world, and fanned them even more. Consider the heavens, the Qur'an exhorted, the seven skies bejeweled by the stars and planets, each of them following a prescribed path. Consider how they are held together—as if by invisible anchors. Do those who will not believe not see how the earth and skies were once fused together—that *We* tore them asunder and made water the source of all life? Consider how man was created, how life arose from a primal muddy ooze, how water springs forth from a rock, how a plant that seems to be dead comes alive. Consider that just as it began, it will also end, but how God can always breathe life into creation. The images weave wonder into ordinary sensory perceptions. Seven skies? A "sewn" world that broke asunder? The water of life gushing forth from dead rock?

Beholding their awe-inspiring surroundings, the desert dwellers were now prompted to consider all that they saw as signs, or keys, for unlocking the secret behind them—a sovereign order holding all things together. Other verses also unsettled standing convictions about natural phenomena, what even counts as natural in the first place: "Behold ye the mountains, that thou believest are frozen, but verily they pass along like the clouds." Could such massive structures really move, just like fleeting puffs of air? The idea defied common wisdom, shaking the trustworthiness of sensory perception. This, in turn, implied the need to change other inherited beliefs and ways of viewing the world.

The parallel to a commonplace experience of the desert is clear. Solid mountains vanishing into the air are like encampments where life has flourished; they disappear without a trace, leaving only windswept dunes behind. The mysteries behind the two images are analogous, perhaps even the same. Indeed, stars and planets also move; they do so, it seems, against the backdrop of infinity. They trace courses just as men follow paths on the desert sands. Yet how does all this occur? What does it mean? Then as now, Qur'anic verses fed the imagination, raising questions and offering a glimpse of what links the finite and the infinite, the transitory and the eternal, appearance and reality. The passage is both a vision and a call to a way of life. The cosmic spectacle exceeds the mystery it presents. It must be to explain it. Desert Arabs *felt*—deep inside, beneath surface instincts—that this image of conduct corresponded to what they knew to be right: acting justly and being good to others, in harmony with the ways of the universe.

The language was beautiful, its form exquisitely poetic, like nothing before; it seemed made to captivate ears already attuned to the magic of poetry. At the same time, it possessed a universal scope and rang forth on a scale without precedent. Instead of unfolding inner, individual anxieties, passions, and emotions, it poured out into the world and reflected transcendent majesty and order. The verses oscillated with the precision of a pendulum, moving between the metaphysical and the psychological, the ethereal and the stuff of daily life. One can imagine how the rhythmical words opened an entire world, disclosing an infinite horizon of wonder and speculation while pointing to the architecture of the cosmos. Now, the inhabitants of the desert had, in their own language, a treasure house of declarations about God and themselves—challenging both intellect and imagination, inviting further reflection and interpretation.

There was much to think about. At any rate, the goddesses of al-Ka'ba had offered little to inspire the imagination or intellect. Nothing much could be said or thought about them that did not concern their ornamental display or role in ritual. To some, they may have been intercessory agents, or angels—but for whom or what? They said nothing themselves. In contrast, the Message urged people to turn their thoughts to what surpassed the confines of the al-Ka'ba, locality, and ethnicity: the extraordinary Being they might have heard the Jews or Christians in their midst discussing and debating as a power above yet also present on earth.

The Arabs had been outsiders to such controversies and disputations, strangers to a conflict that didn't quite seem to concern them. Now, they were no longer mere listeners or onlookers at an unfathomable discourse about the mysteries of the universe—how the skies and the earth are held together, how day gives way to night, and night to day, how the uncertain future yields the immutable past, how life and death each prevail in turn.

Nor did they feel like outsiders to the discourse that presented these mysteries and the manifold phenomena of nature in a unified theory. The news did not come from some extraordinary figure whose origin was itself an enigma, but from an ordinary man who belonged among them—someone who didn't pretend to be more than a messenger, the medium through whom the singular truth about existence and the universe had been revealed. In other words, spectators and outsiders now possessed the means to become participants. They had the material in their hands, and a language, too. More than anything else, this is what sparked the birth of reason in the Arabic-speaking world.

Now, it felt natural to ponder the nature of God by drawing on a message that had been addressed directly to them. The message was pregnant with ideas, guidance, exhortations, images, warnings—above all, with injunctions to contemplate the world and use one's mind to appreciate its complexity and miraculous nature. By entering the holy of holies and knocking down the idols, Muhammad had made his contemporaries see that the goddesses of al-Ka'ba were puny and helpless before the Almighty. Fashioned of dried fig, how could perishable (indeed, edible!) artifacts arranged on pedestals hold power over men? Even if the goddesses' *anima* was believed to be more ethereal than earthly, how much power could they in fact possess? Likewise, how could even the moon, the sun, or the stars be worshipped for commanding mortal fortunes when they simply followed a predestined pattern? Wasn't this order—as the Qur'an affirmed—the predominating feature in the world? It determined how mortals should manage their lives, the change of the seasons, the alternation between night and day; it offered the fixed frame within which to raise cattle and tend one's pastures. Did it make sense to worship mere intermediaries for such an order—or, for that matter, even to worship the order itself—now that they had been enjoined to consider that something stood behind it, which had brought it into being in the first place? What might such a power be?

The Qur'anic verses addressed—in whole and in detail—a range of psychological and existential concerns: yearning for enduring life, a future of comfort and bliss; instinctive fear of punishment or retribution for doing wrong; the promise of reward for doing right. Above all, however, the verses spoke to—and roused—the imagination and the intellect. On the one hand, people were challenged to rid themselves of the limitations in their minds, to break free, and to picture the novel and daunting idea of an almighty and infinite God, somehow one with, and reigning over, the cosmos where the earth seems to move beneath a celestial array of luminous signs. On the other hand, even the tiniest events on earth offered *keys* for unlocking the overall cosmic secret of creation and order; all that *is* calls for people to believe in the reality of His existence.

Such verses, which abound in the Qur'an, shook and challenged perception. One might picture earth-bound desert tent-dwellers suddenly being brought aboard a spaceship that has appeared out of nowhere, then being whisked away to distant skies. From here, they look back at a world they thought they knew, but had never imagined to be anything like the scene that now presents itself. They are duly overwhelmed by the vision—and by the power that surely holds it all together.

But despite the affirmation of the awesomeness of the cosmos and its almighty Creator, does the Qur'an fully explain the relationship of human beings to Him? Do the verses make His nature fully plain, or the nature of the world He created? That is, can these words stand in for our need to reflect on the "big questions"? If the Qur'an stimulates the imagination and prompts us to break free from pre-existing shackles to see the world in a different light, does it not, also, call upon us to cast off our chains as we begin to ponder God's nature, and the nature of our relationship to Him? Does it not enjoin us, not just to imagine, but also to *think* freely, wherever this may lead?

In the context of these speculations, and amidst the major political upheavals that began with the passing of the Prophet, the very first steps in the movement for freedom of thought were made.

3

Free Will and Determinism

Even though a Qur'anic verse warns that their words lead astray, Arabian poets continued to cast a spell on their fellow inhabitants of the desert. Language—both as an artful craft and as a stimulant for the imagination—maintained its role as a medium of sovereignty and individual freedom. At the same time that the Qur'an dispossessed poets of the throne of *meaning*, it coronated a new voice declaring the wonders of the beyond. Lyrical expression yielded to discourse about the mysteries of the world and the models for human life articulated in holy writ. In turn, scholars would follow this rationalist inclination, delving deep into the text of the Qur'an to sound its intellectual depths. Soon, the brazen free-spiritedness of the more outspoken poets would founder on the cliffs of the new religion that was in the course of emerging. At yet another level, others of a mystical bent would attempt to break the bonds of language altogether, considering it too constricting, and seek insight into higher realms. But common to all of these endeavors was the soul's inner yearning to be free, the search for the medium in which liberty might find expression. Eventually, all these different orientations would compete to announce the truth of what was stirring in the desert sands.

The legendary Rabi'ah al-'Adawiyyah (713–801), based in Basra, inaugurated an ascetic tradition in Islam searching for higher reality beyond common sensory perception and language. Hasan al-Basri (642–728) initiated a movement of analytic inquiry stretching language as far as possible by declaring it the medium of rational investigation justified by the Qur'an; later still, law, philosophy, and science would follow suit, each pursuing its own path on the terrain he had opened. Still—and right from the beginning—some of those inspired to exercise their newly discovered intellectual freedom to peruse the Qur'anic text in search of meaning proved intolerant of others who did not share their beliefs; they claimed freedom for themselves alone. When this occurred, freedom was made into a slave. Poets still singing the praises of the sun or stars, or Qur'anic scholars found navigating different waters with another set of concerns, came to be considered trespassers. As soon as it was released, reason was subjected to new limitations.

In a sense, Hasan and Rabi'ah represent the two poles between which the range of freedom founded by the Qur'an extended. On one end, language bounded this domain; on the other hand, it did the very opposite. In her youth, Rabi'ah was a free-spirited young woman—too free, by some accounts. Sources indicate that she was taken captive and enslaved in the course of early Islamic conquests, but that her beauty prompted the ruler of Basra to seek her hand in marriage—which she declined. Legends about Rabi'ah's extraordinary personality and deeds practically make her out to belong as much to another world as to this one. Such was the power of imagination that the Qur'an inspired in Arabia: the world of spirits, whose reality its verses affirmed, were as real as physical matter; they offered "proof" that a mortal, chaste and pure of heart, could move between realms—a hybrid being possessing the qualities of earth and spirit alike.

Much later, in an allegory by a Persian poet (Farid al-Din 'Attar [d. 1220])—which concerns the rise of Sufi mysticism more than it describes actual events—Hasan, the exegete and analyst of Qur'anic language, is said to have encountered Rabi'ah sitting at the banks of the Euphrates one day. Spreading his prayer mat upon the moving waters, he calls out to Rabi'ah and asks, "Shall we offer our prayers here, together?" "Sir," she replies, "Is this your way of showing off the feats of men of this world to one who belongs to the other?" Then, Rabi'ah casts her prayer mat into the sky. Standing aloft, she continues: "Why not come and join me in prayer up here, floating on thin air?" "Surely," she concludes, "the fish can do what you propose, and birds can do what I am suggesting. But what the both of us should seek is a far higher station of the spirit!"[1]

Whereas Rabi'ah became known for her deep piety and almost complete withdrawal from worldly affairs, Hasan chose to assume a public—if understated—role. When not preaching and leading prayers at the main mosque of Basra, he would take a seat on a terrace or patio in the surrounding precinct and offer lessons. Observing what he deemed an essential calling in the Qur'an, Hasan discussed, with friends and students who gathered around him, the meaning and implications of verses that, to his mind, required explication and analysis. The didactic approach Hasan pioneered subsequently became the practice of mosques throughout the Islamic world; eventually, it led to the founding of schools (*madrasahs*) and universities. (The oldest university, dating from around the thirteenth century, was located in a mosque, founded by a woman for this very purpose, in al-Qarawayn [present-day Morocco]; among others, the celebrated Jewish philosopher Maimonides is said to have delivered lectures here.)

For Rabi'ah, Islam meant withdrawing from society completely to devote herself to God and contemplation. Hers was an inner freedom of the soul. For Hasan, Islam primarily concerned human actions—the meaning and measure of free will and responsibility. This meant immersion in the text of the Qur'an to find answers to questions about the new "world system" that had been revealed. Specifically, it entailed addressing issues occasioned by political events, which held deep significance both for everyday life and for the overall message of Islam. The circumstances under which Hasan offered his reflections proved just as important for later scholars as his didactic methods. He was born in Medina, where Muhammad had come to live, just ten years after the Prophet's death in 632. It is said that he met many of Muhammad's companions in his youth. (One account even reports that he was nursed by one of the Prophet's wives.) Therefore, in addition to the authority that his erudition and keen intelligence imposed on others, he enjoyed a special connection, in space and time, to the city of the Prophet and his followers; when Hasan moved to Basra to practice his calling, he brought a certain aura along with him. If the Qur'an had opened the way for people to search for and understand the keys of the universe, the short interval between the Prophet's death and Hasan recognizing his own vocation offered a unique and pivotal opportunity to shape the way the sacred text was understood in the Muslim world.

The *imam* Hasan, as he would come to be called by some, who used this title in the strict sense—"leader of prayer" (or the mosque)—lived in, and lived through, turbulent times. With one eye on Qur'anic verses, he also contemplated political events raging in the newly founded caliphate. Especially toward the end of the rule of the third caliph, Uthman, they involved ever-greater disputes about succession, specifically the claims advanced by the early Houses of Mecca: the Bani Hashem (the Prophet's line) and the Bani Umayya (to whom Uthman belonged). The whole of Arabia up to the Mediterranean (mostly inhabited by Christians in the Levant region) had fallen under Muslim rule by the time of Umar, the second caliph. However, military success and the expansion of dominion only exacerbated earlier rivalries and vendettas.

Hasan had been too young to register the political maneuverings that produced the first two caliphs, Abu Bakr and Umar. However, he had reached the age of reason by 656, when Uthman was murdered by opponents from Egypt protesting what they deemed a corrupt system of government. The discord had fed from—and fed into—standing contests for power. Still in Hasan's lifetime, it would lead to the first military confrontations between Muslims. As a pious exegete, Hasan viewed the Qur'an as the guide to understanding the theoretical and political dilemmas unfolding before him. Are Muslims "free" to rebel against their "supreme authority," the caliph? Or are they bound by his words and edicts? Is the caliph's will that of God, even when he acts unjustly? Can God in fact *be* unjust? If He were, wouldn't this render human responsibility null and void? Indeed, is God's will—as articulated by a caliph or his emissary—supreme, that is, does it eliminate a meaningful sense of human agency? Might it not be that a caliph is unjust, but not God? Might it be that God is just inasmuch as he has endowed us with free will so we may choose to do what is right? And if a Muslim kills another Muslim in the course of a battle for what is right, does he thereby cease being a Muslim? Or should he count as a Muslim who has committed a sin? How will such a person fare in the afterlife? Does he go to hell? In the context of these and related issues, Hasan and his followers formulated two fundamental questions. First, what is the basis for the legitimate transfer of authority in Islam? Second, where does legitimate authority over the lives and freedoms of individuals cease and where does their responsibility begin—if it exists at all?

These central questions—both to Hasan and to the community at large—could receive categorical answers only through analysis of the Qur'an. After all, the Word of God encompasses the whole of human life, including life in society. Resolving the great questions of existence depends on linguistic skill and analytic ability. Intellect—reason, that is—enables one to "unravel" deeper layers of meaning within the sacred text. Doesn't the Qur'an enjoin human beings to exercise their powers of understanding in order to lay hold of the keys to the universe?

Hasan was only two years old in 644, when Uthman, the third caliph, began his rule. He was still too young to know about the disputes attending Uthman's rise to power—to say nothing of previous disagreements about succession. But as we have noted, he was old enough to understand when Uthman was killed. The same year witnessed the first armed conflict between Muslims, "The Battle of the Camel." The conflict, which took place just thirty-six years after the Prophet died, received this name because Aisha, his youngest widow, led her troops mounted on camelback against Ali, Uthman's successor, in an effort to force him to expose and punish those guilty of the third caliph's murder. Did she suspect that Ali and his sons had been involved? Most sources deny this; indeed, they claim that Ali had posted his two sons around Uthman to protect him from the discontented Egyptians. Did the killers, desiring conflict between Ali (who represented the Prophet's line) and the House of Umayya, in fact incite her? Doing so would have covered up their own guilt, and if Ali were to blame the Bani Umayya outright, it would put an end to their claims. Or did Aisha's campaign against Ali and his followers represent a decision to make an alliance with his enemies in the House of Umayya for some personal reason? Many years before, Ali had questioned her fidelity to the Prophet.

The battle fizzled out without major casualties. Aisha was taken back home, with due honors but "broken." All the same, it seems likely that such a confrontation would have made a strong impression on an intelligent twelve-year old, and that, as he grew older, his awareness of its wider causes and ramifications would only have increased. It is easy to picture how a young boy living in the bosom of the Prophet's family would have cringed at the thought of two of Muhammad's closest and dearest relatives—his wife and his cousin/son-in-law—coming to blows. At any rate, the political significance of the battle surely became a source of deep concern as Hasan matured and witnessed its deleterious effects on Islam and the Muslim community. From the very beginning, many had believed that Ali was destined to be the natural successor and carry the prophetic flame. Those who held this position (later to be called Shi'ites) had grudgingly accepted the rule of Abu Bakr and Umar—in part because of their age and status, and partly because of Ali's presumed inexperience. But Uthman's selection was a different matter. Now, a constituency began to emerge that held that the natural line of succession had been wrongly interrupted.

Even as the legitimate successor to Uthman, Ali—who had moved to Kufa in Iraq at the behest of his followers—faced another claimant from the Bani Umayya clan: Mu'awiyah, the governor of Syria at the time (and later caliph and founder of the Umayyad Dynasty). This rivalry occasioned the second armed conflict that Hasan—now as a young man—witnessed. The Battle of Siffin, which occurred just eleven years after the first clash (667), took place on the banks of the Euphrates. This time, an estimated seventy thousand soldiers died. The fighting—in effect, combat between (pro-Ali) Iraqi and (pro-Mu'awiyah) Syrian fighters—weakened Ali's position; it created a schism in his ranks after he was finally forced to accept a judgment calling on him (and Mu'awiyah, too) to renounce all claims to the caliphate. Henceforth, succession was supposed to be determined by some form of election among Muslims. A group of Ali's followers unfairly blamed their leader for having brought this stalemate upon himself. This faction—the Khawaarij (who, as their name indicates, seceded from his ranks) came mainly from the Qurra tribe, which had played the key role in instigating the battle. They would prove Ali's fiercest foes.

Ali's rule did not last much longer. Mu'awiyah's claim to the caliphate—supported by his firmly established Syrian constituency—grew stronger by the day. In due course, a member of the secessionist group killed Ali. This left Mu'awiyah almost entirely in control. But for all that, Iraqi fighting vigor had not vanished completely. The towns and cities (including Basra, where Hasan lived) remained embittered and openly rebellious. Mu'awiyah responded by sending a ruthless general—al-Hajjaj—to quell the revolt. His strong-handed policy aimed at suppressing all forms of resistance to the succession. With an army of informants that spread fear and suspicion throughout the population, al-Hajjaj attacked even the slightest idea that ran counter to what the caliph envisioned. The terrorized people were to think that only one legitimate authority existed—that there was only one political will underwritten by God for all of Islam: the will of the caliph (and, by extension, his regent).

Personal and independent views about actions performed in the name of the caliph—to say nothing of judgments concerning his legitimacy or the validity of the ways his will was imposed (which included beheading and crucifying dissidents and rebels)—counted as nothing less than blasphemous. The conditions amounted to rule by coercion and fear: fear of freedom itself, fear of questioning authority. "I see heads before me that are ripe and ready for cutting," the terrible al-Hajjaj is said to have told the people of Iraq when he first set foot in their country. The Umayyad "doctrine" for suppressing rebellion was simple: Mu'awiyah was the representative of God's will on earth; however bloody or ruthless his acts of repression were, they were all part of a predetermined, divine plan. For ordinary men or women to oppose or criticize them amounted to sacrilege—the rejection of God's will in the name of impious independence. Mu'awiyah had the first and last word. In this context, the belief spread that ordinary human beings had no free will in the first place—especially where politics, the caliph and his commandments, were concerned. What is more, inasmuch as they served as instruments of divine will, neither al-Hajjaj nor the caliph could be accused of unjust actions—however cruel or unfair they seemed to people on the receiving end. Justice, after all, meant carrying out God's own will; surely, nothing He has ordained—or even anything performed in His Name—could be deemed unjust.

These political developments contained, *in nuce*, the themes— justice, free will, and responsibility—that eventually became central to Hasan's thinking; in turn, they came to define different schools of thought in Islam as a whole. The climate of repression provides the best context for understanding how Hasan came to reflect on the political dimensions of his religion, in addition to its metaphysical and ethical aspects. It also explains his melancholy disposition and political reserve. As a pious exegete and scholar, Hasan's natural frame of reference was the Qur'an itself. The Book alone (rather than, say, the declarations of an al-Hajjaj) allows one to determine whether free will or predestination truly prevails. Are all acts decided in advance—even those that seem to be wholly unjust? Could God Himself *be* unjust? Does it follow, then, that mortals are absolved of responsibility for what they do in their lives—and does this mean that they are not called upon to do good and eschew evil? Are they, perhaps, not free in the first place to decide between good and evil? Were Mu'awiyah's orders and actions legitimate and preordained? Was his authority even valid?

The imam Hasan would look at Qur'anic verses and discuss them with his students. Certain questions (such as the legitimacy of Mu'awiyah's succession) he might wisely have chosen not to discuss out in the open. But others, including matters indirectly related to political disputes, he could and did address from a scholarly point of view. After all, even if he did not wish to raise them himself, other participants in the daily meetings could do so. Discussion followed from the circumstances and necessity. The repressive political order, which professed that its authority came from God Himself, invited skeptical minds to sift through His Word to determine whether claims were justified. Hasan combined hermeneutics—interpreting what the Qur'an said—with an approach determined by lived reality. This was no "ivory-tower" debate about academic subjects such as justice, free will, and responsibility based on books picked up from the library. It directly affected peoples' lives. Since the regime of Mu'awiyah/al-Hajjaj claimed to be based on God and the Qur'an, it was only right to look to the Qur'an itself to find a true answer to burning questions.

The matter concerned life and death, the legitimacy of resistance to (and even fighting against) the caliph and his regent, and the nature of just and unjust acts—whether a Muslim was preordained to submit to the caliph's will under all conditions. In the anti-Umayyad climate that prevailed in Basra, members of Hasan's circle—many of whom had ties to movements of resistance—were naturally inclined to develop and promulgate values that suited their political interests. As a matter of course, they affirmed that moral values—especially the sense of justice—are natural, and that they may be discerned by human reason. They contended that unjust acts cannot be attributed to God, for He is just by definition. Furthermore, God has endowed human beings with the capacity to distinguish between just and unjust, between right and wrong, so that they may choose between them; such freedom makes human beings answerable for all they do. Therefore, rebelling against a caliph who has come to power illegitimately and acts unjustly is not only *not* blasphemous, but precisely what merits reward in the afterlife.

Already, then, and in keeping with the demands of the situation, debate among Muslims involved the most ancient and crucial of philosophical questions: whether human beings have free will, and what it means if they do. Because he understood the Qur'an as the intellectual space in which rational inquiry can proceed freely, historians have come to equate Hasan and his way of viewing the sacred text with the birth of reason in Islam. Because he conferred a foundational role to human agency, he has also been associated with the the doctrine of free will, which came to define a subsequent movement arising from those debates.

For all that, the doctrine of free will is associated more strongly with Ma'bad al-Juhani, who frequented Hasan's colloquies. Perhaps this occurred because of Ma'bad's vocal opposition to the Umayyad regime; indeed, his arrest and execution by al-Hajjaj in 699 made him a martyr for the cause. Alternately, it may stem from the fact that Hasan did not go as far as Ma'bad in endorsing free will, at least in the way the latter understood it. Later on, a school of religious scholarship would distinguish between "will" and "free will": the first concerns an experiential or psychological state one cannot deny having (e.g., *wanting* something), whereas the second is divorced from experienced reality inasmuch as "wants" may often be reduced to, and explained by, independent and pre-existing factors. At the other end of the spectrum—at first favored by the ruling authority for the determinist doctrine he represented—stood another famous figure we shall encounter again: Jahm Ibn Safwan (d. 745). Today, Ma'bad and Jahm stand as exemplars of these two opposing doctrines in Islam—free will and determinism.

Scholars do not agree how Hasan himself viewed matters. It is certain, however, that his circle attracted those opposed to the Umayyads, men who sought Islamic guidance and justification for the political and ethical positions they held. The debate about determinism and free will proved both vigorous and grave: different verses from the Qur'an were identified, analyzed, and weighed one against the other in order to delineate the precise boundaries God had set for what is legitimate, obligatory, possible, prescribed, and proscribed—that is, the full range of human action and responsibility.

All who followed Hasan's style of rational analysis and discourse came to be known as *kalam* scholars. Different translations of *kalam* have entered circulation—"dialectical discourse," "theology," and so on. But the literal meaning of the term warrants emphasis: "speech" or, more broadly, "discourse." From the inception, *actual, spoken language* characterized the discipline, the "speech" of the Qur'an itself. Scholars engaged in verbal exchanges with one another using "ordinary" speech—the vernacular of the day. This had a lasting effect on their analytical method, in contrast to the one later used by the philosophers, which was constructed on the basis of technical language translated from Greek.

Eventually, a rift between Hasan and his followers occurred. The off-shoot Mu'tazilite movement is said to have formed after an irreconcilable disagreement with Hasan concerning the status of a Muslim who commits a sin; it is associated with one Wasil ibn Ata (d. 748), to whom we will return in the next chapter.[2] Historians often present the issue as if it had been the only one and tell how Hasan pushed Wasil out of his circle. But while this was a burning item of debate, its significance cannot be appreciated apart from the larger context of political turmoil. Nor were debates limited to the circle at the Basra Mosque. The question of divine justice and its relationship to human will had been raised, and word was spreading. Political and social movements had emerged and continued to gather momentum.

Active opposition to injustice and corruption had started even under the caliph Uthman; it was associated with one of the earliest converts to Islam, the Prophet's pious companion, Abi Dhirr al-Ghiffari. Indeed, the disaffection of the Egyptian parties who killed Uthman belongs in this same context. With Mu'awiyah's ascendancy, the movement broadened and became linked with other questions and groups. Ma'bad (the radical proponent of free will) already found a follower in Ghaylan al-Dimashqi (d. 749)—a known associate of Ibn al-Hanafiyyah, one of Ali's sons, and a contender for the caliphate. Ghaylan, too, was an outspoken advocate of a just social order and free will, and he boldly opposed the Umayyad dynasty. Hounded by the authorities, he fled to Persia but was captured and brought back to Damascus, charged with sedition, and condemned to death. Nor was his execution merciful: first his limbs were cut off; then he was crucified publicly.

A cautious man, Hasan survived the autocratic rule of Mu'awiyah to live under the pious caliphate of Umar Ibn Abd el-Aziz (who ruled from 717 to 720). Muslim historians agree that this caliph should count among "the rightly guided"—a distinction reserved for the first four caliphs. In this less authoritarian climate, it is said, Hasan could express his views more freely. Many of them fell in line with Mu'tazilite tenets, including the radical position (which followed from, and further promoted, the use of divine reason given to man) that the Qur'an had been created by God and was not co-eternal with Him. (This same position, as we will see, led Jahm, the determinist, to meet a bloody end.)

At any rate, the "Hasan method" prevailed. Moreover, the connection between theoretical discourse on divine and worldly matters, on the one hand, and political movements, on the other, was abundantly plain in Basra and its environs. Eventually, practitioners of dialectical discourse would address the topic in more refined philosophical detail. At this early stage, Mu'tazilite tenets were already outlined in specific political and historical terms. Their further elaboration and detailed theoretical defense—in light of opponents' arguments—would mature in due course and yield vast intellectual riches. What is more, alongside Mu'tazilite scholars, others—though neither associated with the political opposition nor thoroughgoing exegetes in the sense of Hasan and Wasil—achieved renown for discussing the issue to which we now turn: whether the Qur'an, the centerpiece of Islam, was created verse by verse, or if it has always existed, in some fashion, as the Word of God.

4

The Qur'an

Created or Eternal?

Some of the most exciting discoveries about Islam's early literary history have been made in Yemen. In the early 1950s, a group of Egyptian archeologists uncovered writings by one of the major Mu'tazilites, Abd al-Jabbar (d. 1025). Until then, all that was known about them had come from a rival school. The discovery was thrilling because the works, by a later representative of the Mu'tazilite tradition, offered an unbiased account of the earlier "masters." In 1972–1973, renovation work at the Great Mosque of San'a led to an even more startling discovery: one of the earliest extant manuscript pieces of the Qur'an, written on parchment. Subsequently, German scholars determined that it in fact consisted of two layers, the lower text containing many variants of the upper, orthodox text compiled by the third caliph Uthman. The lower text is believed to date to before 671—that is, to a period not more than forty years after the Prophet's death in 632. The existence of these variants prompted some scholars to rush to the conclusion that it was the version of the Qur'an compiled by Ali himself, Muhammad's son-in-law. The mosque, first built as a fortress or palace on an ancient site and later turned into a church during the Byzantine period, is said to have been constructed in the Prophet's own day; it was destroyed and reconstructed many times, and often the materials were reused. This explains why parchments were uncovered beneath the plaster of some of the walls.

The discovery of these parchments—which was not disclosed too widely or publicly—caused some alarm among scholars in the Muslim world, especially because of the variants presented by the lower layer of text. The caliph Uthman is said to have gathered the entirety of verses into a single compendium. (Originally, they are supposed to have been memorized by three of the Prophet's companions and/or recorded on different materials; either way, Hafsa—Muhammad's wife and the daughter of the second caliph, Umar—is said to have recorded and preserved them.) Ever since, consensus has held that the Uthman compendium provides the complete and genuine text. Scholarly concern arose because variations now appeared within what counts as the "earthly imprint" of the eternal Word of God. The San'a discovery proved especially unsettling given belief in the text's flawlessness and the tradition in some Shi'ite circles that Ali had kept his own record of the Prophet's revelations; although what has come to be called the "orthodox," that is, Sunni, community does not accept this tradition, there was concern that the San'a parchments might reveal that the Uthman compendium does not faithfully report the Word of God, after all.[1] On further investigation, however, it came to be generally accepted that the "variations" in question were few, involved matters of style, and held no real consequence. Eventually, the drama subsided.

Why should a few variations, or even a handful of different verses, give rise to serious concern? The Qur'an contains 6,236 verses revealed to the Prophet over a period of approximately twenty-three years, from 609 (when he was forty years of age) until 632, shortly before he died. This fact (besides the circumstance that they were recorded with primitive tools and, moreover, often based on the recollections of the Prophet's companions) made the task of collation quite daunting. Uthman[2] reportedly began establishing an authoritative compendium because he feared (or, by other accounts, had actually observed) variations in some of the verses due to different dialects in regions where word of mouth had carried them. Despite the skillful mnemonic tradition among Arabs and the standing account that an original compilation had been completed by the time of the Prophet's death, it is possible that even some early scholars might have wondered whether Muhammad himself had reviewed the verses and verified their accuracy. In any case, one must assume that until they were completed, compiled, and then disseminated in written form, they had been transmitted by word of mouth, one by one. They typically reached people when they were *heard* in oral transmission. (Assuming each verse was written down when revealed, or four complete copies were sent out to the corners of the Muslim world, there wouldn't have been enough copies to circulate among all the faithful; nor, if there had been, would everyone have been able to read them.)

The same was true of statements or sayings by the Prophet which did not number among the revelations but came to be revered, as well: these, too, first came to life orally. There was no way to verify them, except by applying certain standards to their transmission (e.g., which companions heard Muhammad making a statement, how many people had done so, whether other reports existed, to whom they were relayed, how reliable recipients were, whether the ulterior version corresponded to the initial account, etc.). Although we must assume that, over the period of twenty-three years during which he received the revelations—and perhaps a bit later—a similar process occurred as verses and chapters reached people near and far, there was probably a point when followers deemed it necessary to avoid the risk of error by committing the sayings to writing. After all, they constituted the Word of God. Their divine status meant they had to be preserved as an integral whole. The divine message had not come down on a single tablet: its first form was intermittent and oral. The written version came only later. Even assuming that alternate readings (caused by the initial absence of vowel markers to determine how a word should be read) were eventually standardized, the question persisted whether the *text* provided an exact mirror image of the *Word*.

Some early scholars might have questioned whether each and every one of the Qur'anic verses, which were revealed over an extended period, had actually been verified by the Prophet. In his lifetime, "authentication" must have proven difficult—even for Muhammad. How can one accurately remember the exact phrasing of what one heard ten, seven, or fifteen years earlier? After his death, the scope of doubt may well have widened. One can easily imagine how, to counter the spread of doubt, a contingent of loyalists might simply have asserted the authenticity of the whole and denied all claims that a given verse could have been misheard, misplaced, or added.

Had the distinction been made clear, at the outset, between the eternal Word of God and the text, the seeds of controversy might not have been planted. Subjecting verses to authentication through common sense or reasoned judgment would not have detracted from the divinity of revelation. The same would hold for differences concerning "readings": even though meaning would be affected, sentence units would remain intact. It would not necessarily have counted as irreligious to question the authenticity of verses transmitted by word of mouth or copied from earlier versions based on the Uthman compendium. But all the same, this approach came to be viewed as a heretical position. Questioning the veracity of even one verse threatened to undermine the solidity of the structure as a whole. Doing so meant subjecting the text to human reasoning instead of affirming it as the standard for all human judgment. The issue proved sufficiently delicate that scholars—conceivably, even ones who did not necessarily think the Uthman compendium was wholly exact, yet deemed it vital for the emergent Muslim nation to be unified by an official version—encouraged the notion that the text was flawless: it was a genuine record of what was revealed to Muhammad, as permanently fixed now as it had ever been.

The Qur'anic text includes verses affirming that it, the Qur'an itself, has always "been there" as God's Word in one way or another—an eternal tablet coexisting with God Himself. The tradition of "strong" reading holds that what was revealed to the Prophet was scrupulously recorded, collated meticulously under Uthman, and therefore stands as the earthly tablet mirroring its transcendent original exactly. It gained acceptance that this earthly tablet, revealed to the Prophet, had been materially and accurately transcribed into four "exact" copies (none of which is now extant), which Uthman then sent to the four corners of the Muslim World. This tradition holds that the "earthly Qur'an"—that is, the text circulating among Muslims—possesses the same holiness and immutability accorded to God's Word. Over time, the text and the Word became equated: distinguishing between them amounted to heresy.

Still, early scholars might have wondered, and for good reason, whether passages affirming the eternity of the Qur'an were to be taken literally, and whether such statements applied to all its contents. Some verses are certainly general in nature; they may be reasonably considered to present universal principles that apply at all times. Others, however, are very specific and refer to specific incidents or events during the Prophet's lifetime. Do such verses possess the same eternal quality as, for instance, those about the afterlife or God Himself? Surely, these scholars thought, a distinction must be made between the immutable verses of the Qur'an—which are parts of His Sacred Word—and others that, though revealed, are not. The text, that is, need not be viewed in the same way as the Word itself.

A number of considerations encouraged this line of reasoning. Only a few copies of the sacred text were initially available to the Muslim nation, which was in the course of rapid expansion. At the time, most people were illiterate and could only have come to know it in parts, through oral transmission. What is more, Arabic writing had not yet devised a means to differentiate between certain groups of consonants with similar shapes, or between vowels and cognate sounds associated with the consonants determining the meaning of words. Finally, dialects varied from one region to the next, which introduced further possibilities for variation. Even after these linguistic issues had been settled, challenges persisted inasmuch as some important verses—whether orally transmitted or written—seemed inconsistent with others; the matter called for creative interpretation, at the very least. All these considerations must have exercised the minds of scholars who questioned the permanently fixed nature of the Uthman compendium.

Especially toward the end of Uthman's rule, various schools of thought emerged. Most of them formed chiefly for political reasons, but they held different intellectual positions, too. Qur'anic support was needed to legitimize varying positions, and relevant verses were sought to bolster them. Different schools cited different passages to corroborate totally opposite views. As we saw in the previous chapter, the issue of free will provided the paradigm, perhaps the original cause, for such practices. The matter led people to ask how God could be just—and how the rewards and punishments in the afterlife could make sense—if human beings are not responsible for their acts in the first place, if all their acts are predetermined. Some verses in the Qur'an intimate that nothing mortals do proceeds from their own free will; others affirm that God has endowed mankind with the ability to distinguish between good and evil and choose between them. Human agents are therefore answerable for their actions, and rightly deserving of reward and punishment.

In this context, some scholars concluded that inconsistencies could only be resolved by distinguishing between God's Word and the text of the Qur'an. This would make it acceptable to propose that some verses in the text contradicted others, which stood as "correct," and disregard them as human errors. God's Word would continue to stand as eternal and immutable. To underscore the distinction (and justify tampering with some verses), it was affirmed that whereas God's Word is co-eternal with God, the text represents an act of creation given over to time: whatever inconsistencies it seems to contain may be ascribed to human error and therefore eliminated by skillful exegetes. To view the Qur'an as a temporal product (and not as the immutable original) makes questioning, or even excluding, parts of it—with a view to rounding off some of its edges, as it were—a legitimate enterprise. That said, such an approach raises another contentious issue: the "duality" one is left with, which conflicts with the pure monism of God.

Other scholars took a further step. Why should the text be created but not the Word? After all, if one affirms that the Word is eternal, doesn't this amount to positing another eternal *something* that exists besides God? As for inconsistencies in the text, why should one assume that an eternal standard holds for judgment? Couldn't they simply be human distortions or errors in the (created) text? Early determinists and proponents of free will saw eye to eye on the matter of the Qur'an having been created. But whereas the former did so as part of a blanket denial that anything at all can be co-eternal with Him—including, above all, justice—proponents of free will insisted that *being just* and *being one* were the only "states" coexistent with God. Over the ages, these early positions evolved; ultimately, determinists upheld the eternality of the text. But at this early stage, as we will see below, pro-authority scholars (i.e., those who were favored by rulers and argued in favor of determinism) sought to deny the eternality of the Qur'an.

From the preceding, one can already see how the different lines of argument would evolve. Questions about the authenticity of some verses first led to questions about the immutability of the Word and its relation to the text; in turn, questions about the immutability of the Word raised questions about whether or not God could be ascribed properties at all. And so, heated debate arose concerning God's unicity and the qualities ascribed to Him. Some properties mentioned in the Qur'an are physical, for instance dimensionality and visibility. Perhaps the existence of such attributes was relatively easy to accept or reject. Others, however—say, omniscience and omnipotence—required more involved arguments. Many verses suggest or state outright that God has these "features." At the same time, other passages deny that even these categories apply to Him: God defies all description, period. The matter held political implications. In parallel to the thesis (endorsed by the early Umayyads) that men are not free to determine their actions, one could also argue—invoking various Qur'anic verses while discounting or reinterpreting others—that God Himself cannot be described as having the property of justice. What is more, inasmuch as He cannot be described at all and has no features knowable to mortals, it is presumptuous to claim to understand His thoughts—that is, the Divine Mind animating the Qur'an itself.

As we saw in the previous chapter, the doctrine of free will (and its relation to God's justice) was identified most strongly with Ma'bad al-Juhani and Ghaylan al-Dimashqi, both of whom were associated with the Basra-based "opposition movement." Two scholars initially patronized in the Umayyad courts, Ja'd bin Dirham (d. 774) and Jahm Ibn Safwan (d. 746), have come to be identified with the opposing doctrine of determinism. Jahm and Ja'd, who are known to have spent time together in Kufa and to have influenced one another, also came to be associated with the view that the Qur'an is created.

The scarcity of early sources makes it difficult to work out the exact genealogy of different views of the Qur'an's createdness. By and large, however, there are two major lines of thought. The determinism doctrine exemplified by Jahm denies that God possesses the quality of justice—indeed, any properties at all. To show this, Jahm distinguishes between God and His effects, arguing that all our claims to knowledge about Him are really about the effects of His *actions*. He is not—as we and other entities in this world are—made up of an underlying substance or essence endowed with qualities or properties whose existence is eternal in the same way, and insofar, as He Himself is eternal. In other words, He is not a composite of substance and accidents, as we are. Moreover, His actions—such as the creation of the world—not only are *not* properties; they are manifold, unlimited, and *external* to Himself. Indisputably, they include the act of creating the Qur'an; this, whether understood as a text or as abiding meaning, should not be considered an eternal and immutable *something* attached to, but different from, Him. Viewed in this way, it does not possess the kind of sanctity accorded to Him. Like all of God's effects or actions in the world, including nature itself, it admits human intervention.

What would such "intervention" involve? Both of Jahm's tenets—the denial of divine properties and, especially, the createdness of the Qur'an—led him to a conclusion that proved earth-shaking both in its own right and in historical context: the claim of "reason before hearing." It is significant that he formulated his "rule" by using the word for "hearing" (*sam'*). The matter involves deciding between verses that seem to contradict each other, and, more specifically, opting not to accept a verse (or interpretation) underwritten by an authenticated chain of transmission, but rather choosing the one consistent with common sense—the one aligned with human reason, that is. Is it possible that Jahm was referring to all the verses in a complete written compendium before him and questioning their validity as transcriptions of exact oral histories? Or was he questioning what was still a matter of oral transmission, not yet recorded in a text, whether in part or in full? Without detailed information, it is hard to tell. But either way, Jahm's claim represents the first clear challenge that reason posed to faith in the history of Islamic thought. This position did not challenge faith in God, His prophets, or the revelations made to Muhammad. It challenged the view that what has reached us from—or about—them should simply be accepted at face value and not examined in light of our own reason. Questions and doubts about conflicting Qur'anic verses or interpretations could now be raised and addressed from a different perspective. Wasn't it possible, due to a scribal error or a lapse of memory, for mistakes to have been made, or that certain verses had been intended in ways other than those now understood? Being temporal phenomena—and therefore lacking the sacredness of divine eternity—verses may be questioned. Indeed, isn't it necessary, especially when facing manifest inconsistencies or seemingly unrealistic claims, to question the meaning—and even the authenticity—of problematic verses, and to adjust (or even reject) them as not being a genuine part of God's Word? Aren't learned and pious scholars allowed to interpret verses in such as way as to make them consistent with one another? Surely, this is what God intended.

We can imagine a situation when—in presence of the Prophet or one of his close companions (or even in the days of Abu Bakr, Umar, and Uthman)—a meticulous process of reviewing verses to be included in the compendium must have seemed natural and necessary. Indeed, within Muhammad's circle, neither revelation itself nor its meaning stood in dispute. Furthermore, according to tradition, verses were being "recorded" on various materials by Hafsa even as they were being revealed. However, this material could not have been copied and disseminated right away, nor could it have been read by everyone, even if copies were made. It is more reasonable to assume they were transmitted orally. As the circle of readers and listeners broadened, the impulse to scrutinize verses and engage in speculation about them must have come to seem necessary, especially with the passing of time. The practice was not directed against the revelations themselves, as they had been heard and recorded, but against human conjecture about their meanings. In time, and once the Uthman compendium was disseminated, Muslim scholars eventually reached agreement on a framework for interpreting verses. However, this was not Jahm's approach: for him, *hearing* the repetition of a given verse, even one confirmed by transmission or in writing, still meant its validity should be subjected to reason.

This meant that verses and statements going back to the Prophet (even if they had been written down in the interim) should not be taken at face value. God Himself had enjoined believers to evaluate words in light of reason; this holds for any verse that seemed to conflict with human understanding, even if it has been authenticated by a line of transmission that had been properly examined. From an orthodox point of view, the idea was shocking; it seemed blasphemous to reject the standard employed by countless jurists and scholars: the "fact" that verses were first revealed and then transmitted by reliable sources, which authenticated them as the genuine words of God. But for Jahm there was nothing impious about scrutinizing what counted as divine, for he considered the verses of the Qur'an to be mere effects, or acts; the process needed to be completed, as it were, by judgment through reason.

Later, Abd al-Jabbar (935–1025), like other Mu'tazilites before him, would uphold the doctrine of free will, which he derived from the basic principle of God's justice.[3] He would have considered affirming the primacy of reason a further logical step. When his works were uncovered (also in the San'a Mosque), a fuller statement of his "heretical" doctrine became available: reason (or "intellect," *al-'Aql*) represents the ultimate principle both for faith and for life, because man can distinguish between right and wrong only by this means; moreover, it is by reason alone that what stands in the Qur'an can be demonstrated and achieve orthodox consensus (*sunnah*). This argument might seem strange—he continues—inasmuch as proofs appear to lie only in the sacred text and *sunnah*; alternately, one might think that reason performs a validating role and must therefore "come later." This is not the case, however, for God addresses only men possessing full reason, and since *sunnah* can be validated by reason alone, it must come first and provide the foundation for all determinations. (Abd al-Jabbar was not averse, in another context where he argued against the obligatory nature of imamate rule, to claiming that it was a matter of the text, not reason).

Jahm reached the same conclusion from the opposite angle. As noted, his determinism made him deny that God had any properties or qualities at all—in particular, the attribute of justice prized by the Mu'tazilites.

God's revelations to Muhammad were divine acts; therefore, they are similar in kind to other effects proceeding from Him, all of which are subject to our understanding and interpretation. Either way—that is, both from a Mu'tazilite perspective and from Jahm's deterministic viewpoint—the Qur'an counted as created, not an immutable divine tablet immune to fault, error, or inconsistency (and therefore incompatible with the judgments of reason).

Determinism is primarily associated with Jahm. In part, this is due to the "strong" version of determinism he espoused, which likens our actions to fluttering feathers in blowing winds. Equally, the connection came about because Ja'd, though himself a determinist, and building on the groundwork laid by Jahm, advocated an even more controversial theological position, affirming not only that the Qur'an is created, but that it does not possess the same sanctity as God Himself.

Jahm's reasoning may have concerned only the distinction between substance and property: God is substance with no property, and the "tablet," like the world, is just the product of His action rather than something affixed to Him, as it were; therefore, like many things in the world that are products of God, it does not stand beyond human influence or industry. For his part, Ja'd, although he shared Jahm's position regarding God's (absence of) properties, chose a different route for affirming the createdness of the Qur'an and the fact that its contents admit human arbitration: he simply denied it the kind of sanctity ascribed to God. How did he arrive at this idea? Especially in the northern provinces, Arabia stood under the influence of the Byzantine Church; indeed, parts of the population had converted to Christianity. In the fourth and fifth centuries, the controversy about whether God and Christ were one (and the related issue of how to view the status of the Virgin Mary) had already given rise to sects— Nestorian and Monophysite/Jacobite—with conflicting views.

Ja'd is reputed to have been a Nestorian convert to Islam. If so, he would have been inclined to view the Qur'an and the Prophet, in Islam, in terms similar to the way Jesus and Mary were regarded in Nestorian Christianity. Nestorian belief held that the Word (Jesus) came from a divine source but was not consubstantial with God Himself, and, furthermore, that Mary, as a normal human being, had simply served as a medium. She was not possessed of sanctified status personally. A parallel mode of argument would replace Jesus with the Qur'an and Mary with the Prophet. The analogy may have been encouraged by the fact that, unlike the (monophysite) Christian tradition affirming Jesus' divinity and Mary's sanctity—indeed, perhaps in purposeful contrast—the Qur'an repeatedly stresses that Muhammad was a "regular" human being. (The Nestorian view of the Virgin held that she was also "normal.") Nothing about the Prophet suggests that he was in any way sanctified or divine. He was simply a messenger, like others before him, called to remind men and women to believe in God and the afterlife, and to deal righteously with one another. Even if something special had prompted Muhammad to be chosen as the medium for the Word of God, an exalted status had not passed to him personally.

Ja'd may have reasoned that, just as a major branch of Christianity of the time wrongly accorded consubstantiality to the person of Jesus—whom the Qur'an also describes as the Word of God—Islam wrongly ascribed divine sanctity and eternality to the Qur'an, which incarnates the truth already inscribed in the early tablets or books of Abraham and Moses. Both were miraculously created—Jesus through the medium of Mary and the Qur'an through the medium of Muhammad. Both may be said to be *of* God, but neither one is consubstantial or co-eternal *with* Him. Just as Jesus, though the Word, is *of* God rather than His embodiment in human form, so, too, the Qur'an, though also of God, is an earthly artifact that does not share His eternality or sanctity.

This seems to provide a plausible genealogy for Ja'd's view that the Qur'an was created. In contrast, when Arabic sources address the origins of his "heretical" doctrine, they allude to a certain Jewish connection. The agent in question is said to have taken the idea from someone who had received it from the nephew of one Labid bin A'sam, a contemporary of the Prophet. Labid was the centerpiece of a legend—made famous in our times by Salman Rushdie's *Satanic Verses*—telling how he cast a spell on the Prophet and caused him to recite verses inspired by the Devil (instead of ones relayed to him from God by the angel Gabriel). Clearly, such a view is consistent with the doctrine that not all Qur'anic verses should be taken at face value! In any case, Labid evidently believed that the Qur'an was a temporal creation—perhaps in keeping with the position of second- and third-century Talmudic scholars who had debated similar matters with reference to their own sacred writings. (Like Maimonides, the great Jewish thinker and authority who lived some thousand years later, they concluded that the Torah itself was created.)

Of course, it is not inconceivable that Jewish sources influenced Ja'd. For all that, it seems rather contrived to link the influence with a "conspiratorial" chain reaching back to someone whom Muslim literature (and right from the beginning) had consistently identified as an "evil magician" associated with enemies of the Prophet. We must bear in mind that much of our knowledge about the period in question depends on records which were based on oral accounts; the more these accounts concern peripheral and controversial figures, the less reliable they become. For a Muslim who, on the one hand, believed that God's holy books were one in kind and came from a single source (as the Qur'an affirms), but, on the other, came to hold that the sacred writings of Judaism and Christianity were temporal events, it would have made sense to conclude that the Qur'an must also have been created in time. For a Nestorian Christian who acknowledged Muhammad's prophecy, the logic would have been even more compelling. Such may well have been Ja'd's line of reasoning when he proclaimed—counter to the orthodox view that the eternity of God means the eternity of His Word—that the Qur'an was created.

Needless to say, both Jahm's doctrine of "reason first" and Ja'd's claim that the Qur'an is not eternal and does not share God's own sanctity suited parties who wished to fit the text to their own (ideological) concerns. As we have seen, many conclusions can be drawn from the tenet that the Qur'an is not eternal—including the argument that it is not sacrilegious to question the veracity of its revealed proclamations, or even to suggest that it contains errors. The halo surrounding the Qur'an, which makes it seem intrinsically untouchable, simply vanishes once subjected to the scrutiny of reason. In this light, one could theoretically imagine a scenario whereby Muslim scholars, still drawing their religious and moral inspiration from the Qur'an, convened at regular intervals, whether over decades or centuries, to review what still counts as valid and what does not—what reason dictates that one should retain, and what now offers only historical interest. Such formal convocations might prevent the religion from falling into the hands of individuals or parties using it for selfish or bigoted ends. In fact, however, the Qur'an came to count as an eternal document of truth (even if it was generally acknowledged that the text did not equal the Word). Consequently, scholars, jurists, and exegetes stuck to the letter of the text, opposing any deviation from what stood written and insisting on a strict adherence to its every verse.[4]

The Mu'tazilites did not consider Jahm or Ja'd precursors; even though their positions on the primacy of reason and the question of the Qur'an's createdness resembled each other on many points, the matter of determinism interfered. Indeed, Jahm and Ja'd had both enjoyed Umayyad favor in their lives and were employed to teach the young princes. Even so, neither of them met a happy end. Jahm was executed in 743 after being arrested and brought back from a remote corner of Persia. Historical records do not indicate the reason, but it was presumably his "creation doctrine." In turn, Ja'd was brutally executed in 774—on the first day of a feast in the precinct of the main mosque of the Wasit region in Iraq—in full view of worshippers gathered for the occasion. This is said to have happened on orders from the caliph, at the hands of the local ruler, Khaled al-Qusari. Sources do not mention the reason for this execution, either, but it likely occurred on the same grounds that Jahm had been killed. Ja'd is said to have been avenged by a later caliph, whom he had taught as a young prince; reportedly, both eyes of al-Qusari's son were gouged out in retribution! Even though the two scholars' determinism had appealed to the Umayyad caliphs, their position on the createdness of the Qur'an, which brought them close to the Mu'tazilites, was not viewed with the same appreciation.

The Mu'tazilite School founded by Wasil—the scholar who left Hasan's circle in the Basra mosque to form a group of his own—had not yet hit its stride. Over time, it replaced the position advocated by Jahm and Ja'd, who separated reason from free will, with subtler arguments along dialectical lines. In due course, the opposing, determinist doctrine yielded to views that granted a role to human agency—what, today, one might call a "soft-determinism" doctrine (which yet another school advanced). Eventually, refined arguments also developed about matters such as substances, properties, and actions. If, in the early days, the Mu'tazilites had been outsiders living in insecurity and in terror of the Umayyad caliphate, the tables turned under the Abbassids. As we will see, when their ideology gained the upper hand, something like an inquisition was launched and rival scholars—most famously, Ibn Hanbal—were forced to adopt their views.

From Wasil to Ibn Hanbal

Today, the issue of the eternal or created nature of the Qur'an does not seem to garner much philosophic or religious interest. Consensus holds that printed[1] or handwritten copies of the Qur'an faithfully reflect the original revelations made to the Prophet. As a mirror of the Holy Message, the very language of the text possesses sanctity in it own right. For all that, this *linguistic* "sanctity" now constitutes a field of debate. The question arises whether it continues to offer a liberating force for intellectual progress, as it has done in the past, or now restricts it. Since the early days, the spoken language has changed dramatically; the spreading gulf between written language—which is rooted in the spoken Arabic of that early period—and spoken "Arabics" has been offered as an explanation for the notable decline of intellectual progress in the Arab world over the past few centuries. At the end of this study, we will return to this controversial issue: the possibility that the sacredness inherent in the original language has constrained the living Word that flows within and out from the Qur'an.

As we observed in preceding chapters, most "literature" was passed along orally in the early days of Islam. Arabic writing is thought to derive from Phoenician or Aramaic script (upon which Hebrew writing is also based). The Nabataean tribes dwelling in and around the present-day Jordan Valley are thought to have been first to use it, although traces remain from only the sixth century on—scarcely a hundred years prior to Muhammad's birth. Before favorable conditions for the widespread use of writing emerged, memory transmitted speech. This held both for the pre-Islamic and for the early Islamic poems we still have, as well as for the verses of the Qur'an and the sayings of the Prophet. Many conditions had to be met for an orally transmitted saying (*hadith*) to qualify as authentic. One needed to determine whether the original source was one of the Prophet's trusted companions and had been physically present, whether each person in the chain of transmission was a pious and trustworthy believer, and, finally, whether there was disagreement about the words as they passed through different lines of transmission. Today, when editors establish an ancient text on the basis of conflicting manuscripts, they pursue an analogous process of authentication: they draw up a "family tree" of extant versions to determine the various chains to which texts belong, and they decide which one of them is most reliable and most directly tied to the original source.

The sacredness invested in the Qur'an meant that due care was given to proper oral transmission—a practice at which the culture of the day excelled: we still have entire odes from pre-Islamic and later poets. The poetic style of the Qur'an helped in this process. Of course, it proved even easier to memorize and disseminate short statements and aphorisms. At the same time, it is worth remarking the divergence between poetry and speculative discourse (that is, the method of argumentation pioneered by Hasan). All that has been handed down to us of the vibrant intellectual exchanges between early jurists and theologians consists of aphorisms and fragments; logical arguments were not transmitted in their entirety. One often has the impression that the brief statements we possess either provided the seeds for arguments to be developed in the course of further discussion, or that the oral tradition of the day could not yet "handle" intricate arguments and disputations the way it could manage poetry. Therefore, a perverse twist of fate would have it that we now have almost nothing of substance from the pious imam himself or early proponents of free will. In contrast, we possess a complete poem by Bashar, a poet of Persian descent with an explicitly Zoroastrian religious bent, whose licentious style aligned him with the free-spirited and rebellious movement to which Ma'bad al-Juhani and others belonged. Hasan expelled Bashar from his circle; later, Bashar's ways cost him his life when the Umayyad dynasty yielded to Abbasid rule (750).

Bashar's story also provides an instructive lesson in light of what we have remarked about the role of poetry in Arab culture as the medium of intellectual freedom and, therefore, as a harbinger of reason. Whereas

Hasan excluded Bashar from their circle, Wasil Ibn Ata (700–748) and his companions drove Bashar out of Basra altogether. From today's perspective, the friction that arose looks like a test of liberal values. It seems that Bashar's unorthodox beliefs, licentious poetry, and brazen sexuality (to say nothing of the earring he wore) exceeded what the self-professed movement for free thought and rational inquiry—which it might have seemed natural for him to join—was willing to tolerate. From the very beginning, then, the champions of reason in Islam took a dim view of values in conflict with their own. The attitude only hardened when the movement gained ascendancy under the Abbasids and its doctrines were adopted as the official tenets of Islam (see later in this chapter).

Historians believe that the cause for Wasil's displeasure with Bashar did not involve his many eccentricities, but rather a couplet Bashar composed. Standing before the scholars gathered at Wasil's theological seminary, Bashar declared, in verse, that the sun has reigned supreme for all time and commands worship; the earth and the rest of the heavens occupy the positions of lowly suppliants. The incident is telling, for it underscores the line that early Muslim advocates of free thought and reason set for themselves and others. It marked off a space within which they could comfortably pursue their own inquiries. It did not extend so far that others could think as they wished.

Hasan is said to have lived a very long time, from 642 until 728. Some sources claim he almost reached a hundred, even if he retreated from society in later years. Most scholars associate the Mu'tazilite school with Wasil, who studied under Hasan before defecting and starting his own group, but there are Shi'ite accounts—for example, the history of the Mu'tazilites provided by the Yemeni Murtada in the fourteenth or fifteenth century—that credit the elder man as its real founder. To legitimate this view, the doctrine is linked with the first caliphs and the companions of Muhammad himself; indeed, its proponents suggest that Hasan was nursed by Umm Salameh, one of the Prophet's wives, when his mother worked for her in Medina. Such accounts draw attention to a well-known pronouncement by Muhammad that more than seventy forms of Islam will eventually arise—with the implication that Mu'tazilism represents the true path.[2] Toward the end of his days, either Hasan or his close followers struck some of the more "Byzantine" arguments dating from the earlier period of his life out of the repertory of discussion. Reportedly, they had been meant only as mental exercises to sharpen students' argumentative skills, not as actual intellectual positions (e.g., questions concerning the state of inhabitants of Heaven and Hell—whether their continuous movement meant they would *never* achieve ultimate happiness). Hasan's aphorisms in this area might seem more like clever sophistry than serious arguments, but this may be due to the fact that we do not have a complete record of his teachings.

Wasil was only twenty-eight when Hasan died. Given the difference in age, it is understandable that the younger scholar proved more outspoken in expressing views directly opposed to the Umayyad regime—and also that he braved his master's self-imposed reserve by venturing to formulate, in explicit terms, opinions later described as Mu'tazilite. Many scholars believe Hasan entertained these views, too, but that he never expressed them openly for fear of how the repressive authorities might react. Reports that may be true—or not—about Wasil and Mu'tazilism also connect directly with Shi'ite activism, that is, with political and military opposition to the Umayyads; such activism proved a major factor when the Abbasids finally toppled the Umayyad caliphate altogether.

One source maintains that Wasil stood close to Muhammad Ibn al-Hanafiyyah and his son, Abu Hashem. From the very beginning, Ibn al-Hanafiyyah—the son of the Prophet's cousin and son-in-law—had been deemed the rightful heir to Ali by his supporters. (Early Shi'ites disagreed about whether he or one of Ali's other sons, al-Hasan and al-Hussein, should inherit spiritual rule of the Muslim nation.) Ibn al-Hanafiyyah was also a religious scholar, and his views were sympathetic to the forerunners of the "school" or "movement" advocating free will, as represented by Ma'bad and Ghaylan al-Dimashqi. He is said to have stood especially close to the latter—one of the early martyrs of freedom in Islam—and to have walked at his funeral in open defiance of established powers. Both Ibn al-Hanafiyyah and Abu Hashem stood close to members of Hasan's circle and are said to have had a good deal of influence on Wasil himself. At any rate, Wasil likely attended school with Abu Hashem at the first-ever *kuttab*—an educational institution for younger scholars reportedly founded by the latter's father. Abu Hashem, even more than Ibn al-Hanafiyyah, was known for association, both intellectually and in terms of active political involvement, with the movement of armed opposition (*al-Kaysaniyyah*) that eventually took over the Kufa region, then extended its rule into Persia, India, and Armenia. The rage of such opposition groups against the Umayyads was understandably exacerbated by the killings of Ibn Hanafiyyah, al-Hasan, and al-Hussein during the early battles against the caliph's armies.

The official foundation of Mu'tazilism is associated with Wasil—specifically, with the position he took in the dispute about what becomes of a Muslim who commits a grave sin. However, it is probably safe to assume that he owes this distinction more to having articulated, explicated, and elaborated views and sympathies that were current among opposition groups at the time (e.g., freedom of the will and the createdness of the Qur'an) than to having originated these views in the first place. Inasmuch as such positions were also connected to the Prophet's rightful succession line, they may be regarded as political, too. Indeed, what we know about Wasil's history confirms that he was an ideological activist in addition to being a theoretician, for he sent his students to carry his teachings to places as far away as Persia and Armenia (where anti-Umayyad princedoms had begun to spring up). Later, his followers and admirers fondly recalled two qualities that distinguished him in addition to his keen intelligence: his inordinately long neck and his inability to pronounce the letter *r*! His neck would hardly have impeded his speaking abilities, but his enunciation impediment certainly might have. Even this feature added to his renown, however, for he is said to have commanded language so skillfully, and to have possessed such verbal artistry, that he could rephrase an entire poem, and express its full meaning, while avoiding sounds he could not voice eloquently.

Only two years after Wasil's death, the Abbassids toppled the Umayyads and assumed power. Initially, they made Kufa (Iraq) their capital, but then moved it to the newly built metropolis of Baghdad. In both early and later battles, they received the aid of Shi'ite opposition groups already in existence, which joined Abbas's armies in the hope that their rightful leadership over the Muslim community would finally be restored: after all, the Abbasids descended from the Banu Hashem—that is, the Prophet's line—and therefore stood closer to Ali's constituencies than did the Banu Umayyah (Umayyads). However, the Abbassids clung firmly to power once it lay in their hands—for over five hundred years; eventually, they became the target of Shi'ite militancy themselves.

Wasil's school, once marginalized and harassed under the Umayyads, could operate more freely, and even flourish, under the Abbassids. In due course—especially after paper-mill technology was introduced from China (see the next chapter)—the debates conducted at Basrah could be recorded more fully, and their incredible logical rigor made plain. When the Abbassid caliphate officially relocated to Baghdad, members of the Mu'tazilite school moved there, too. In the following decades, they were free to pursue their calling as dialecticians and philosophers.

As the center of the vast Abbassid dynasty, Baghdad witnessed rapid urban and cultural development. Home to the celebrated caliph Haroun al-Rashid, the majestic city provided the setting for wondrous fables told during and after his rule. (Tales about Sinbad, as well as *The One Thousand and One Nights* are associated with this period, in addition to the famous lyrics of Abu Nuwas about love and wine.) What is more, Baghdad became the "mecca" of intellectuals and scientists from near and far. Significantly, they included Christian scholars from Nusaybin. One of the more enigmatic figures in the history of science, Jabir Ibn Hayyan—who played a key role in founding experimental chemistry and identifying the elements that would later yield the periodic table—is said to have lived and worked under the auspices of Haroun. Under the reign of the latter's second son, al-Ma'mun (who ruled from 813 to 833), Baghdad acquired the title that has decorated it ever since: the capital of Islam's "Golden Age."

Perhaps Mu'tazilite scholars sensed that a new breed of empirical and technical thinkers was slowly beginning to overshadow, if not replace, them at the House of Wisdom in Baghdad; perhaps they felt they were now so firmly established within the hierarchy of political power that they could transpose their tenets into official dogma. At any rate, the once-suppressed rationalists and supporters of free will repositioned themselves to become the voice of an authoritarian ideology. In yet another of the many religious crises in Islam's history, what came to be called *al-mihnah*—"examination," sometimes referred to as "the Muslim version of the inquisition"—occurred. Now, it was anti-Mu'tazilite religious scholars who were pursued, harassed, and forced to renounce their views. The main item of contention was whether the Qur'an was created or co-eternal with God. Al-Ma'mun initiated the *mihnah* during the last year of his reign (833)—a surprising event inasmuch as he otherwise demonstrated great tolerance for different beliefs—and his successors continued it. Its victims included Ibn Hanbal (780–855), an esteemed scholar to whom what later came to be known as the orthodox (Sunni) school of Islam owes a major part of its codex. (By the same token, he was "responsible" for the backlash against the Mu'tazilites that occurred later, when their books were burnt and they were forced to hide—ultimately, almost disappearing from the Sunni world altogether.) Reportedly, he was tortured so that he would renounce his opposition to the createdness of the Qur'an.

Well-respected for his piety, Ibn Hanbal considered himself an exegete and a legal scholar; he had devoted his life to the explication of the Qur'anic text and the sayings of the Prophet for the daily use of believers. That was all Muslims needed in order to live their religious lives. He did not think—as the Mu'tazilites did—that he had earth-shaking doctrines or a philosophy of his own to propose; indeed, he would probably have considered anyone making such claims an intellectual impostor. Equally—and as his predecessor and the other great figure of this tradition, Abu Hanifa (702–772), saw matters—he did not believe that the political realm held sovereignty over the religious realm. Indeed, Muslims answer only to the Qur'an and the Prophet's sayings, not to political rulers. In contrast, the Mu'tazilites (and likeminded contemporaries) were political players and took it upon themselves to develop a vast body of theoretical doctrines both to expound their own beliefs and to defend them against others (among others, Zoroastrians, Manichaean dualists, Christians, and Jews, in addition to Muslim rivals). Unlike Abu Hanfia and Ibn Hanbal, who concentrated on legal interpretation, they were concerned with the "meta-problems" of religion; the more down-to-earth matter of what believers needed in order to conduct their daily lives interested them little. These divergent points of focus eventually developed into the two disciplines of *kalam*, speculative discourse about God and the world anchored in speech, and *fiqh*, the explication of Islamic law; both disciplines are rationalist, but they apply to different fields and address different needs. As an independently minded religious scholar, Abu Hanifa died in prison for refusing to place his religious scholarship in service to the caliph; Ibn Hanbal met with the same fate for refusing to legitimate a caliph's religious ruling concerning the Qur'an's createdness.

Scholars have observed that the full body of orthodox (Sunni) belief that eventually emerged represents an outgrowth and systemization of responses to the different legal and theological challenges posed by various schools ultimately deemed to have strayed from the right path—including, first and foremost, the Mu'tazilites. Standard accounts present Ibn Hanbal as the heroic forerunner of this systematic articulation. In time, four main schools of orthodox jurisprudence developed in Islam; their foundational principles (*usul*) may represent the first-ever systematization of what we would now call a theory or philosophy of law (see Chapter 9). All the same, the *mihna* crisis continues to occasion wonder to this day: did the extreme measures taken to rationalize the faith backfire and leave the Muslim world with a religion that resists modernization? Did the *politicization* of religion (from either end, whether by rulers or Mu'tazilites) set the tone for it to become an item of public contention rather than evolving more naturally and tolerantly as a code of ethics in the private sphere?

Early Islam

Literacy, Conflict, and Expansion

So far we have sketched, in broad strokes, the evolution of ideas across a fairly long period—some two centuries—from the Prophet's death in 632 to the *mihna*, which was instituted in 833. Over the same course of time, political conditions underwent drastic, even revolutionary, change. Needless to say, the developments had an impact on both the form and the content of intellectual history. A quick overview of the radical transformations follows.

Ibn Hanbal's *mihna* took place under that Abbasid caliphate. This is paradoxical inasmuch as it occurred during what is known as the beginning of Islam's most glorious epoch, which witnessed a flourishing intellectual climate, the establishment of the famed House of Wisdom in Baghdad, and the rationalist pursuit of knowledge in different fields. All of these developments drew on an influx of translated material from ancient Greek, Persian, and Indian civilizations, facilitated by a new medium that allowed professional writing to flourish. The intellectual drama of the age unfolded thanks to the use of paper—one of the major turning points of intellectual history on a global scale. Invented in China (and broadly used there by the seventh century, at the latest), it was taken up throughout the Islamic world within a hundred years. Records extant in China today confirm that the Umayyads and the Abbassids entertained alliances and vigorous commercial relations with the Tang dynasty. Paper mills—and, with them, vast professional and trade activity (scribes, librarians, "paper shops," etc.)—spread along the Tigris and further still. While the number of volumes housed in the House of Wisdom (established in the early

ninth century) is not known precisely, collections in twelfth-century Muslim Spain (including the library attached to the Great Mosque of Cordoba)
boasted over a million titles. Annually, some sixty thousand manuscripts of
varying lengths were produced; in contrast, the largest Christian libraries
of the day, in Paris and Avignon, held only two thousand "books."

By the end of the ninth century, Baghdad production facilities using
primitive assembly lines had made it possible for customers to visit over a
hundred "paper shops" in one suburb alone; here, one might find a religious treatise, a translation of *Kalilah and Dimnah*,[1] Aristotle's *Topics*, or
the works of Ptolemy. A new milieu emerged where philosophers, translators, poets, and jurists could meet by chance, engage in long or short exchanges, or merely catch sight of their peers (as still occurs today in the
handful of university bookshops that remain). Matters of interest for later
historians abound—for example, the mention made by the famous Ibn
al-Nadim (d. 990) in his invaluable *Fihrist* (in just a few lines, as he did
not yet know the intellectual worth of the party in question) of a young
student of philosophy going through manuscripts for sale in one of these
stores, a certain Alfarabi; it would be another two hundred years before
this scholar came to be recognized as one of Islam's most important philosophers—the "Second Master," after Aristotle.

The importance of the "paper revolution" is impossible to overem-
phasize. Indeed, it bears comparison to two major industrial leaps later in
history: the invention of moveable type in the sixteenth century and digital
technologies today. The quantitative and qualitative strides made as a result
of the dissemination of knowledge on paper had an incalculable effect on
intellectual history. (Chapter 24 will tell the somewhat sad tale of printing
in the Muslim world.) The discovery of paper and its many uses changed
the proverbial game. Prior to this point, practices of writing—that is, the
materials and instruments involved—resembled a child's movements before it learns to walk. When the dominant medium of transmission was
still memory and spoken language, the scribes who wrote down the Qur'an
had relied on camel bone, animal hides, and parchment.

Indeed, the oldest known copy of the full text of the Qur'an on paper
dates from 971 or 972; it was found in Persia.[2] Of course, Arabic script
predated the age of paper mills; as we have noted, it is believed to derive from the Nabatean, Phoenician, and Aramaic alphabets. But the oldest extant parchment containing the Arabic text in its final form is dated

25 April 643, eleven years after the Prophet's death; this short excerpt, which has the form of an exchange receipt, was found in Egypt. Presumably, the same script was used in the lost Uthman compendium.

The introduction of paper revolutionized the use of writing. Like the Chinese, the Umayyads adopted the medium of paper for administrative and financial recordkeeping[3]; naturally, it also served in correspondence. However, only in the Abbasid period did its use become "public"; now, the focus fell on translating and disseminating literature. This application proved instrumental in the development of Arabic analytic and logical skills—as reflected in the fertile creativity of the rationalist literature of the day: jurisprudence, theology, philosophy, and the various sciences. Poetry alone remained unaffected, perhaps. At the time, the verbal art depended more on sound than on script—indeed, the same still holds in our own times.

Just as breathtaking as the story of literacy is the spread of Islam from Medina—the city to which the Prophet and his companions escaped to avoid persecution after an attempt on his life. By the reign of the second caliph, Umar, the entirety of Arabia (including Jerusalem) already lay in Muslim hands. By the time of Mu'awiyah I, the founder of the Umayyad dynasty (651–650), Muslim rule spanned the broadest territory the world had seen until then, reaching west from North Africa to the Atlantic Ocean, and eastward onto the Indian subcontinent.[4] The Arabic of the Qur'an provided the *lingua franca* of intellectual discourse, even though Arabs were now vastly outnumbered by the populations of the countries that had fallen under Islamic rule.

From the beginning, many who raised their voices and achieved fame and status were of non-Arab descent, *mawali*. Like Hasan's mother, their families were "brought back" to provide services to the conquerors. Although the Umayyad dynasty enacted politically repressive measures against Muslim opponents, it is said to have shown tolerance toward non-Muslim communities and to have let them live in relative security. In some places—such as Greater Syria, where Christianity prevailed—these groups constituted the larger part of the population. Indeed, Mu'awiyah's wife was Christian. Local Monophysite and Nestorian Christians (as well as Zoroastrian troops) helped Mu'awiyah to victory in his maritime battles against the Byzantines. (An especially significant combat was what has come to be known as "The Battle of the Masts," in which more than seven hundred enemy ships are reported to have been sunk.) Some historians have argued that Umayyad rulers showed tolerance at least partly for financial reasons—that the tax (*jizya*) levied on non-Muslim communities in return for their security and nonintervention in affairs was incentive enough not to encourage conversion. At any rate, the policy was reversed in the Abbasid era.

Under the second Islamic caliphate, accomplishments in administration and architecture proved just as impressive. The mosques in Damascus and Jerusalem still stand as prime examples. Here as elsewhere, the Umayyads spared no effort in recruiting and employing the most skilled professionals, including Christians and Jews (many of whom had gained experience serving the Byzantine Empire).

These early achievements are all the more remarkable for having occurred in the midst of internal conflict and feuds over the legitimacy of succession. The battles raged so fiercely that the site of Islam's early rise—Medina itself—was besieged by Mu'awiyah's son, Yazid; if they escaped the slaughter, the city's inhabitants died of the diseases that followed. Nor was Mecca—the holiest of holies, the birthplace of the Prophet, and the home to al-Ka'ba—spared the wrath of Yazid and his engines of destruction. These shocking events seem to have amounted to a revolution turning against itself, bent on destroying its origins, even as military exploits abroad announced triumphs reaching farther than could ever have been imagined.

In this context, it is worth remarking the split that occurred within the selfsame rationalist movement which had been inspired by freedom and courageously called for free will. One might have expected freedom and rationalism to form a pair, neither part of which would allow the other to be discarded. However, from the inception, they were torn asunder. How this early split influenced the ways Islam evolved in practical terms—becoming a more and more restrictive system—remains a matter of conjecture. Let us recall that Muhammad's message, in many ways, was nothing less than a cry for freedom—both intellectually, as a call to break out of confining beliefs and mental habits, and an inspiration to seek, in rational fashion, an explanation for how the world functions. Early religious scholars rose to defend doctrines of justice and free will against the standing political authorities, and they drew upon Qur'anic sources to do so. Ma'bad and Ghaylan are exemplary in this regard, as are the Mu'tazilites. All the same, and as we have seen, Bashar was expelled first from Hasan's circle, and then from

Basra itself. Moreover, when the Abbassids assumed power in Baghdad, the libertine poet was done away with altogether—and at the instigation of the Mu'tazilites, at that.[5] Above all, the ideological campaign which was waged against religious scholars to force them to declare that the Qur'an had been created stands as a grim reminder of how religious authority, when it occupies a position of political power, can restrict freedom of thought; the same holds for later backlashes against the Mu'tazilites themselves, which led to their banishment and their books being burned.

On the other hand, one should hardly characterize the Umayyad era as a time when freedom flourished. On the contrary—and despite the indulgence shown to non-Muslims—the ruthless treatment of ideological opponents, the executions of Jahm and Ja'd, the sacrilegious destruction of Medina and al-Ka'ba, and the carefree debauchery of some of the caliphs all reflected the fruits of authoritarian government. As has occurred on many other occasions in history, a clique reserved for itself the right to live above the law, breaking every rule the population assumed it was held to observe.

Notwithstanding its military, architectural, and administrative feats, the Umayyad government was corrupt and authoritarian. As such, it could only provoke an opposition movement calling for freedom. However, it also follows that this movement was by necessity puritanical—imposing rules and restrictions on belief and behavior. In this light, one must read the fate of Bashar—and others—contrived by Hasan and Wasil (whose positions later Mu'tazilite doctrine affirmed) as a puritanical reaction to the excesses of the Umayyads. It is only logical, perhaps, that the leaders of the movement for free thought set out to impose strict moral rules and limitations from the outset. Even at this early phase, then, the "cyclical" pattern of alternation between opposites in the history of Islam may already have been set. Muslim societies are still plagued by this "tug-of-war"—between secular nationalism and Islamism, for instance—which marked the last century. A balance, such as the Qur'an itself calls for (and which prevails in some other cultures), still has not been struck; Muslim society—especially in Arab countries, if not in other places such as Indonesia or Turkey—remains undecided about the margin of freedom to allow for difference.

Needless to say, history's twists and turns make a mockery of sweeping generalizations. The caliphs (whether Umayyad or Abbasid) were not all cut from the same cloth. But the founders of the doctrine of free will were not concerned with propagating individual moral freedom or liberal values: their teachings concerned only religious responsibility and the just-ness of reward and punishment. Consequently, we should not be aston-ished that when the Mu'tazilite movement gained the upper hand, its leaders and followers did not protest the *mihna*—the inquisition that sub-jected scholars like the pious Ibn Hanbal to torture (discounting the even worse possibility that Mu'tazilites had in fact instigated and campaigned for such practices). Umayyad battles against Ali and his descendants, bra-zen disrespect for the holy cities of Mecca and Medina, and the dissolute lifestyles of many rulers amply justified popular support for the Abbasid uprising. However, the question remains whether Islam did not lose, in the midst of that early political turmoil, what then as now guarantees a healthy social order integrating the two elements of progress: freedom and reason.

The Abbasid caliphate started with the final defeat of the Umay-yads in 750. It lasted—with internal political turmoil and dissension of its own—until its capital, Baghdad, was sacked by Hulagu Khan in 1258. The library, housing untold treasures from both the Arab and classical worlds, burned to the ground; only a few manuscripts, reportedly saved by the fa-mous astronomer and philosopher, Nasir al-Din Tusi (d. 1274), survived. The Abbasid system of government was so decentralized that when Bagh-dad fell, for all intents and purposes the last, overarching Islamic caliph-ate vanished. The Muslim world came to be ruled by different, contending dynasties in different regions. The Umayyads, though defeated in the east, managed to reorder their ranks in the course of time and revive their old glory by crossing the Strait of Gibraltar. In Andalusia, the brilliance of their civilization shone forth, untainted by the excesses of their ancestors and augmented by the patronage of scientific pursuits. At the same time, Islamic rule in Spain was marred by internecine conflict: different dynas-ties (the Almohads and the Almoravids) vied for power, while Christians rose against the Muslim raids now reaching deep into the European con-tinent. For all that, politically unstable Muslim Spain brought forth intel-lectual titans such as Averroes and Maimonides, whose mark on posterity proved enduring.

Elsewhere, the Islamic world had begun to disaggregate. Princedoms, kingdoms, and even self-proclaimed caliphates—some of Sunni and others of Shi'ite origin—shot up in the vast expanse that had formerly been united under single rule. The major caliphates were the Fatimids (tenth to twelfth centuries), the Mamlukans (thirteenth to sixteenth centuries), the Ayyubids, and the Ottomans; the latter lasted until Ataturk declared it dead in 1924. In the process, other countries and regions came to adopt versions of Islam, with inflections that varied according to native systems of theology and legal interpretation. Surveying the Islamic world today, from Africa to southwest Asia, one still finds the remnants of these schools of thought: Ibadiyyas and Zaydiyyas in Oman and the Yemen, Shi'ites and Alawites in Iran and Greater Syria, and new forms of Sunni belief such as Wahhabism in Saudi Arabia.

However, somewhere in the course of these developments—most likely in seventeenth-century Persia, with what has come to be known as the school of Isfahan—Islam's story of reason reached its end.[6] To arrive at this point, we must trace its journey, which began in Basra and then proceeded from the Abbasid capital of Baghdad. In so doing, we will also need to look more closely at the story's contents.

Speculative Discourse

A Style

The *mihnah* subjected Ibn Hanbal—and other religious scholars—to torture and trial to make them declare, against their beliefs, that the Qur'an had been created. This "inquisition" brings into relief the divergence between two very important rationalist disciplines in Islam: *kalam* (speculative discourse) and *fiqh* (law). Scholars in both fields began with the analytic study of religious texts. Above all, they consulted the Qur'an; experts in jurisprudence also looked closely at the Prophet's sayings. Legal thinkers pursued the down-to-earth matter of trying to systematize human relations within the community of believers: how the law ordains that people should live, and why this is the case. In contrast, *kalam* set its sights higher and asked questions broader in scope. Here, the task was to understand the relationship between God and the world: to articulate, in rational terms, a universal system consistent with religious belief and to develop a holistic theory of knowledge. Ultimately, then, the difference between the two disciplines concerns theory and text. Although a few later Mu'tazilites, such as al-Jahiz (d. 869), were drawn to empirical study, practitioners of *kalam* never really developed a serious interest in "science" comparable to the attention it received from a third school of rationalism, *falsafa* ("philosophy"), which Nestorians in Baghdad facilitated. While legal scholars focused on how to translate scripture into regulations governing the everyday lives of Muslims, speculative discourse scholars focused on how to develop a theory of knowledge that would rationally explain God's relationship with the created world.

Different translations have been proposed for *kalam* (which is the term the scholars themselves used for their discipline): "theology," "speculative dialectics," and "dialectical theology." The translation here—"speculative discourse"—is meant to capture the broadness of the endeavor. On the one hand, it distinguishes *kalam* from *falsafa* (which derived from Greek sources, as we will see in later chapters), whose practitioners for the most part also drew inspiration from the empirical sciences of the day; on the other hand, "speculative discourse" highlights the fact that *kalam* sought to offer ontological and epistemological theories about the world distinct from theology in the strict sense (even if they ultimately depended on it).

If interest in "science" set *falsafa* apart from *kalam*, is it possible to identify a feature that distinguished *kalam*, as its practitioners defined it, from *falsafa*? To be sure, its dialogical method of argument stands out. Strangely, what has gone relatively unnoticed is—as we have noted—that it called itself a science of *speech*. The analytic methods employed to determine meanings and devise theories—unlike those that came to typify *falsafa*—drew chiefly on the contextual use of language. In particular, as we will see in the next chapter and later on, practitioners of *kalam* shied away from granting existential status to the referents of abstract nouns (for example, "justice," "knowledge," and "will")—unlike the "philosophers," who did so gladly. Instead of constructing their theories by hypothesizing metaphysical levels of existence thought to "house" such meanings, they examined usage and context; the task was to determine, say, what *being just* means in common speech—in both behavioral and psychological terms. In so doing, they pursued what, at the time, counted as a natural method for evaluating significance among speakers. They likely took their cue from the fact that, to understand what the Qur'an says about the world, one has to focus on meanings within language, as it were. Even the abstract noun *'aql* ("reason" or "intellect"), prized by philosophers as the instrument for gaining knowledge, is not mentioned once in the Qur'an, whereas related forms—verbs, adjectives, and participles—occur in abundance; this indicates an emphasis on *actions*, or human behavior, as reflected in and performed through speech, rather than ontic entities.

A *kalam* scholar could also be a jurist; thereby, he would enlist the doctrines of the school to which he belonged. As a legal thinker, he would rely on the text of the Qur'an and follow the guidance afforded by his *kalam* background. He would strive to determine specific judgments on different particular issues either by applying general rules, if these existed in the Qur'an, or—as was more generally the case—by eliciting judgments from particular examples: specific incidents in the life of the Prophet, or specific edicts in the Qur'an itself. As we will see, different schools of jurisprudence evolved in the course of time. They all adhered to traditional transmission, but some hewed more closely to the letter of the text than others. Ibn Hanbal, for example, was more of a literalist than others; the clash that occurred between him and his supporters, on the one hand, and with Mu'tazilites (as well as practitioners of speculative discourse more generally), on the other, was of singular intensity. But however much they disagreed, both sides affirmed the eternal nature of the sacred text.[1]

The necessary point of departure for, and ever-recurring focus of, all rational discourse in the *kalam* discipline was God: His will as opposed to human will, and His attributes as distinct from His transcendental, unitary nature. All the same, speculation soon extended to areas of inquiry that may be described as philosophical in a broader sense—for instance, the question of what it means for human beings to act, and for such actions to qualify as good or evil; what it means to acquire and possess knowledge; how a body is constituted as physical matter, and what it means for it to occupy, and move in, space—or how its dimensional or accidental properties (e.g., taste, smell, and shape) relate to its unchanging essence. Mu'tazilites did not necessarily always agree. Theoretical differences manifested even between father and son (for example, between the famous Jubba'i scholars in the tenth century, whom we will meet in the next chapter). What is more, once translation made philosophical works and other writings from abroad available, the scope of inquiry naturally expanded; some thinkers even incorporated Greek theories into the corpus of texts meriting analytic attention and critique.

The common denominator uniting all scholars of *kalam* was their style: a mode of discourse that involved the labyrinthine, crisscrossing interplay of ideas expressed in ordinary language and exchanged by interlocutors, whether imagined or real. Where did this style come from? Did it simply and straightforwardly copy the dialectical method of a preexisting tradition (e.g., Greek philosophy, as some historians have suggested)? It seems more likely, in my view, that it was a "homegrown" method dictated by practical necessity more than a ready-made template imported from elsewhere. The dialogical style originated in real-life situations (e.g., the discussion sessions of Hasan's circle), using the common language of the day—when the lively discussion of ideas could neither be tape-recorded nor written down; it was both easy and instructive to remember "argu-ment-bytes" and pass them along orally. The process came to constitute a distinctive feature of written heritage, too. Typically, an author would develop his thesis argument by argument (instead of outlining it in a complete, self-contained piece of prose). At each step, a hypothetical op-ponent's response is interposed, and then shown to be invalid. The line of argumentation moves forward and is then interrupted again by a question, challenge, or attempt to show a contradiction in what has been said.

If the works of Abd al-Jabbar are representative, discourse practitio-ners of later generations adopted a specific point of view, position, or argu-ment; then, they addressed all the objections raised by their predecessors. In so doing, they carved out space for their own, new contributions or objections. Over time, a massive battery of *kalam*-specific concepts devel-oped in this manner; each part building on the other, it yielded a coherent theoretical edifice. To be sure, many of these concepts admit comparison to related concepts from Greek or other sources. All the same, basic catego-ries such as motion and rest, cause and condition, divisible and indivisible, and so on, must provide the operative concepts for any culture interested in knowledge.

The method, or style, distinguishing *kalam* likely derived from oral records of debates in what we would now call "discussion groups." The scene one should picture is not a solitary scholar seated at a candle-lit desk well into the night, writing in academese, and answering only the ques-tions that occur to him as he writes one line after the next. A more apt image is a master class: the teacher or facilitator leads discussion in real-time and in language as it is spoken, with interlocutors who may be physi-cally present or not. All the while, he seeks to develop the thesis he wishes his students to accept and, in addition, tries to sharpen their ability to present ideas in their own right; when confronted with objections, they should be able to defend them. Accordingly, it was only logical for argu-ments to be presented one by one and step by step; in the process, par-ticipants could raise questions on their own initiative, or do so when the discussion leader called for pause and reflection before moving on. The lectures, monologues, and public readings of scholarly papers so famil-iar today would not have achieved the results desired; nor would such ap-proaches have been realistic in a group meeting held at a quiet corner in a mosque's precinct.

We can also imagine how, as the practice became more established, students would sit in a circle around the prominent scholar leading them, each holding a writing pad on his knees and taking notes as the teacher ran through the arguments as convention now dictated. When a new idea was presented, or when they remained unconvinced by an answer, one of them would interject a question or a voice a challenge. Many sects—including Mu'tazilitism—are reported to have arisen under such circumstances.

However, this is not the way that all schools of thought originated. Other rationalist disciplines dating to this period—for example, *usul al-fiqh* (jurisprudence), *falsafa* (philosophy), *usul al-lugha* (linguistics), and Ibn Khaldun's "science of society" (as it called itself)—for the most part retained conventional forms of discourse. *Fiqh*, which focused on the actual rules prescribed to the community of believers, represented a practice of discourse inasmuch as it addressed specific issues of proper behavior that a believer might ask about; like *kalam*, it involved questions and answers, but was not actually dialectical. To a certain extent, it remains the same today. An example being debated at this very moment involves what to do when the new moon has not been observed by the naked eye to verify the end of Ramadan and the beginning of a new month. What happens when fasting has lasted only twenty-eight days and everyone concurs that, scientifically speaking, the new moon must have already risen, *but* the moon was observed late the previous month and the sun has now set too late for the new moon to be seen? Should believers continue to fast for the twenty-ninth day, thereby fulfilling the injunction to fast the whole (lunar) month? And what if, by some chance, the new moon has indeed been observed? Are believers then required to stop fasting and begin their feast? These, and similar legal conundrums, are the province of religious legalists to whom believers turn for guidance in daily life. Accordingly, the style in this discipline is often dialogical, but it tends to take a question-and-answer form, rather than presenting a sequence of arguments. Jurisprudence, on the other hand (and as we will see in detail later on), adopted a conventional prose style.

Kalam began as a discursive practice among scholars, exegetes, dissidents, political activists, poets, and other seekers of knowledge; it developed as a mode of oral argumentation in Basrah, where it expressed an intellectual community's efforts to delineate parameters for pressing ethical and metaphysical questions. Its origin in common speech granted it a natural and spontaneous quality no other discipline possessed, which must have invigorated the evolution of the inquisitive and analytic frame of mind associated with the "Age of Reason" in Islam. In the further course of history, its unique style continued to define, preserve, and promote inquiry. As writing and literacy spread and its practitioners moved to Baghdad and elsewhere, different schools of thought branched off and became established in their own right. Even though it is impossible to present a complete account of the intellectual expanse the practice achieved, the next chapter will provide a few glimpses into this (largely uncharted) territory.

8

Discourse

In Pursuit of the Ultimate Answers

(I) Attributes

Kalam began, as we have seen, by espousing and developing views about God and His relationship to the world. The two fundamental questions were whether the Qur'an was created, and whether human beings are responsible agents—that is, whether they possess free will. Quickly, speculation extended to other areas of inquiry. Throughout, the guiding principle was to arrive at a rational understanding of the world and our place within it as moral beings. This issue immediately raised the question of what it means to affirm that God is just. From the outset, then, scholars debated whether, and in what manner, God may be said to have attributes. Are His qualities or properties indistinguishable from Him? Are they constitutive of His essence? Would it be better to affirm that He "is" some of them—or none of them at all?

In this context, the most elementary distinction concerned physical properties (e.g., dimensionality or visibility), on the one hand, and qualitative descriptions (omnipotence, omniscience, benevolence), on the other. In the Qur'an, God is described in both ways. Unlike their later opponents, Mu'tazilite scholars did not believe that God has physical properties, and they interpreted passages in the Qur'an that suggested He had them—for example, when He is described as having a face or sitting on a throne metaphorically. All the same, they faced the problem of accounting for qualities that bear on matters of free will and responsibility. God does not "sit" anywhere; still, He *is* just.

But in what sense may God be said to have justice or to be just? Clearly, one first has to determine what *justice* means. How does one do so?

Rather than assuming (as Plato did, for instance) that some abstract meaning exists which one has to search for by way of a mental process, scholars turned their attention to situations where human beings are described
as being just, to see whether an account for justice could be provided at
this level. In other words, they sought to explain the matter without first
conferring existence on some kind of abstract entity or property called
"justice" which they could then ascribe to human beings by saying they
somehow "have it." A major concern was to avoid granting some kind of
independent existence to justice, which they would then have to account
for as *something else* when describing God as just. This would be anathema
to them, given their belief in His pure unicity. Accordingly, another approach was required to explain how attributes may be predicated of subjects. The approach that scholars took—examining the sense in which
justice is ascribed to human beings in order to explain what it means to ascribe justice to God—is telling. Basically, their method involved refusing
to accept a discourse about God that did not make sense in terms of reason at the level of human experience. (Needless to say, their considerations
took for granted that, even though He did not possess properties, he was
both One and just "by nature.")

One early attempt—typical of this "reductionist" method, which allowed matters to be interpreted in terms of human conduct—involved the
claim that when we are said to act justly, or to be just, only two matters
stand before us: the particular behavior or action that is deemed just, and
the cause or circumstance that motivates it. Muʿammar al-Sulami (d. 842)
proposed the term *maʿna* to introduce what we might understand as a
"function" or variable: a circumstance or cause (other than justice itself)
which accounts for someone being just or for being described as exhibit-
ing justice or acting justly. As a function—a cause external to the property or behavior described, which is different from what might otherwise
be claimed to be the abstract meaning of justice—*maʿna* shifts the focus
from the level of second-order ontology (whereby justice would be a primary idea or meaning) and reduces it to the level of the specific behavior
or disposition being explained; here, it is something other than the behavior or disposition at issue, namely, what causes it. As a variable, any such
explanation must change in keeping with the given situation. Why we are
said to be just on any specific occasion may differ based on any number
of circumstances. In each case, the conditions affording an explanation

are specific: so-and-so is just because she returned to someone his due, or because she refused to take what she was not entitled to claim for herself. Although the action and the cause are separate from one another, they are laterally correlated at the primary level of human behavior. Where God is concerned, however, the Mu'tazilites argued that He Himself—simply by "being who or what He is"—provides the cause or condition for His being just. In this instance, God and the *ma'na* are one. Thus, whether justice, omniscience, or life stands at issue, the concept of *ma'na* reconciles the matter of attribution, on the one hand, and the affirmation that God does not possess properties, on the other.

Of course, one might claim that shifting the focus in this way (from reified properties to accounts or causes) simply means pushing the same problem to another level of abstraction—that it amounts to a linguistic or technical ploy rather than a substantive logical argument. Indeed, the proposal was challenged even within the Mu'tazilite tradition. However, the objection did not hold that the proposal was simply a linguistic game; rather, it was argued that introducing a function of this kind entails a process to be repeated *ad infinitum*: each *ma'na*, opponents held, requires another *ma'na* to explain why this particular account—and not a different one—is needed in the first place. No particular account can be self-explanatory; it requires justification in turn, and so on, repeatedly. (Significantly, although such iteration would not apply to the relationship between God and justice—the real reason for introducing the theory—the approach was deemed inadequate because it proved problematic when explaining things at a human level.)

A later Mu'tazilite, the elder Jubba'i (d. 915) did not accept Mu'ammar's proposal fully. However, because it showed a possible way to avoid affirming the existence of abstract entities or nonphysical properties in subjects, he agreed that it pointed in the direction to be taken. In lieu of a function entailing the need for further functions without end, Jubba'i proposed that a particular condition or state (*hal*) in a subject explains the manifestation of the relevant conduct. That is, when such a state holds, the party in question will be said, by virtue of this state, to have a will, to possess knowledge, to be just, and so on. If Mu'ammar's *ma'na* seemed ungrounded (inasmuch as each explanation requires another), Jubba'i's *hal* sought to affirm the connection between behavioral display (e.g., an act of justice) and what explains it by attaching the latter to the acting subject as some kind of condition or state. For example, when we say someone is angry, this is the case because a certain state or condition holds for him or her, which makes him or her exhibit what we identify as "being angry." The person is angry in the sense that, or because, a state of anger grips him or her.

Jubba'i's proposal did not catch on. It was rejected by even his own son—who belonged to the same Mu'tazilite school. The younger Jubba'i (d. 933) considered the idea of a state or condition too "physical," which made it difficult to apply to God—the ultimate reason for pursuing these debates. (*Hal* implies the related word *mahall*—the physical location where this state holds.) All the same, the general concept of a condition or state (e.g., the condition or state by virtue of which someone may be said to *have* knowledge) remained in use. This may have occurred because, like Mu'ammar's *ma'na*, it means something other than a property or quality: it refers to a psychological or behavioral frame of experience that may be identified in people. It may also have continued to be used because it provided a way to "tie down" what the party in question displays by proposing that a mode of *being* makes him or her act as she or he does; this avoids the residual externality implied by Mu'ammar's theory.

All the same, one wonders what defines the condition posited by Jubba'i. How does *being* in a state of knowledge differ from *having* knowledge? More important, what is the exact relationship between the state and the behavior to be explained? Is the state a *cause* for the behavior, as *ma'na* is supposed to be—for instance that my being in a state of anger causes me to be angry when someone steps on my foot? Surely, having my foot stepped on is what has made me angry, not the state. Moreover, if a state or condition obtains in a person, wouldn't it be an attribute or a property the person can be said to *have*? In other words, wouldn't the person have a condition, instead of the property it supposedly brings about? Worse still, wouldn't the person have, as properties, both the condition and what it brings about?

While perfectly legitimate, these questions lose their urgency (for us) in light of the gradual shift within the tradition of speculative discourse, away from attributing predicates to subjects in ontological terms toward a psychological viewpoint.[1] Rather than assuming that something called "justice" must exist concretely, one can attribute "being just" to a subject by simply focusing on behavior in evidence, which can be referred back to a cause/circumstance or to a psychological state/condition.

Both Muʿammar's *maʿna* and Jubbaʾi's *hal* make having-a-property into a state-of-being, through which particular behaviors are in turn displayed. Whereas *maʿna* still seemed vague (that is, not clearly connected to a particular agent), *hal* tied the condition or circumstance in question to what the agent actually experiences—even though many questions remained unanswered.

In this context, the question arises to what extent classical Arabic, language as spoken at the time, was invested in discourse about the existence of abstract entities—as held, for example, in traditions imported from Greece (e.g., Platonic forms and Aristotelian verbal accidents). During the same period, ideas of this kind came to animate philosophical discussion in Baghdad. Alfarabi, for one, exerted great effort to explain how the Greek verb "to be" (which has no cognate in Arabic) was semantically embedded in subject-predicate statements irrespective of natural language; thereby he affirmed the *existence* of the predicate *in* or *for* the subject (see Chapters 10 and 11). Given that the Arabic these scholars employed (in contrast to the language of Alfarabi, for example) did not have any conceptual stakes in the existence of second- and third-order substances (e.g., those referred to by abstract nouns) and connected directly to everyday, practical interactions, it may have been more natural for them to focus on the normal behavior of speakers (i.e., context-based language practices) when trying to explain what it means to say someone is just, knowledgeable, or virtuous; this pragmatic focus dispenses with the need to affirm the existence of one thing in, or for, another.[2]

At any rate, Abd al-Jabbar combined the two functions introduced by the two Baghdad Muʿtazilites and offered what arguably represents a more comprehensive and mature theory. For him, states are not physical properties or attributes that require corporeal "containers"; nor, for that matter, are they esoteric or abstract forms or entities. They are simply psychological conditions or experiences. As he explained it, one simply finds oneself in (i.e., experiences) a particular state—hope, belief, or wonder, for instance—that one can readily distinguish from being in another state. States are what one experiences. One intuitively knows that one is experiencing this state and not another one. There is no reason to distinguish between *my being angry* when someone steps on my toe and *my state of anger*—no reason to think of the latter as a *maʿna*, or cause, for the former: they are one and the same. Furthermore, the entire project of seeking to define what being angry is (is it a state, a property, a cause?) as a prelude to determining whether I am angry (or just, or wondering, etc.) is misguided: it is mistaken to think we are required to posit and define what justice or anger are before experiencing being just or anger. We know, directly and intuitively, what being just is, just as we know, directly and intuitively, what anger is, simply from experiencing such states. Post-experientially, we form our ideas about states and what they mean. Ideas do not precede experiences. As for these experiences, they are just what is there: no reason exists to distinguish the state experienced from its particular manifestation on a particular occasion—as the elder Jubba'i had tried to do.

Significantly, Abd al-Jabbar's approach did away with another feature of human existence that the philosophers of the day prized: intellect. This followed naturally from his understanding of the nature of ideas—that they are not independent abstract entities subsisting in metaphysical space that in turn lend themselves to intellectual cognition (as many Baghdad philosophers maintained). Instead of positing a cognitive relationship between the intellect, on the one hand, and matters such as justice, on the other—that is, instead of understanding the mind as the cognitive subject of *intelligibilia*—the subject of experience is the *person him- or herself.* Experience is not a predicate of the body, as the elder Jubba'i seems to have held. Nor, as earlier philosophers claimed, does it represent a predicate of the mind. The integral self, the person, is the primary subject of experience. The person is the subject of predications.

However, explaining anger as a state of experience does not preclude the need to explain what causes it. What is it, then, that makes one enter one state as opposed to another? Here, Abd al-Jabbar invokes (Mu'ammar's "first-order") *ma'na*: a given state occurs by virtue of some specific cause, which varies from case to case. In a sense, therefore, his account draws upon both the notion of *hal* (state) as well as that of *ma'na* (cause), but it treats both concepts in a way different from that of predecessors in his own school.

Abd al-Jabbar did not abandon the effort to identify what such a circumstance or cause might be. On the contrary, he took stock of philosophically relevant states (e.g., willing and knowing) and tried to determine what must attend the state in question. He was fully aware of how the matter related to other aspects of his overall theory. Thus, he denied that knowledge—in contrast to a physical condition such as pain, for example—comes to inhere as a property in a specific physical location (such as the mind or the heart). Likewise, he denied that knowledge itself represents the object of immediate experience. As we have already observed with respect to justice and anger, he held that one first finds oneself in a state of knowing; on this basis, the concept of knowledge then is formed. This meant that he had to give an account of what *knowing* is—what makes us able to say that one is in a *state of knowing*. (We will consider his thoughts on the subject in the following section.) Likewise, he had to account for what makes us able to say one is in a *state of willing* (a sensitive issue, as we saw in previous chapters, which we will revisit in Chapter 12). On the whole, however, the distinction between *state* and *entity*—with the accent placed on the former—served the *kalam* scholars' purpose of accounting for God's justness and unicity without needing to posit abstract entities or qualities associated with Him; in general, this ran counter to the Aristotelian tradition that prevailed among contemporary philosophers.

Besides states and entities, *kalam* scholars addressed many other topics, such as what the world is made of. As we have seen, ninth-century Baghdad—to whose Mu'tazilite school Mu'ammar and Jubba'i, father and son, belonged—abounded in "paper shops" where translations from Greek philosophy, including the works of the Pre-Socratics, were readily available (to say nothing of other types of literature). The Aristotelian notion that the material world consists of infinitely divisible matter was common currency among the philosophers of the time. In contrast, practitioners of speculative discourse for the most part opted for the contrary theory that the world is composed of indivisible particles or atoms. Most researchers contend, quite reasonably, that scholars derived the notion of atomism from Greek texts. All the same, it is reasonable to assume that these opposing views represent speculative perspectives that came naturally. At any rate, many practitioners of speculative discourse considered atomism to be more in line with their views about the world, which were largely anti-essentialist; this theory could be enlisted to argue that the material world had been—and is constantly being—"put together" by God.

And yet, even in the context of "atomistic" theory, scholars adopted different perspectives. One particularly fascinating example is the discussion that occurred in Baghdad between al-'Allaf (d. ca. 840) and his student al-Nazzam (d. 836): Is the world made up of an infinite number of indivisible particles, or a finite quantity? Al-Nazzam, who held the first view, contended that the infinite set of particles we call the "world" was created by God all at once—in one fell swoop, so to speak. If this is so, then nothing that is or ever will be is created anew or within time; everything was already there at the beginning.[3] But how was it "there"? Al-Nazzam—who was recognized by his peers as somewhat of a genius—answered by proposing an early form of evolutionary theory: that all that exists can be divided into what is manifest and what is latent. What is latent already exists in what is manifest; over time, it may become manifest itself. Al-Nazzam's theory sought to reconcile determinism and freedom, for not all that is latent necessarily becomes manifest. We may view what is latent as the unlimited possible combinations of particles constituting what is manifest; whatever a manifest body is or does brings out one or more latent "things." The matter does not concern only biological, or living, phenomena. Al-Nazzam included all objects, animate and inanimate, in his theory. Bodies are what God has brought into existence as manifest objects. However, He has not brought about (i.e., made manifest) the accidents or properties that they display. For all that, these features are already latent within them.

How, then, does it happen that they show themselves—that one particular combination of latent particles becomes manifest? Al-Nazzam's imaginative answer held that these accidents are produced/made manifest by the bodies themselves. In a world made up of infinitely indivisible particles—where these particles are in constant, self-propelled motion, and where the general principle is evolutionary development—physical bodies activate the latent possibilities they harbor within. Such a "division of labor" between God and Creation allowed al-Nazzam to affirm that although God has made the conditions that enable us to act, it is still up to us to choose what to do; we are the authors of our deeds. If one accepts this argument, it resolves the question of whether God determines human action or if we bear responsibility.

(II) Knowledge

Al-Nazzam influenced many of his contemporaries in Baghdad[4] before dying at the young age of thirty-six. Whereas another of Natham's Mu'tazilite contemporaries in Baghdad—al-Jahiz—showed interest in the empirical study of the animal world and made it a point to study available Greek texts before writing his own compendium in which he explicitly expressed the view, *inter alia*, that this world can be observed to exhibit an evolutionary pattern, *kalam* practitioners favored a speculative, or theoretical, approach in their studies. They did not investigate the stars or elements. Instead, they focused on the human condition. Thereby, their speculation revolved around, and was framed by, ordinary speech. Although the ultimate item of interest was God, they had adopted the view that one can only make sense of what is said about Him if one understands one's own behavior and what one says about oneself. How, then, could they argue that such analysis and speculation yields knowledge about the world? This, after all, was exactly what they claimed to be pursuing.

Before addressing the matter, two issues require our attention: the Aristotelian logic favored by philosophers, and the prevailing consensus about how to define knowledge. By this time, of course, Aristotle's logic had received numerous interpretations and contributions (e.g., the Stoics' discussions of conditional statements). For all that, philosophers generally held that demonstrative syllogisms assured certain knowledge. The operation proceeds as follows. The material we have to work with consists of the full array of statements we can make on a given topic. Any two of the propositions on our "list" may be combined and yield a third statement for evaluation. If, for example, one of the first two statements is universal (e.g., that only crocodiles—as opposed to alligators—open their upper jaw) and the second confirms that this particular reptile has its upper jaw opened, then the third statement (that this reptile is a crocodile) necessarily proves true. (Though in common use by philosophers at the time, this example has actually been revealed as a myth.) The "system" relies on positing, for any given pair of categorical statements (at least one of which has a universal form), a conclusion that follows by virtue of the syncretic relationship between the two premises.

The system looks so neat and tidy that one is tempted to liken it to a computer or a factory. However, it has many shortcomings. One of them—as the famous legal scholar Ibn Taymiyyah pointed out (see Chapter 17)—is that we cannot be certain whether a universal statement (for example, all crocodiles open their upper jaw) is true unless we verify it inductively or employ analogical reasoning. If the system's deductive strength assures consistency, the inductive dependency embedded within it represents its Achilles' heel. A further weakness of the Aristotelian system is that its conclusions derive from already-acquired premises (the data programmed into the system, as it were). Even though the "contemplative faculty" is at work, it simply goes through the various pieces of information that have been entered and recognizes which of them fit together to produce a conclusion. Indeed, as if to corroborate this factory-like quality, Islamic philosophers often used the word for "production" (*yuntij*) when referring to the deduction of a valid statement (conclusion) from two given premises. In the tradition of *kalam*, on the other hand, *nazar*—approximately, "reasoning" or "theoretical speculation," which corresponds to Aristotelian contemplation (although it yields a different kind of activity altogether)—is the term employed when a new piece of knowledge is "born."

Lexical differences often prove telling. The difference between "to produce" and "to give birth to" (*tawleed*) points to the fundamental divergence between the Aristotelian approach and the methodology of *kalam*. If demonstrative syllogism involves looking for a concept that bridges two propositions, and the conclusion reveals how they are in fact related, *nazar* seeks a wholly *new* proposition. Here, one contemplates one or more known facts with the aim of discovering another one, which is unknown. In a syllogism, conclusions are embedded in, and deduced from, the system, which proceeds analytically. What *kalam* pursues, on the other hand, is a synthetic inference—which, all the same, is still meant to count as certain. In other words, it means inferring a new fact. (We will return to this point in the next chapter.)

But what does *tawleed* imply? What does it mean to say that facts are born, that new items of knowledge come into being? Demonstrative syllogisms simply concern the truth or falsehood of statements: two true propositions produce a third, which, if procedure is observed, is also known to be true. In *kalam*, it is not enough to be told that a statement is true or false: it is one thing for a statement to be true, and another *to know* that it is true. Even if the system of demonstrative proofs functions properly, one must still explain what the knowledge of a statement means—what it means to know that it is true.

Accordingly, the literature of *kalam* devoted a great deal of attention to epistemology. This focus involved theories that were partly logical, but also partly psychological in nature. Many of the debates were made available in the 1950s, when an Egyptian archeological team discovered compendia made by Abd al-Jabbar, in Yemen.[5] The volumes reveal how much progress the tradition of speculative discourse had charted since its earliest days in Basra and after many of its scholars moved to the Abbasssid capital in Baghdad. The primary concern of these discussions was to identify what it means to possess knowledge—in particular, how to assess claims when they involve matters that are as yet unresolved. On the whole, scholars acknowledged the distinction between immediate knowledge[6] and acquired knowledge; the challenge was to account for the latter. This meant explaining, first of all, what knowing means, and then, in a second step, what it means to acquire new knowledge that is not experienced directly. In contrast to the view that knowledge involves grasping or cognizing the truth, they proposed that knowledge belongs to the same order as belief: to say one knows something essentially means describing a psychological state; that is, it means affirming that the party concerned believes the matter to be so (experiences him- or herself believing). For all that, declaring knowledge a subspecies of belief is not enough, for one often believes something to be the case only to discover that it is not.

Even so, Abd al-Jabbar argued, one cannot claim to know that something is the case and, at the same time, deny that one believes it to be the case. Therefore, he held that knowing and believing go hand in hand, and that the former displays an additional feature distinguishing it from simple belief. This feature is the psychological condition by virtue of which one *feels* that one knows—what he called "repose of the soul." This sense of calm involves certainty that no action is required to validate the truth of what one believes to hold true. Repose means, according to Abd al-Jabbar, that one is in a state of mind wherein denying the belief in question, or entertaining another belief opposed to it, is not even possible. In this account, therefore, we are presented with two psychological or experiential states: believing and "repose of the soul." In an initial step, we can represent his definition of what it is for A to know X as follows:

1. A believes X (to be the case), and

2. A believes that it is not possible for him to believe (not)-X.

A word about (2): the formulation tells us that the agent believes (a positive state) and she cannot believe (x to be) otherwise. There is repose in his or her soul—a sense of quietude and rest concerning the item of belief—and so much so that a change of mind on the subject is deemed impossible. The modality (not possible) in this formulation does not modify

the whole statement—in other words, it does not affirm that it is not possible for the agent to believe not-*X*. (After all, she or he *could* believe not-
X.) It simply refers to the individual person, describing his or her *particular*
state of mind, not the truth-value of the statement.

Presumably, by adding the feature of repose, Abd al-Jabbar was simply trying to raise the degree of subjective conviction to its highest possible
level, given room for variation within the spectrum of belief. It is at the level
of certain belief that the agent's psychological state comes closest to that of
knowing. Yet this is not enough. Abd al-Jabbar conceded that a person experiencing such repose may turn out to be mistaken. Repose does not, in
itself, guarantee that one in fact knows what one thinks one knows—it provides a necessary, but not a sufficient, condition. Further circumstances can
show one to be wrong. Even so, the argument seems to be that even if it
turns out that one is mistaken, this does not change the fact that one experiences the same repose when one is right: the condition is an integral part
of what feeling-one-knows *means*. The psychological state of rest provides
a necessary component of what it is to have knowledge.[7] Confidence represents a necessary feature of our claims to knowledge (even if it offers no
guarantee).

Is all this enough to explain what knowing means? Earlier Muʿtazilites,
and *kalam* scholars belonging to other schools, did not all agree, but for
Abd al-Jabbar what ultimately decided the matter is the "objective" satisfaction of the belief in question: when one believes, in a state of repose,
that something is the case and it happens to be just as one believes it to
be.[8] Thus, the third and final component required to explain what knowing means is:

3. *X* is as *A* believes it to be.

Whereas (1) and (2) describe epistemic states, and are by themselves
sufficient to describe such states, (3) extends beyond the subjective thresh-
old and describes an objective condition.

But even so, the question remains *how* a person comes to have
such an experience if it does not occur immediately. I may "find myself" knowing that a stranger is walking toward me—a direct, experiential kind of knowledge similar to other knowledge I have from sensory,
mental, or emotional impressions (such as being angry or bewildered, or
seeing and hearing). But how do I "find myself" knowing that the per-

son walking toward me is, say, a scholar? Clearly, one must distinguish between *intuitive* and *acquired* knowledge and account for how passage occurs from the former to the latter. This can only be done, Abd al-Jabbar declares, by an act of speculation or reasoning: *nazar*. This act takes into account other data or experiences I have had. I have to look into other information to be able to make the required inference—for example, what the person is wearing or holding in his hands, or what I heard earlier about a new scholar who has just arrived in town. For all that, the act of reasoning does not itself guarantee the acquisition of new knowledge. It is a necessary (I have to consider the evidence), but not a sufficient, condition. Once further knowledge is gained, my action (*nazar*) has brought it about. But the mere fact that I have performed the action guarantees nothing. The distinction between two relations of implication is clear: that whenever *A* occurs, then *B* does, too; or, conversely, whenever *B* occurs, it is because of *A*. The second kind of relation is exactly analogous to the process of giving birth—*tawlid*. Reasoning/speculation provides the only means by which to acquire (give birth to) a "secondary" item of knowledge; such knowledge *presupposes* reasoning instead of being its necessary result. (Among scholars at the time, it was common to make this distinction between these two kinds of implication.)

The act of speculation does not guarantee the result, but the result presupposes the act. *Kalam* extensively employed this type of causal relationship in other areas of inquiry, too; its use in this particular sphere simply confirms that speculation is an activity like any other, physical or mental. Unlike the rules of implication that hold in Aristotelian syllogism, where conclusions follow necessarily (and even automatically) from their premises, the rules developed by Abd al-Jabbar remain closely connected to psychological processes. The act of reasoning is very much a subjective operation; a conclusion to speculation is not automatically guaranteed; and once it has been reached, it is distinguished by the state of mental repose. Clearly, this is not a *deductive* or mechanical approach to the acquisition of knowledge.

So far we have covered important steps in the theory, but there are still more. What is it we speculate about, and how is it that we can—through our speculation—*cause* knowledge to come about? In typical cases, Abd al-Jabbar affirms, there is a question to be answered and a specific "lead" to explore.[9] The trick is to examine the lead in such a fashion that the answer to the question will follow from it. As we know, however, this does not always work. The operation requires further refinement: "bringing to birth" (i.e., inference) succeeds only if what we look into is the *right lead*, and we look into it in the *right way*. For instance, if I hear that the new scholar who has arrived in town is riding a white mule, and that he is wearing brightly colored clothes, I will focus on these facts as ones that might single him out from other people in town. Until this point is reached, the answer remains indeterminate and judgment hangs suspended. But once I have made my inference—now believing with certainty that this man is the scholar in question—the answer becomes determinate. Now I can claim that I believe that matters stand as I see them, and that the repose of the soul I am experiencing represents the condition (*hal*) by virtue of which I feel confident that they are as I believe them to be. It is clear what this *hal* is at the level of immediate knowledge (i.e., we know with certainty how it feels to know something). Likewise, we can recognize the same feeling at the level of acquired knowledge—that is, when we have found the correct lead and, by looking into it in the right way, make the correct inference. *Verification* is correct inference (the third component of the formula): when the man introduces himself and confirms who he is, it confirms my knowledge—that is, what my speculative reasoning has already supposed.

These reflections remain on the level of psychology, however. It is only natural to ask what knowledge itself *is*. Does it, as some of Abd al-Jabbar's contemporaries held, possess some kind of independent ontological status? Abd al-Jabbar's view falls in line with the account given above about justice. It is simple and straightforward: while *knowing* that one knows represents an immediate experience, knowing what knowledge is is something that must be acquired. I form a *notion* about knowledge based on my immediate experiences. This does not amount to circular reasoning, he claims, because immediate experience, by virtue of its directness, does not depend on prior knowledge. In other words, what we know, on the whole, is constructively formed from our experiences. Abstract nouns such as justice, virtue, knowledge, and so on, refer to concepts we come to form on the basis of our interactions with others; they are not independent entities subsisting in an abstract world which our intellects somehow "grasp" through logical abstraction (much less through the rigid methods favored by the philosophers).

As we have seen, Abd al-Jabbar did not confine these experiential states to knowledge. He would claim that one experiences the state of knowing just as directly and immediately as one experiences thinking, believing, desiring, and so on. In all such cases, one simply "finds oneself" knowing, desiring, willing, thinking, or believing; distinguishing one state from another poses no difficulty. These direct, or immediate, experiences occur in the same way as sensory or perceptual cognition. It made sense for him, therefore, to claim that some instances of cognition or experiences that are immediate could, on second thought or after further investigation, be determined to have been misleading.

For Abd al-Jabbar, the key to acquiring knowledge is the act of speculation: following "the right lead in the right way." (As we will see, this holds for the discipline of jurisprudence more generally.) Reasoning represents an *inferential* act rather than an application of deductive rules. Deductive reasoning is analytical; conclusions proceed from what lies embedded in the premises. In contrast, Abd al-Jabbar stresses the process by which a "new fact" may come to be known with the same level of certainty (and with the same provisional conditions) by which "objects" of immediate knowledge are supposed to be known. Of course, a new fact that is not analytically deducible is not something that was formerly untrue, and now is. One may understand it as a fact one arrives at *laterally* rather than *vertically*: instead of moving down from one statement (fact) to the next, one makes the (reasoned) jump to a statement (fact) at the same level as the first one.[10]

The preceding account offers a mere sample of the great lengths to which the practitioners of speculative discourse went in applying reason to their inquiries. Arguably, our minds are more inclined to infer (connect facts laterally) than to practice syllogism or deduction. The contrast between the two types of reasoning set apart philosophers influenced by Aristotle, on the one hand, and scholars of speculative discourse and jurisprudence, on the other.[11] In trying to develop an inferential system of "giving birth" to facts, Mu'tazilites were searching for a way to demonstrate that one can arrive at new knowledge which is not already presupposed. The extent to which they succeeded may be debated, but it cannot be summarily dismissed.

Other groups in this tradition formed before and after the Mu'tazilites, but none held as much intellectual weight. Under Abbassid rule, the Mu'tazilite school even exercised impressive political influence. Then came the backlash. The elder Jubba'i not only had an independently minded son, but also another student who, in time, rose up to challenge his master and found his own school: al-Ash'ari (d. 936). Al-Ash'ari's brand of speculative discourse soon relegated Mu'tazilism to the margins of orthodox Islamic society, where it languished. The Mu'tazilita' effacement was so severe—their writings were probably burnt or destroyed—that, for hundreds of years, practically the only information about them came from their opponents (including al-Ash'ari). It is no surprise, then, that the announcement of the Yemeni discovery caused an intellectual earthquake among scholars in the field.[12]

For Mu'tazilites, discourse meant healthy disagreement on a wide range of subjects. Their ideas ranged so broadly that they eventually deemed it necessary to provide a definitive articulation of their main tenets, lest they be confused with others with related views. The position commonly held to explain the name of the group concerns the debate surrounding a Muslim who commits a grave sin: is such a person a believer or a nonbeliever? One view, advanced by the Khawaarij, held that this kind of person is not a believer and will therefore go to Hell. The opposing position, advanced by the Murji'ites, declared that the sinner is a believer; pending repentance, he could end up in Heaven. The Mu'tazilites contended that he is neither and will therefore end up in Hell. However, they argued that he would not land at the same level of Hell as unbelievers. This in-between position, which was one of their main tenets, came to define them in the eyes of contemporaries and posterity.

Two other tenets qualify as distinctive, too. On the one hand, Mu'tazilites affirmed God's unique nature and, on this basis, denied that He had attributes. On the other, they upheld His justice (and its corollaries, free will and human responsibility). As we have seen, they developed arguments that made sense of these ascriptions without deviating from their belief in God's unicity or from their belief that He has no properties. Over time, they formulated other, complementary tenets concerning the nature of morality: the first holds that God cannot break his word (which follows from His innate justice), and the second holds that human beings are obligated to call for good deeds and condemn evil ones (a matter related to free will and responsibility). These additional tenets basically balance the obligations between God and His subjects: we may be sure that He cannot but reward us if we act properly; and we do our part by spreading righteousness. The good, they claimed, is natural, and may therefore be discovered by human reason. Things are not good because God says they are; God says they are because they *are*! (As we will see in the next chapter, this defense of *natural* morality did not go unchallenged.)

. . .

To its credit, Mu'tazilism represents the most daring voice of rationalism in Islam. If members of this school felt uneasy about accepting the authenticity of all Qur'anic verses wholesale, they expressed greater doubts about the other pillar of orthodoxy: the Prophet's sayings. They articulated such strict conditions for accepting that a text is genuine that they admitted only eighty (out of hundreds). It is worth observing that many inhumane injunctions (e.g., female circumcision) that are still carried out in some parts of the Muslim world derive their justification from what the Mu'tazilites rejected early on. For all that, the school stands out less for the subject matter it addressed than for its (epistemologically) daring spirit. Arguably, the Mu'tazilites—far more than "rationalist philosophers" such as Averroes, later on—bore the torch of intellectual freedom in Islam.

Law and Morality

Is it good because God says it is so, as orthodox religious scholars held? Or does God say it is good because it is so, as Mu'tazilite scholars claimed? This central point of contention fed directly into a practical issue for a class of legal scholars, now in emergence, who sought to understand an ethical injunction deriving from the three sources that define life for Muslims: the Qur'an, the Prophet's sayings, and "consensus" (originally defined as how Muhammad's companions had conducted their own lives).

Seeking to understand both what the sources said and the implications to be drawn from them, legal scholars addressed a wide range of questions. What are members of the Muslim community obligated to do? What are they prohibited from doing? Are there degrees of commandment and prohibition? What consequences does it hold to do as commanded (or not)? How strong is the injunction in each instance? Scholars who undertook such studies had to excel in their knowledge of Arabic to explain or interpret (*tafsir*) Qur'anic texts, and they needed to establish which sayings of the Prophet (*hadith*) were authentic.

We have already encountered Ibn Hanbal, who suffered at the hands of the Abbasids. Another major figure who preceded him, with whom the new class of legal scholars (*fiqh*) is also associated, was Abu Hanifa (d. 772). He was born in Kabul, but his life ended inside an Abbasid jail, where he had languished for years—reportedly, for declaring that it is lawful in Islam to rebel against an unjust caliphate. These scholars devoted themselves to studying tradition with the aim of categorizing the commandments relevant to daily life—whether explicitly declared or merely implied. Eventually, four main schools of legal thinking evolved that, in one form or another, still govern life in Sunni communities the world over today. Shi'ites, on the other hand, generally follow the codes of two other major schools.

Behind the *what*-questions stood a more fundamental question: *why*? Do ethical injunctions express moral values that are valid independent of what transmitted tradition says, or do these values derive from it? Either way, what, exactly, are they? Is it possible to identify a core set of values? In other words, is there a solid moral basis, following from tradition or otherwise, for legal commandments? It is significant that scholars deemed it necessary not only to identify the full range of injunctions and the legal consequences they entail, but also to discern the underlying reasons they had been made in the first place. Is the basis of the law simply the fact that it exists in a community (however this community has come about)? Does it lie in moral principles? If so, are these principles natural or conventional? Does compliance with the law derive from political or from religious authority?

Abu Hanifa initiated, and jurists of different schools in turn contributed to, what may be considered a fairly advanced project of identifying a prudential purpose underlying all law. Significantly, this purpose was the good, or the interest, of the individual human being. These different schools' emphasis on the individual human being as the "unit of interest" of God's law immediately established a clear-cut separation between matters of religion and affairs of state. Although political rulers (caliphs) may have wished to be charged with overseeing both spheres, orthodox jurists viewed matters differently. If "the state" was responsible for collective concerns within the community, religion involved the concerns of human beings as individuals. Therefore—and unlike the Church in Europe—jurists did not claim political power for themselves. "Separation between Mosque and State" never posed a problem—in contrast to Europe. Needless to say, matters stand otherwise today, as religious movements (Muslim Brotherhood, the Islamic State, etc.) vie for political power.

Modern scholars identify different phases in the development of legal scholarship in the orthodox tradition of early Islam. A vigorous first generation immediately following the Prophet's contemporaries included Abu Hanifa, Malik Ibn Anas (d. 795), and others. During the "middle period," their concepts and ideas were collated and organized. The third generation is associated especially with the speculative thinkers al-Juwayni (d. 1028) and his student al-Ghazali (d. 1111). Finally, a later, "resurgent" phase is ex-emplified by al-Shatibi (d. 1388) in Andalusia. The genealogy of the differ-ent legal schools (Shatibi belonged to the one associated with Malik bin Anas) more or less followed the same pattern.

Besides questions of *what* and *why*, legal thinkers addressed the ques-tion of *how*. How are inferences to be drawn? What method should one adopt for doing so, and what rules of adjudication should be employed? To address these issues, as well as those relating to questions of *why*, another field of study developed over time: *usul al-fiqh*—that is, the principles (or foundations) of *fiqh*. In today's language, the best translation of the term is probably "jurisprudence," or "philosophy of law." This branch of study treated the general principles of law; legalists, in contrast, focused on prac-tical interpretation of what the law says.

While it was primarily legalists themselves who developed the sci-ence of jurisprudence, they did so in an environment where *kalam* set the general intellectual tone. Of course, *kalam*, the science of speculative dis-course, reached back to Jahm's doctrine of "reason before transmission" and to the Mu'tazilites. The latter held that one could discover moral val-ues by employing reason, and that such values held independent of the fact that they were divine commandments. In retrospect, one might call this tradition a kind of "moral naturalism." Even scholars who did not agree thought there must be a purpose intelligible to human beings behind God's commandments—and that reason would reveal it.

As we have seen, the Mu'tazilite school was eventually pushed to the margins of the intellectual establishment. Speculative discourse continued in the more conservative form that a certain al-Ash'ari (himself a former Mu'tazilite) lent it. Reason was not abandoned altogether, yet it was no longer sovereign—the standard against which the transmitted tradition had to be tested. Speculation still occurred about God and the world, but the tables had been turned: now, the orthodox view of moral values was defended against the Mu'tazilite position. Legal scholarship continued as well, leading to what may have been the first comprehensive and coherent system in the history of the philosophy of law.

In general agreement about what to regard as the sources of the law—the Qur'an, the Prophet's sayings, and consensus—scholars identified five main *purposes* (*maqasid*) that the law holds for securing or preserving the interests of individual human beings. Typically, they are arranged: (a) religion, (b) life, (c) mind, (d) human issue or procreation, and (e) wealth. The order is as significant as the categories themselves. The first item of interest on the list is religion—that is, the values that should guide human conduct—and the last is material possession. "Life itself," the fact *that* one is alive, occupies second place relative to moral quality: *how* one lives. (Arguably, the primacy accorded to moral life and education holds implications for state policies when determining what its primary role should be: moral life and education, or armed protection.) "Mind," the faculty that enables the individual to achieve knowledge and make informed choices, is less important than religion, that is to say the moral system of values by which one lives. The fourth purpose, concerning biological reproduction as an extended "good" or "interest" of the individual that the law must protect, stands above strictly material goods.

Of course, one might argue (and, indeed, arguments did occur) about what constitutes the defining "goods" of individual human life and which ones should be prioritized. However, given what has been written about law—in both ancient and modern times—it is impossible not to be impressed by the vast system these scholars developed. Their point of departure was that (even) God's law has a purpose; on this basis, they ultimately determined that the moral life is what must be preserved above all.

In addition to debates about "the purposes of the law," more work was required to translate these purposes into legally binding adjudications. It was necessary to draw on the three sources—Qur'an, *hadith*, and consensus—to work out different degrees of "bindingness" extending from what is absolutely obligatory to what is absolutely prohibited. To this end, thorough understanding of Qur'anic language was required. Extrapolating the proper adjudications from the different sources required jurists to command the subtleties of lexicon and syntax. Likewise, it was necessary to develop a set of guidelines for applying adjudications on a case-by-case basis. Finally, in order to complete such an edifice, jurists had to distinguish between three main ways of determining "benefits" in specific instances: those considered necessary, those deemed complementary, and those that are merely advantageous (in order of priority). Other jurists elaborated subsidiary rules, as well. They included provisions for attenuating a duty or obligation by measuring it against the circumstantial burden to be borne by the person who carries it out, the intention underlying an action in dispute, the conventional meaning of words when a statement stands at issue, the inadmissibility of doubt or suspicion in judgments (or the presumption of innocence), and so on. All these rules—in addition to the principles and purposes already identified—were meant to provide the basis for pronouncing judgment. The "resurgent phase" of jurisprudence, perhaps exemplified most fully by al-Shatibi, testifies to a very advanced and vigorous understanding of what a coherent system of law should look like.

But even after taking great pains to lay this groundwork, jurists faced a problem: how to arrive at judgments in cases not explicitly covered by the three canonical sources. In a sense, a method was required for acquiring new knowledge (that is, knowing the right thing to do in a given case) based on knowledge one already possessed. Employing the term *qiyas* (which, for philosophers, meant the syllogistic mode of reasoning developed by Aristotle), jurists chose the inferential method—current among *kalam* scholars—of analogical reasoning as the tool for arriving at new knowledge. As we will see, the decision would give rise to dispute between proponents of deductive (syllogistic) and inductive (analogical) approaches. Developing a method of reasoning for concrete application amounted to affirming the need for the law to develop continuously. Some, like al-Shatibi, went even further in this direction by proposing that *qiyas* is not just a methodology, but represents a fourth *source*; he meant, in other words, that the adjudications of earlier jurists should be incorporated into the body of the law, too. Not everyone agreed, of course; some, like the Andalusian Ibn Hazm (d. 1064), steered the opposite course, affirming that legal rules should be restricted to matters based on explicit textual evidence. (However, some contemporary scholars have argued that Ibn Hazm's "liberal" project was meant to challenge what had become an "authoritarian" class of jurists—the *'ulama*—who claimed to be the only legitimate interpreters of the Qur'an: his aim, then, was to restore interpretive right to the individual, which required that the text itself be the standard rather than the *'ulama's* interpretations.[1])

For all that, these "intra-jurisprudential" issues did not settle the challenge the Mu'tazilites had posed concerning the place of reason—that is, the question whether reason itself is the ultimate standard or measure of all the sources the jurists upheld; even with this array of principles and rules in place, the validity of components within canonical sources was not put into question. Mu'tazilites, on the other hand (and as the case of

Abd al-Jabbar illustrates), would regard reason as decisive for validating a dubious verse, *hadith*, or matter of received consensus. In particular, the question persisted whether canonical sources had set moral values or simply corroborated them—whether "what is good" is so because God says it is, or because this is the way it is "by nature." The other critical question that came into relief concerned *qiyas*: is the jurists' understanding of such "reasoning by analogy" reliable as a rational method, or is the philosophical approach—"syllogism"—better?

Among the Mu'tazilites' opponents numbered a scholar who commanded all the disciplines mentioned above. He was so brilliant he had mastered them all—including philosophy.[2] Al-Ghazali (d. 1111)—who was also schooled in Ash'ari *kalam*[3]—is said to have given up a prestigious appointment at the Baghdad House of Wisdom, the foremost academy of the time, to go forth into the world and seek answers he could not find in the vast library at his disposal. His knowledge of philosophy was so great that, when translated into Latin, an introductory book he had written was thought at first to be by the same philosopher he meant to attack in the work.[4]

Al-Ghazali's numerous writings include a discussion of jurisprudence (*al-Mustasfa*); it is preceded by his philosophical perspective on the fundamentals of logic. Here, he challenges the main Mu'tazilite tenet concerning moral truth and the knowledge it admits. But since he was hardly a run-of-the-mill legal scholar, he does not spare members of the profession criticism for faults in their methodology. In general terms, he held that one can neither rely on (analogical) reasoning alone, nor can one rely exclusively on what has been transmitted (from the sources) in order to validate moral truths and legal judgments. Reasoning (especially syllogistic reasoning) and transmitted sources must be used in concert. Accordingly, he argues that neither the legalists were right to rely solely on transmission, nor were "rationalists" correct when they invoked reason alone. Al-Ghazali illustrates his claim with a straightforward example. Could legalists properly infer a prohibition on wine consumption from the prohibition on intoxicants found in transmitted tradition? Conversely, could the conclusion that wine is prohibited be drawn from the empirical fact that wine is an intoxicant? Clearly, he observes, one cannot reach this conclusion unless one combines the empirical premise that wine is an intoxicant with the transmitted injunction that intoxicants are prohibited. Hence, neither the literal legalists nor the strict rationalists are right to ignore the other side's claims.[5]

In brief, al-Ghazali argued that although some statements are self-evident and necessarily true, and although some concepts are primary and necessarily cognized, they do not include moral concepts or statements. Accordingly, the latter must be inferred or deduced. But for all that, they cannot be deduced or inferred rationally. Therefore, an "out-of-the-box" element proves necessary: transmitted tradition.

The distinction between primary and secondary truths was well known among philosophers, as was the distinction between single concepts and their elaboration. (As we have seen, Baghdad paper shops had made the works of Aristotle readily available to scholars). Al-Ghazali reformulated the familiar corpus of philosophical doctrine to address contemporary issues, taking into account points of agreement and disagreement with the Mu'tazilites. Counter to purely Aristotelian tradition, both sides held that, given the human limitations declared in the Qur'an, all items of knowledge are to be subsumed under the heading of belief. Al-Ghazali, however, denied the Mu'tazilite condition for knowledge: that our object of belief should be as we believe it to be. This position was in line with that of the Mu'tazilites' opponents, the Ash'arites; indeed, he had studied under one of their masters (al-Juwayni, d. 1085) early in his career. Al-Ghazali compiled a list of items the *kalam* tradition generally held to constitute knowledge (i.e., truths about the world) that fall under the heading of belief-with-certainty. The first is knowledge of primary principles, which is informed by reason alone[6]; significantly, at the top of the list, al-Ghazali features knowledge of one's own existence. Given his rejection of the Mu'tazilite view that knowledge implies the objective satisfaction of the object of one's beliefs, there is reason to wonder how al-Ghazali would have explained self-consciousness. He did not try to do so, however. Second are certainties about "inner sensations" or feelings (for example, hunger, thirst, fear, joy, and so on). All animate beings experience these sensations as directly and as surely as rational beings know the "primary principles," even though they are not experienced by way of the five senses or reason. The third group consists of cognitions we have of the world of appearances that derive from sense perception (such as the whiteness of snow, the roundness of the moon, particular measures or distances, etc.). We also take these truths to be certain, even though they are subject to error. (After all, further observation allows us to modify them.) Fourth are statements containing empirical generalizations—for example, knowing that fire burns, heavy objects fall, and so on. They differ from the third category in that they are generalizations, whereas observations of sensible objects are particular perceptions. (The particular observation that the wine one has drunk is intoxicating differs from knowing/claiming that wine in general is an intoxicant.) Fifth comes knowledge acquired indirectly—for example, what a famous figure we have not met believes, or that a place we have not visited exists. Beliefs acquired in this way are confirmed by repetition or when information is passed along through different channels; like what we know empirically, they gain consistency and become more concrete over time.

Al-Ghazali adds two further items to the list, neither of which—he tells us—can (or should) be used as premises in demonstrative arguments or syllogisms, because they do not admit the degree of certainty such proofs require. The first of these (i.e., the sixth of the seven categories) concerns beliefs reached by the faculty of imagination—for example, that everything that exists must occupy a physical location, in other words, that no space (or vacuum) exists beyond the world we inhabit. Instinctively, one may feel that believing such matters resembles *a priori* knowledge. However, al-Ghazali affirms, once we subject these beliefs to a rational test, we quickly realize they cannot be maintained—indeed, some of them can be proven to be flat-out wrong. One should not rely on instinct. By excluding such objects of "knowledge" from the list of certainties, al-Ghazali declares it impossible to determine synthetic *a posteriori* or metaphysical truths about the world such as one might achieve through rational inquiry. As we have seen, the entire Mu'tazilite project was based on this very principle.

The final category of knowledge-claims—which holds particular interest in this context—concerns "common beliefs." Moral statements fall under this heading (for example, belief that lying or killing are wrong, or that saving someone from drowning is good). These claims are neither self-evident *a priori*, nor do they derive from the imaginative faculty. Rather, one believes in the correctness of the statements (or the validity of these values) by learning them from the community, being taught by righteous people. Children are brought up to internalize them as indisputable principles, and then come to consider them on par with *a priori* truths (which they are not). Repeating an argument by Avicenna (without acknowledging his source), al-Ghazali observes that if one were brought up in total isolation, without any moral teaching whatsoever, and considered, in such a state, the validity of statements such as "justice is good" or "lying is bad," one would experience doubt that one would not entertain about a statement such as "two is greater than one." Indeed, one would doubt these statements even more than statements concerning the absence of space beyond the created world (which one arrives at by way of imagination and therefore may believe instinctively).

In sum, al-Ghazali excludes moral statements from *a priori* (analytic and synthetic) and *a posteriori* (synthetic) categories, and he does the same for metaphysical propositions. Notably, when he identifies informational statements (which provide us with what he calls "acquired knowledge") as matters belonging to the (conditionally) reliable five categories employed in reasoning, he expresses a clear preference for received transmission (information that reaches us from reliable sources) over the rationalist tradition. However, it is not clear how he can justify this preference inasmuch as he also affirms that "reliable" sources teach us moral statements. Why should one category be considered more trustworthy than the other (unless, of course, he is referring specifically to *hadith*)?

Before challenging the Mu'tazilite doctrine in full—and also in order to guide legalists in their work[7]—he outlines his view of syllogistic reasoning (*qiyas*), that is, what it means to draw a conclusion from two premises. His explanation takes us back to the concepts used by Mu'tazilite *kalam* that we have already encountered, especially concepts of "giving birth" and "following a lead."

The Mu'tazilites' concept of the lead involves what the party engaged in speculation looks for to facilitate reaching a conclusion. One must "hit on" the right lead—a medium logically connected with the conclusion being pursued—so that the process of thought may arrive at a desired conclusion; until this point, its truth or falsehood is indeterminate. In contrast, al-Ghazali portrays the lead (the Arabic term, *daleel*, is the same) as the middle term of a syllogism: the common denominator in two premises made up of subjects and predicates, which then, having served its purpose, is dropped in the conclusion. This may also be illustrated with the example of wine: the first proposition is that intoxicants are prohibited, the second is that wine is an intoxicant, and the conclusion is that wine is prohibited; hereby, being-an-intoxicant serves as the lead: the middle term that is ultimately dropped.

Al-Ghazali anticipates the objection that such a conclusion does not really differ from its premises—nothing new is being discovered or reached. He admits it is true that the conclusion is already embedded in the premises (wine is already included in what "intoxicating beverage" means); on the other hand, however, the conclusion differs from the premises because of how the statements are defined: each one concerns the relationship between a specific subject and a specific predicate. In this case, the conclusion consists of a subject ("wine") and a predicate ("is prohibited")—a combination that is absent in the two premises (that wine intoxicates, and that intoxicants are prohibited). When occurring as parts of a syllogism, these subjects and predicates are called "terms"; the one that occurs in both and then is dropped in the conclusion represents a "middle term." Thus, while the conclusion is already *almost* stated in the two premises, it is not the same inasmuch as the two terms now brought together in the conclusion were not stated together in either of the two premises. This response falls in line with Aristotle's understanding of the deductive system, yet it cleverly avoids the Mu'tazilite effort to portray the "lead" (*daleel*, which al-Ghazali treats as the middle term) as proceeding toward something entirely new—that is, amounting to an inference rather than a deduction.

By appropriating the concept of lead (i.e., interpreting it as a middle term), al-Ghazali reduces the Mu'tazilite idea of "giving birth" to just another word that stands for a concept bridging two other ideas, whose cognition may be explained in any number of ways (including, he observes, by the philosophical theory of emanation[8]). Al-Ghazali points out other ways that jurists and practitioners of speculative discourse have explained how the middle term is cognized—including the possibility that the terms of the syllogism are logically connected by way of implication or presupposition. In the process, he mentions the view of causality he elaborates in other works: such relations are *coincidental* rather than *causal*. Although anything can happen on the heels of something else, which we then assume to have provided a direct cause, we need not expect "just anything" to happen: God has given us knowledge that such a plethora of possibilities will not, in fact, be realized. Al-Ghazali's wording when describing such "coincidentality" (our habit of expecting only the "appropriate" or "right" thing to occur in the context of something else, whether concurrently or subsequently)—*'adat*, *'bi'littifaq*, and *'bi'liqtiran* (by habit, by coincidence, by association)—has prompted many scholars to observe a resemblance between his theory and that of David Hume, who also reduced causality to a natural intellectual habit.

Having defined first principles in terms of cognition without demonstration, and having shown that demonstrated conclusions may be reached analytically (or through some form of divine intervention), al-Ghazali takes up the Mu'tazilite doctrine that moral values are natural. According to this school, actions are divided between those that are good/agreeable and others that are bad/repugnant. Reason immediately recognizes many of them for what they are.[9] Mu'tazilites claim, moreover, that further moral judgments occur through rational speculation—for example, one may realize that a disagreeable truth implies harm, or that an agreeable lie suggests benefit. A final category concerns actions whose moral value derives from religious sources, which is neither rationally self-evident nor deducible by rational means (for example, acts of worship: prayer, pilgrimage, and so on). For the Mu'tazilites, the moral value of some actions is akin to the truths of primary principles —like those of logic and mathematics— whereas the moral values of other actions may be deduced from first moral principles by way of speculative reasoning.

Al-Ghazali takes the Mu'tazilites to task by arguing that actions called "agreeable" or "repugnant" are simply a matter of what seems to fit (or not to fit) with the speakers' intentions: those that match are viewed positively, and those that do not are seen in a negative light. The same action that appears "good" may appear to be the opposite from another perspective; indeed, the same person may view the same matter differently at different times. Goodness and badness are not natural qualities that inhere in actions, nor are they qualities that admit absolute definition. There are no essentially constitutive qualities of a bad act: descriptions vary according to context and the parties involved. In contemporary parlance, al-Ghazali proposes a utilitarian version of a consequentialist theory of moral action.

Let us recall that practitioners of speculative discourse never wavered in their concern for fitting human thought and action into a comprehensive theory centered on God (or what they believed of Him). In this context, holding a naturalist or a consequentialist view of moral action bears directly on God's justice. Are God's acts just because He wishes them to be so, or because that is how they simply *are*? If the latter is the case—and He is just by definition—then it is as impossible to conceive of Him committing injustice as it is to imagine something being what it is not. And yet, doesn't such a definition of God confine Him? Moreover, isn't *this* confinement inconsistent with His nature? Against the Mu'tazilite position, Ash'arites argued that God is wholly unrestricted. Of course, He wouldn't commit an injustice, but surely He could—after all, He is omnipotent. The argument was never settled. Still today, philosophers disagree whether moral values are natural and universal.

At any rate, the fact that such arguments were debated *pro et contra* with rational rigor attests to vigorous intellectual life during the early centuries of Islam. Unfortunately, a comparable climate generally proves lacking in the Arab world today. Why did this rigor and vibrancy disappear? And why—with a few exceptions we will consider in due course—did this intellectual discipline not preserve the freedom of thought that had called it into being in the first place?

Many Western scholars attribute this intellectual rigor to Greek thinking that was imported into Arab culture. But while Greek thought undoubtedly found use as an instrument, it was by no means what inspired the genesis of the movement—nor, on the whole, was it what guided it. What inspired the flourishing culture of early Islam was surely the Qur'an itself. The Message fired the imagination, prompting human reason to follow suit in attempts to formulate, rationally, the vast horizons that had suddenly opened up—a development for which the Peninsula was already ripe. Yet if imagination moves swiftly, reason tends to plod. Once the flare of imagination begins to fade, reason is impeded by its own circumspection. Finally, it closes in on itself and becomes immobile. When this occurs, it is confined by literalism. The text turns into a prison and no longer offers a window onto the vast expanses of the universe. Language becomes an obstacle, not a bridge.

Early practitioners of speculative discourse viewed matters differently—almost as the poets had seen their task: to break free from the limits of language by means of language itself. Whereas the poets drew on their inborn faculty of imagination when exploring the meaning of the universe, speculative scholars relied on reason fired by the message of the Qur'an. Later, when reason seemed to lag far behind the imagination, the Sufism of Rabi'ah sought an escape. Later still, even full-blooded philosophers such as Avicenna saw fit to convey their thoughts through poetic imagery.

There are two major points at issue. The first concerns the Qur'anic text. Initially, it provided the source of intellectual inspiration. However, as time passed and vernaculars slowly evolved, a gap emerged between the text and language as it was now spoken—with the classical form still providing the standard for new intellectual discourse. Arguably (see the last chapter), this meant that the classical text, once the catalyst of innovation, came to act as a limiting force. The second, related item concerns freedom—more specifically, freedom of thought. Though joined at first, freedom and reason quickly separated, leaving less and less room for creative thinking. The same, holy book (and language) that once had inspired free thought and intellectual progress may have become—especially in recent times—a source of limitation. As we have seen, freedom in the sense of "freedom to differ" proved a victim early on. This occurred right at the beginning, with Hasan and Wasil's treatment of Bashar. We also saw it with Jahm, Ja'd, and others—and yet again with Ibn Hanbal and Abu Hanifa. Nor did it stop here. In the present day, atavistic followers of Islam have minds so shackled by a literal understanding of the text that they have toppled marvelous statues of the Buddha in Afghanistan and the Twin Towers in New York; girls seeking to be educated and even worshippers in mosques fall victim to their efforts to erase difference.

But our story continues. This time, we will visit Baghdad once more under the reign of the Abbassid caliph al-Ma'mun (d. 833), the son of Haroun al-Rashid (whose times came to be associated with the famous tales of the *Arabian Nights*). During this period, difference promised enrichment; it was not seen as threatening. Scholars with different intellectual positions and religious beliefs gathered at his (and his regional *wazirs'*) nightly banquets to discuss their ideas freely. This is when Nestorians and others were busily translating works from Syriac and Greek, and the paper mills ran at full speed. But even al-Ma'mun, toward the end of his reign, reached beyond due measure by trying to formalize Mu'tazilite tenets (which once had been banned) as official doctrine. This is when the *mihna* started—which inaugurated the slow erosion of the caliph's authority in religious matters.[10] However, let us return to our story of reason in order to consider a point of friction between transmitted (now Greek) and indigenous sciences: language and logic.

Al-Ma'mun and the Devils' Banquets

All erroneous sects, ideas, and creeds can be traced back to the Devil.
So declared al-Shahrastani (d. 1153) in the introductory remarks to his cata-
logue of the origins of deviant belief systems (*Al-Milal wa-l Niḥal*).

"Why bow to Adam when he was created of earth, whereas I was created of fire, a loftier element?" the Devil makes bold to ask. By questioning
a divine injunction and, worse still, finding it irrational and therefore unjustified, he disobeyed God. The scene al-Shahrastani describes expresses
how the orthodox saw Mu'tazilite doctrine, which put reason above (blind)
faith. One can imagine, then, how he and likeminded clerics would have
viewed the banquets the caliph al-Ma'mun had held some 250 years earlier,
where representatives of various creeds and sects—devils all—gathered to
discuss metaphysical subjects.

Had al-Ma'mun sought to emulate the ancient symposia that Socrates
attended (as reported in the works of Plato, which were now available
in Arabic)? Perhaps. Legend holds that he beheld a gray-bearded sage in
a dream, who identified himself as Aristotle; the vision inspired him to
sponsor a translation movement, which reached great heights under his
patronage. Legend also holds that he made it a condition of peace with
the emperor of Byzantium that a copy of Ptolemy's *Almagest* be surren-
dered. Yet it is also possible that al-Ma'mun simply sought to centralize religious authority; in this case, his efforts paralleled those of the speculative
tradition, which sought to create an atmosphere of open debate with the
ultimate goal of arriving at consensus. This would explain why his court
stood open to proponents of all sorts of beliefs and sects: perhaps he hoped

they would come to share the same point of view. At any rate, the caliph is known for having tried to centralize political authority in his fractious empire.

Yet al-Ma'mun does not seem to have been interested in Plato's dialogues so much as science, pure and simple. It fired his imagination so greatly that he ordered—and, what is more, personally directed—an excavation of the pyramids. A tunnel was dug into the largest one in search of the hidden astronomical or geometric secrets it might contain. Under his reign, the House of Wisdom—essentially a library—became a bustling center of research; it was frequented by translators, scientists, doctors and engineers, all immersed in the study of scientific texts translated from Greek, Persian, Indian, and other sources. Empirical research, inventions, and constructions were also pursued. During this time, the first observatory in the Islamic world was constructed.[1] The ancient desert fascination with the skies and stars could now be pursued using scientific instruments and mathematical equations.

Under the rule of al-Mamun's father, the famed and elusive Jabir Ibn Hayyan lived and worked—the founder of experimental chemistry, who came up with the idea of a periodic table (later made reality by Lavoisier). Spherical trigonometry—an essential element for astronomical models later on—algebra, and the logarithmic tables constructed by the famed Persian scholar Khawarizmi (who also introduced the Indian decimal system to the Arab world) belong to this period, as well—as do the mathematical works of the Sabian Thabet Ibn Qurra. This is when the enterprising Banu Musa brothers authored the *Book of Machineries*.[2] The caliph himself commissioned the work, in addition to treatises on chemistry, geography, optics, and countless other fields. The Mu'tazilite Jahiz (the speculative discourse scholar who turned to the study of animals[3]) pursued his studies in the House of Wisdom, as well.

Indeed, the Mu'tazilites—the forerunners of speculative reason in Islam—may have experienced their best years under this caliph's reign.[4] It was truly a "golden age"—as many scholars and historians came to call it. Whether al-Ma'mun held discussions with the scholars at "the House" or hosted them in the evening in his *majlis* (court) at the palace, whether discussions concerned the stars, the circumference of the earth, or metaphysics, it was a climate in which scholars of different hues and colors could present their opinions freely and without fear of intimidation. A truly scientific spirit prevailed. In this climate, the new discipline of *falsafa*, or philosophy, emerged. Above all, it is identified with one al-Kindi (d. 873), a man of the same tribe as the poet-prince Imru'al-Qays. Al-Kindi also engaged in scientific research and produced works on subjects ranging from color dyes to music and mathematics. This orientation may mark the initial divergence, in the story of reason, between philosophy and the discipline of speculative discourse, *kalam*.

Not all philosophers in Islam were scientists, yet most of them seem to have considered empirical research of one kind or another (rather than the analysis of language) to constitute an indispensable part of their activity. This may well have had to do with Aristotle in particular, whose works reflect the integral continuity between empirical observation and metaphysical speculation. More generally, it may have followed from the nature of material translated from Greek—the works of Euclid, Galen, Ptolemy, and the like, alongside those of Plato and Plotinus. "Knowledge" came to be viewed as a single and comprehensive corpus containing all these disciplines; to be "a person of knowledge," or a philosopher, one had to demonstrate the ability to work with all of them. In addition, al-Ma'mun and other rulers were interested in technology—innovations that would increase human mastery of nature. Already, then, human reason had begun to be fascinated by sources other than the Qur'an, and the imagination by subject matter other than "speech." At the same time, however, the empirical aspect of Islamic philosophy must also have stemmed from the personal characteristics of the men who took to this pursuit—often, they seemed less mindful of indigenous disciplines than of the new sciences beginning to filter into the Muslim world from abroad.

In his writings, al-Kindi (like other philosophers, later on) made sure to emphasize that the new fields provided by Greek sources should be studied alongside native disciplines. The two pursuits complement each other, he affirmed in *On First Philosophy*. In lineage, al-Kindi may be compared to Plato, descending from what might be considered an aristocratic background from the Arab tribe of Kindah. In his philosophical approach, however, he stood closer to Aristotle, for he was not content with theoretical argumentation and speculation. Some scholars have suggested that he must have learned some Greek to write on philosophy. But given the line of celebrated Christian scholars at the House of Wisdom—whose main task involved translation into Arabic—he would have had no need to study the other language. The work was performed for him (and for others, too) at the behest of al-Ma'mun, who even sent envoys abroad to acquire whatever works they could from other cultures and languages so that they might be made available in Arabic.

It is impossible to overestimate the contribution that Syriac Nestorian Christians made to the development of "the House." The project of translating the major Greek works preserved by the Eastern Church of Byzantium was formally inaugurated by the "sheikh of translators," Hunayn Ibn Ishaq (d. 873), and continued by his son and others. The same occurred with works in Persian and other tongues. In addition to translating, most of these scholars authored studies of their own in fields ranging from medicine to ophthalmology. Qusta bin Luqa (d. 912), a Melkite Christian of Greek origin from Baalbeck in Lebanon, authored and translated in fields ranging from astronomy to medicine. The first translation of Ptolemy's *Almagest* is attributed to him. It is primarily thanks to the efforts of these scholars that the Greek heritage was preserved for the Latin West. In the process, they earned the distinction of laying the foundations of philosophical Arabic in Islam.

Alfarabi (d. ca. 950)—the second major figure of Islamic philosophy, typically referred to as "the second master" (after Aristotle)—is reported to have studied logic with the Nestorians Youhanna Bin Haylan and Abu Bishr Matta ibn Yunus; in Baghdad, the latter continued the scholarly tradition of earlier Nestorians at the House of Wisdom. In a supposedly autobiographical narrative reproduced in the work of a later historian,[5] Alfarabi traces a direct lineage for the transmission of philosophy from Alexandria to Edessa and Nusaybin; finally, it reached him (through his teacher) in Baghdad. Whether authentic or not, the report reflects the common view of how the discipline of philosophy originated in Islam: essentially, it was understood to represent an "imported science," unlike the disciplines of speculative discourse and jurisprudence. The fact that it was imported would have been only too apparent, for the Arabic used to write it was initially at pains to incorporate foreign terms and concepts. Phrases that seemed cacophonous offended traditional ears and sensibilities. Indeed, orthodox scholars derided al-Kindi's philosophical Arabic. It must be said that such scorn was not entirely fair. While some of al-Kindi's extant writings in metaphysics may have sounded strange, other writings that have survived—for example, his essay on sorrow—are beautifully written. At any rate, it wasn't until Alfarabi that philosophical language assumed "indigenous" form. By the time of Avicenna, it had become sufficiently established for traditionalists to view its "naturalization" as a threat.

Many years later, Ibn Khaldun (d. 1406), the founder of the "science of society," distinguished between two kinds of science in Islam, which he called "transmitted" and "rational," respectively. The latter term was reserved primarily for philosophy. The former included speculative discourse and jurisprudence, in addition to other disciplines. Al-Ghazali[6] had distinguished between "religious" and "rational" pursuits. However, it is important not to be misled by these classifications—it is not as if one category employed reason and the other did not. On the contrary, both speculative discourse and jurisprudence were essentially rational sciences—as was the study of language, which we will discuss in a moment. What set philosophy apart was not so much its "rationalist approach" as the metaphysical views its proponents held (at least in part) and, significantly, its independent genesis as a comprehensive body of knowledge in which the natural and other mathematical sciences formed important parts. From the very beginning, scholars pursuing theoretical philosophy studied and wrote about the sciences, too; in the case of medicine, they practiced the profession. In the latter capacity, scientists would remain highly regarded in Islam.

However, philosophers faced a significant problem when they claimed that their theoretical investigations possessed the same kind of precision as their scientific discoveries, practices, and inventions. This claim in particular was what al-Ghazali, for example, rejected: although he couldn't argue against the practical value and accuracy of scientific practice, he considered that affirming the same of divine and worldly speculations was unjustified.[7] Nor was his charge extravagant. Many philosophers seem to have held that speculative metaphysical truths could be demonstrated as readily as the truths of positive science. The attitude must have originated, at least in part, in the way Aristotle's works were presented in the Arab world: as an integral series of investigations beginning with the analysis of language and ending with metaphysics. Evidently, the unitary nature of the enterprise, both as a body of knowledge and as a methodology, seemed so complete that it made sense for enthusiastic parties to claim that the philosophical truths of metaphysics were on par with truths offered by the hard sciences—assured by a logical methodology that was free of any possible error: the proper analysis of thought as expressed in formal language. Such a claim, of course, would immediately jar with the received tradition that the source of all knowledge is to be found in Islam's Holy Book.

It is difficult to know whether figures answering to this coarse characterization of the philosopher actually existed. Still, it was sufficiently widespread that it featured in the literature of the time in the form of real or imaginary discourse between a logician and a linguist at a salon of one of the regional wazirs. The episode, which has captured the attention of recent scholars of Islamic philosophy, is included in a work written by Abu Hayyan al-Tawhidi (d. 1023). The author's depiction of the event holds interest for two reasons. First, it represents the atmosphere of open debates that took place among intellectuals at the time; the second point of interest concerns the subject matter, which holds real and symbolic significance inasmuch as it addresses the pressing question of the day, whether the formal language of logic or the natural language of ordinary speakers holds the key to understanding and analyzing the world. The exchange involves two major figures who stand for opposing orientations: on the one hand, the grammarian al-Sirafi, and Matta, Alfarabi's colleague (and probably teacher), on the other.

Aristotle's oeuvre, let us recall, was taken to constitute a single edifice of learning. The foundations of language and logic occupied the two ground floors. The middle levels were devoted to the physical and natural sciences. Above them stood speculation about the principles governing all inquiry into nature. This uppermost level (metaphysics) is what al-Ghazali warned against. Other critics of the "alien" body of work found fault even at the ground floor, however, where the methodology—logic—is presented as a universal formal language, a medium for discovering truths about the world that replaces natural language. This critique followed from the fact that, alongside (and, in their eyes, in opposition to) "native" analytic efforts such as *kalam* and *fiqh*, which were based on the Qur'an and articulated in the natural, spoken Arabic of the time, Aristotelian philosophy proposed a logical system that seemed to be based on a totally foreign language. The matter concerned the utility of Arabic as an appropriate vehicle of reason, which was quickly becoming the *lingua franca* of the Islamic world.

Scholars took interest in language for various reasons. Above all, Arabic is the language of the Qur'an, which was considered the basis for all conceivable knowledge, whether practical or theoretical. Especially as time passed and usage changed, knowing the pure Arabic of the Qur'an proved essential. The growing distance from language as it had been spoken meant that specialized knowledge of Qur'anic Arabic was required of jurists and religious scholars in order to determine what Muslims should believe and how they should live their lives. Simply put, the law could not be understood correctly or practiced otherwise. Significantly, many scholars did not have Arabic as their native tongue. They not only had to learn it, but also to excel at it, if their claims were to prove credible. First, however—and as we have seen[8]—grammarians had to study aspects of Arabic (what is known as diacritics and *I'jam*) and devise a script that would facilitate reading texts—including the Qur'an—in the correct manner.

Scholars of language did not limit their focus to the rules of spoken Arabic (which hitherto had been unwritten and undefined). They were equally interested in analyzing the foundations of language, just as *fiqh* analyzed the foundations of law.[9] As occurred in *kalam*, the discipline developed along the lines of two major schools. The first, which was associated with the speculative discourse scholars in Basrah, displayed greater interest in what we would today call "linguistics." Scholars sought to define Arabic in terms of rules—in other words, to formulate a grammar describing how the language should be spoken, much in the same way as rules of logic reflect correct manners of reasoning. The second school considered that actual usage, rather than rules, should remain the standard for what is grammatically acceptable—even if such practices seem to conflict with rules derived originally from them. These scholars did not think "the science of language" should probe these practices in order to generate underlying rules. Needless to say, the "rule-based" approach attracted parties who wished to introduce new kinds of discourse (e.g., science or philosophy) into the common tongue.[10]

In the context of what was to become an intellectual "tug of war" between advocates of the Aristotelian "import" (above all, Christian translators and philosophers) and "native" linguists (who called for "purity" and held that actual usage—rules and practices—provided the proper means for reasoning) we can appreciate the interesting debate that Tawhidi reports.

11

The Language-Logic Debate

Almost genetically, one might say, Arabs are intoxicated by the beauty of their language, its alluring blend of rhyme and its broad semantic range. Poetry would not hold the exalted status it has enjoyed since pre-Islamic times if linguistic mastery—the ability to strike the right chords in the listener—were not so revered. The form of Qur'anic language, as much as the divine nature of the Message, still inspires awe. Its captivating qualities include the shades of meaning conveyed by the vocabulary: semantic subtleties that become apparent only as elaborate syntactic constructions unfold. In the exchange Tawhidi recounts to the wazir, the linguist Sirafi affirms that even a conjunction such as "and" (the single vowel, *w*) can hold as many as five or six significations, depending where it falls. Nor does the "dance of meaning" depend on syntax alone. Arabic is so rich, Sirafi declares—and it has spread so broadly in different regions, where the same word can have different senses—that the full significance of words emerges only in light of the manifold contexts they come to occupy.

Legend holds that Tawhidi was an unlucky, impoverished individual with an ugly build and few social graces. Clearly, this is not the sort of person one expects to encounter in stately courts where "gentler" men of letters and intellectuals are found.[1] All the same, he was knowledgeable and well read; a later historian describes him as the philosopher of *littérateurs*, and the *littérateur* of philosophers.[2] The wazir who entertained him is said to have had an insatiable appetite for the sciences of the day and to have been equally curious about the men associated with them. In recounting these meetings with the ruler, Tawhidi chose a genre akin to the famed *One*

Thousand and One Nights. As is well known, Scheherazade told Shayrayar erotically charged and phantasmagoric tales so he would stay awake until dawn—to prevent him from fulfilling his vow that he would kill his companion of the previous night when he rose. Tawhidi's life did not hang in the balance, and his nighttime tales concerned current debates among intellectuals; all the same, they were narrated in captivating fashion (if over the course of forty evenings, and not a thousand).

Not unexpectedly, the first night focuses on the subtleties and intricacies of the Arabic language. Further stories and accounts follow, addressing various topics of the day. The wazir is interested in mysterious and unsigned writings that have been distributed in paper shops by a clandestine group calling itself "The Brethren of Purity." It seems they are calling for some kind of religious renewal under the cover of philosophy. Yes, Tawhidi, answers. Indeed, he knows who these people are—and by name, at that![3] He adds that he has given their "letters" to the famed logician Abu Sulayman (al-Sijistani), but that the latter found them wanting in real philosophical depth.[4] What about philosophy and Islamic law, the wazir asks? What do philosophers and jurists have to say? Is it possible to reconcile these two fields of study? And what about Christian philosophers—Matta, his pupil Yahya bin Adi, and others? Tawhidi describes the character of these men: those who are pious, ribald, smart, or studious but dull. The exchanges continue. What about the soul? The afterlife? Sometimes, Tawhidi takes the questions back home to reflect on them, or to confer with his friend Abu Suleiman, before returning with a response. The end product, *The Book of Enjoyment and Companionship* (*Al-Imta' wa-l Mu'anasa*), is an educated man's literary delight, as the title promises. But for all the rich information Tawhidi left about the period, the author himself died old, forlorn, and poor. The wazir upon whom he might have relied for a decent living was deposed from office—due to the endless court conspiracies that were typical of the time—after only two years of service.

The famed Sirafi-Matta debate that Tawhidi recounts on the eighth night is said to have occurred in 940 at another wazir's *majlis*. The logician and philosopher Matta, we recall, occupied a high position at the House of Wisdom in Baghdad; he oversaw the translation of the Aristotelian corpus and is said to have taught (or, by other accounts, to have studied with) Alfarabi, the "second master," as well as Yahya bin Adi. As Tawhidi describes him, however, he seems no better than a bumbling idiot:

he proves able neither to defend logic, nor to rise up to Sirafi's challenges and arguments.[5]

The debate begins when the wazir asks whether Matta is correct to claim that the science of logic alone enables one to distinguish right from wrong, truth from falsehood, good from evil, a valid argument from a fallacy, or certainty from doubt. The question is clearly loaded, for it combines the seemingly straightforward matter of distinguishing between true and false statements with more problematic issues of epistemology and ethics. After other participants "conveniently" cajole him into taking up the wazir's challenge, Sirafi asks Matta what he means by "logic." Matta answers that logic is an instrument that can differentiate proper from improper speech—just as a scale distinguishes between light and heavy weights. Sirafi responds that what distinguishes proper from improper speech are the rules of grammar. He then observes that even if logic were to differentiate between weights, it would still fail to identify what the matters being weighed *are*: this can only occur through language. And if this holds for matters that can be observed with the naked eye, how much more must it be true of unobserved meanings and ideas within the mind. Finally, he says, if the logical rules that you propose have indeed taken this obvious need for language into account, they derive from what the Greeks have said. So what relevance do they hold for us? Why impose upon Arabs logical rules that are based on a foreign tongue?

At this point, Matta is forced to claim that, though derived from language, logic is universal—like mathematics. Meanings and ideas are not specific to any one language in particular. The new rules of logic define relationships between them. To pursue the discipline of logic, all that one needs of a given, natural tongue—in this case, Arabic—is to take a few basic words (e.g., *noun*, *verb*, and *letter*) which can then serve to represent universal logical rules. At a later juncture, Matta claims that if a logician were to look into matters of grammar, he would do so only accidentally or in a secondary way; and if a grammarian were to look into matters of logic, he would do so in like fashion—meaning, of course, that logic does not fall within the natural domain of grammar, and vice versa.

The extreme view of language Matta is made to advocate here places him in an awkward position. Even though he proposes logic as a scientific language, he cannot simply dismiss its rootedness in natural language—as might occur, for example, in the formal languages of chemistry or mathematics. As Sirafi points out, the relations between ideas or meanings that logic investigates are the very same ones that language reflects. Moreover, such relations and meanings are distorted by a system of logic that has taken to tinkering with Arabic to make it fit rules that are imported: introducing strange terms and phrases and trying to redefine what Arabic words mean. To illustrate his point, Sirafi observes that logicians have attempted to redefine the preposition "in" (*fi*) to make it fit their definitions of what "present in" means—as one says of properties[6]; in so doing, they have completely destroyed the word's meaning in Arabic. Sirafi does not deny the need to investigate meanings. He simply argues that to do so, inquiry must rely on a natural language. It is wrong to presume that meanings can be so abstracted from context and use that they become ethereal, universal entities (the issue being whether such entities have an existence analogous to the one affirmed of physical objects). They are integrally bound to the language in which they are expressed. Matta has to maintain that ideas, in the final analysis, are somehow independent of language.

This basic discussion, of course, calls to mind the major developments that have taken place in "ordinary language philosophy" over the past century—especially in reaction to a tradition (particularly in German and continental thought) that often proposes theories unrelated to ordinary speech. In parallel, major strides were made in the development of a formal language of logic for articulating and analyzing meanings and the relations between them. For all that, at no point in history, perhaps, was the challenge of understanding the problem of natural and formal languages expressed more clearly than when it arose in the Arabic context, some thousand years ago. It resulted from the tension between indigenous and imported traditions—above all, from the passion and pride Arabs had in their (now classical) language; they thought it the foundation of all possible knowledge—in contrast to a new system of thought (which presented itself as "more rational"). Arguably, this circumstance—the magnetic pull of Qur'anic, or classical, Arabic—still proves relevant for the "arrested" state of intellectual progress in the Arab world today (see Chapter 24).

Tawhidi's narrative mocks the philosophical Arabic into which Nestorians were translating Greek and Syriac texts, as well as the "jargon" of al-Kindi (with whom Arabic philosophy began). Indeed, such writings must have been extremely strange to read: while they claimed to discuss matters both rational and divine, they employed figures and words that—

though seeming to be in Arabic—must have felt totally foreign. Speculative discourse, as we have seen, had developed its own style, indigenously grown from actual speech practices. By the time later speculative discourses came to be written down or recorded, the language and style of *kalam* had been sufficiently naturalized that it did not give rise to linguistic challenges. In contrast, philosophic Arabic seemed to be imposed from without. Although the example cited above—the preposition "in"—seems trifling, it opens onto a vast debate about whether properties can be said to exist *in* subjects (e.g., whiteness in snow, or "horseness" in a particular horse). Clearly, this claim reaches far beyond giving a "twist" to a single word's meaning.

Needless to say, the picture changed as philosophic Arabic became naturalized over time. In his commentaries on Porphyry's *Isagoge* and Aristotle's *Categories* and *De Interpretatione*, Alfarabi addressed the matter head on, explaining the need to develop a formal, specialized language—as occurs in other sciences and professions. Although he explains, very "logically," why a particular lexicon is necessary, it becomes clear that the new science does, in fact, require that categories be "parachuted in" to support its claims. One of the major points concerns the absence in Arabic of the present tense of "to be" in predicative statements such as "The horse is white." This verb, Alfarabi explains, has cognates in many other languages—for example, Persian, Zogdian and Greek. Its role of relating the predicate to the subject is already implied by the syntactical circumstance in Arabic whereby the noun is followed by the adjective that modifies it ("The horse white" = "The horse [is] white"). Therefore, it is irrelevant whether the word actually exists in Arabic or not: its function is assumed by syntax.

So far, so good, one might say. All the same, the question persists about what we mean by "The horse [is] white": does whiteness *exist*, whether *in* or *for* the horse (i.e., are we to confer ontology "on it")? Indeed, we have been told that the verb "to be" (which is not concretely given in the Arabic phrase) is syntactically implied. On the other hand, Alfarabi's claim is that a particular existential relation is indeed implied. To show this, he argues that Arabic sometimes uses a pronoun in place of the existential verb: "The horse, it white." Here, the introduction of the pronoun—we are to understand—"makes up for" an existential affirmation that somehow "sits" between the original noun (as subject) and the adjective (as predicate). Therefore, he adds, we might as well use the adjective "existing"/"in existence" (*mawjud*), since this is what "it" stands for in this context: "The horse, existing white."[7] Here, Alfarabi's account begins to lose its credibility. By the rules of grammar, the adjective "existing" might stand on its own (as when we say "the horse is in existence" [i.e., "here"]), or it might take a prepositional clause ("the horse is existing in the stable" [i.e., "present in the stable"]).

Alfarabi proposes that this same, adjectival construction could be used in place of "it"—in other words, as the "is" of predication. Thus, one might say something that would amount to "The horse, in existence, white." Alfarabi seeks to emphasize the existential sense of predication. However, this is much easier to do in languages with the verb "to be," and he stretches the limits of syntax too far when he claims that his argument falls in line with the normal (Arabic) subject-verb-object construction. As it stands, Arabic grammar requires that the initial adjective ("white") not be nominative in this case, for the word would no longer modify the subject; instead, it should now be in the accusative case because, in this new construction, it has come to modify the verbal clause describing *the state* of the subject. And now that verbal clause itself must become nominative in order to match the subject. Otherwise, the sentence does not make sense in recognizable terms. Translated into English, it would read something like "The horse exists as white," whereby "as white" modifies "exists" rather than "the horse": "the horse has a white mode of existence," as it were. In other words, Alfarabi's linguistic ploy does not offer a plausible interpretation of the predicate as affirming the existence of a property in or for the subject. What comes to be affirmed, instead, is the property of white or whiteness of the verb "exists," or the construction "exists as."

For all that, Alfarabi's *Book Of Letters*—where he discusses the aforementioned issues—was probably the first detailed treatment in Arabic of the need for, and value of, constructing a formal language. More than the works of any other scholar, his careful and insightful reflections are responsible for the fact that a specialized, philosophical language eventually developed—which, by the time of Avicenna, became as "naturalized" as the Arabic of *kalam*.[8] Through the study of Greek commentaries of Aristotle (e.g., those of his student Theophrastus and his later commentator Themistius, as well as the Stoic treatment of conditional sentences) and by making full use of post-Aristotelian developments, Arabic logic attained unprecedented rigor.

When Avicenna came to write his compendium (*Al-Shifā'*), philosophical and logical Arabic—including Alfarabi's manipulations of language, which had failed to convince many of his contemporaries—seemed like "second nature." Building on this foundation, he was able to make major advances not just in the fields of logic and modal logic, but also in other areas of philosophy. Indeed, Avicenna's context-based treatment[9] of language displays such self-assurance that he was in a position to offer a perspective wholly different from that of his predecessors with regard to the meaning of statements—that is, the elements that provide the building blocks for logical models. Breaking with Nestorian Aristotelianism, Avicenna inaugurated a new approach to philosophy.

Back to the Human Will and Language

The example of the preposition *fi* ("in") Sirafi proposed had a philosophical objective, as we have seen: to question Matta's interpretation of subject-predicate sentences as concerning the existence of properties in objects. In the type of syllogism Matta had in mind, the units of discourse involve reference to abstract entities—for instance, "animalness" and "humanness"; by declaring in one statement that an entity is related existentially to another, we affirm, first, the independent existence of that entity, and second, that it exists in (or for) the other term. Alfarabi, in turn, took the operation a step further by arguing that this interpretation is logical, irrespective of the grammatical idiosyncrasies of particular languages.

In effect, Matta and Alfarabi claimed that subject-predicate sentences judged true or false in fact express what, in today's technical language (and following Bertrand Russell's terminology), are called "propositions." If sentences are the linguistic currency traded by speakers, propositions represent how matters in the world are (supposed to be) *per se*, in themselves. The latter are the "genuine" bearers of truth-values, rather than the sentences that express them. The logical distinction between a proposition (a logical entity) and a sentence (a unit of speech) stood behind the Matta-Sirafi debate: Matta claimed that units of logical discourse are essentially different from units of linguistic discourse, and that they follow universal rules independent of the grammar of any particular, natural language.

At first, this claim seems to involve what it means when two sentences from two different languages "say the same thing"—that is, the abstract meaning, or the proposition itself as distinct from the sentence.

However, further reflection reveals that such a view is problematic. Is "the same thing" (which, after all, we "know" only as the proposition itself) a concrete entity somehow subsisting independently—in a purely logical universe, as it were? Or should we presume it to be a concrete reality existing in the "real world"? For example, when we say, "God is just," are we talking about God and justice themselves, or does our statement represent a logical proposition occupying a medial space somewhere between us, on the one hand, and God and justice, on the other? In other words, should we understand our propositions as second-order "sentences"? If these propositions constitute the units of logical discourse and are the fitting bearers of truth-values, should we assume that the "logical universe" harbors both true and false propositions—including those that have never been expressed in any language? Finally, when we declare that "God is just," should we assume that a concrete relationship exists between God and justice at yet another level of reality, to which our proposition "refers" (as Frege understood the term—in contradistinction to "sense")?

These are questions philosophers debate to this day. The problem does not concern making propositions or considering them to constitute the units of discourse in a formalized logical grammar. Rather, it is about what we claim these propositions to be: whether they are constructs bearing on our own needs and purposes for organizing interaction in and with the world, or whether they amount to independent facts in logical space that reflect, or refer to, another level of metaphysical reality. The philosophical position Matta and Alfarabi took on such questions is clear, especially given their logical motivations. However, Sirafi's position is never really developed; even though the debate lends it prominence, it fails to provide an argument concerning the full range of implications. As a linguist, Sirafi is content to point out the shortcomings of the logical argument. The debate resurfaces in later treatments of the subject, when actual acts of speech are again held to bear directly on logic in particular, and on knowledge more generally. The matter comes up in the works of Avicenna and the philosophical tradition, which define propositions in a way that grounds them in contexts requiring the fulfillment of certain speaker-audience conditions. It also features in the works of Abd al-Jabbar, to which we now turn.

In the simplest terms: should sentences communicating information of the subject-predicate type be understood as human endeavors and, therefore, as bounded by language? The alternative means holding that they reflect relations in logical or metaphysical space. The question is whether meanings should be viewed as a function of linguistic usage or independent of language altogether. If one views them only as human endeavors, the sphere of logic they "mediate" amounts to a construct or theory, not an independent, concrete reality. In the philosophical tradition, Avicenna steered this course, which meant departing from the earlier Matta-Alfarabi position.[1] Another path focuses on the psychological underpinning of the speech act, seeking to explain what makes a sentence a sentence. Abd al-Jabbar took this approach. Curiously—and this is the reason for this particular chapter—he did so when discussing the will.

We encountered the issue of will right at the beginning of our story. It was a subject of major concern, bearing on whether human beings determine their own actions and what it means for God to be just. In light of the new context, where *falsafa* and *kalam* pose two competing approaches to knowledge, an example will prove instructive. As we observed in Chapter 8, Abd al-Jabbar's theory of knowledge centers on the state one experiences—for the matter at hand, the experience one has of believing with certainty that something is the case. In all instances of believing, suspecting, wishing, wanting, and so on, one knows oneself to be in the state that one is experiencing; it is possible to distinguish being in this condition from other states. Moreover, all such states are ascribable to one's self or person. The subject of experience is one's very self, not some physical part or location within the body or mind. If knowledge means "to be in a state or condition of believing something to be" (instead of meaning there is some entity, however defined, that appertains to, or "exists for," the epistemological subject), no need exists to pin down or localize such knowledge—for example, in the brain or heart; rather, it counts for the subject as an integrated whole.[2]

For Abd al-Jabbar, it was equally self-evident that having a will means experiencing a state such as believing and thinking. "Having a will" means having the experience of willing something to be. I have the experience of willing something—I know this to be the case and find myself experiencing it—in the same way I know and find myself in a state of thinking, worrying, wondering, and so on. To deny that I experience myself as being in a state of believing or wanting would be absurd or mere sophistry, Abd al-Jabbar claims. In keeping with the conventions of speculative discourse, he entertains objections and responds to them. One of the first objections involves the claim that "to *have* a will" means no more and no less than the fact that I find myself in a state of simply knowing or believing that I can derive some benefit from a particular action—such that, were I to carry it out, I would be described as having willed it. While explaining the word "have" in this fashion agrees with Abd al-Jabbar's general approach of explaining knowledge and belief in psychological terms, it elides or obfuscates a more fundamental matter. Abd al-Jabbar responds by observing that one may know something to be of benefit and yet not will it, or one may know that it will cause harm but desire and will it all the same (although he also points out the difference between these two situations); likewise, one may will something but not carry it out.

As expected, Abd al-Jabbar's approach to explaining the will does not invoke metaphysics—a frame of analysis that posits meanings with an independent existence, separate from human behavior. Rather, it addresses states we experience, which we can directly set apart from other experiences. Here, he stresses that willing is no different from other states we experience directly, and which we can tell apart simply by experiencing them. We directly experience our own sense of intention and will for bringing about a particular act. We directly experience *wanting* (to do) something, in the stronger sense of experiencing the *will* to do it. (The Arabic noun, *irada*, covers both senses; unlike the verb from which it derives it carries a stronger sense of "having a will"). Emphasis falls on experiencing a psychological state, or feeling, that constitutes a particular kind of action. By shifting discussion from the realm of abstract ideas to human behavior, Abd al-Jabbar can argue at the level of directly experienced human feelings or psychological states, which are hard to deny. In this light, the matter of willing something—or the conscious feeling of deciding what one wants to be the outcome of an action—admits comparison to other states or conditions one experiences, such as wondering or thinking. If the matter remains opaque, it is not more so than anything else one experiences.

The *example* Abd al-Jabbar employs holds particular interest. It would not be surprising if he had picked any number of commonplace acts to illustrate his point. However, Abd al-Jabbar chooses *acts of speech*. In fact, this brilliant approach should not astonish us, especially given that field of inquiry, *kalam*, literally means "science of speech." Here—in contrast to what contemporary philosophy affirmed—meanings are not abstract entities; instead, they lie in the sentences themselves, or, more precisely, in the ways speakers *use* sentences. In other words, Abd al-Jabbar argues that the use of a sentence represents a form of activity—that some acts, specifically those in speech, occur as they do precisely because of the agent's will (for example, when giving an order or sharing information in a statement). If the speaker does not intend or wish for a sentence to impart information about someone (or something) in particular, the utterance may be said to have the generic form of an informative declaration, but it does not count as a declarative sentence.[3] Here, Abd al-Jabbar distinguishes between the statement's form, on the one hand, and its concrete instantiation in a specific context, on the other. Only if it is attached to a context—in this case, that of the speaker *intending* to be understood as imparting information—may we understand the statement to be declarative. Indeed, we may glean information from the sentence spoken by the speaker; but this does not necessarily correspond to the *purpose* of the speaker (as she or he may tell us in turn). As speakers ourselves, we can tell (we *know*) what the purpose of a statement is when we make it, and we can distinguish between this aspect and information that is conveyed unintentionally.

There are two interrelated and very important points to be made about this perspective. First, sentences are *acts* performed by the speaker. As such, they offer the *paradigm* of what *will* means: we need only look as far as our own use of language and states of mind we experience directly. Needless to say, not all acts are performed volitionally, but Abd al-Jabbar seems to consider this matter self-evident. Even so, he considers efforts to identify an abstract meaning for will (which then could be used to distinguish between voluntary and involuntary acts) to be a pointless enterprise. Instead, he focuses on linguistic usage: the way we employ language offers the most direct means for explaining what "will" is. To avoid confusion, we should note that Abd al-Jabbar goes far beyond distinctions that philosophers, from Aristotle on, have made between "speech acts" such as promises and orders: even informative ("constative") sentences, commonly deemed bearers of truth-value, should be considered acts performed by the speaker. In other words, *meaning* is embedded in *use* at all times.

What holds when we are speaking also applies when we are addressed. Being an addressee involves understanding the sentence spoken to us as an act involving the speaker's will. For example, we could not understand being praised or insulted if we did not assume that the speaker *means* to praise or insult us. A sentence is not an insult if it is not intended as such.

It may take the *form* of an insult, but it is not an *act* of insult. Abd al-Jabbar applies the same reasoning to other kinds of statement: orders (whether positive or negative), questions, threats, and so on. Only inasmuch as they are understood as intended or willed for a specific person by the speaker do they make sense. Otherwise, words and their arrangement would be purely schematic and empty; they would not fulfill the function that grammar gives them. Abd al-Jabbar's basic argument holds that all of these functions (informing, questioning, ordering, threatening, etc.) make sense only if we understand them as *acts* associated with an intention and will on the part of the speaker, who wants them to work in a particular way.

In concrete fashion, then, the foregoing explains how scholars who anchored their view of language differed from those, like Matta or Alfarabi, whose investigations focused on abstract meanings. Although Abd al-Jabbar often adopts views expressed by earlier Mu'tazilites—in particular, those of Jubba'i, father and son—he also parts ways with his predecessors. The issue at hand offers a case in point: the elder Jubba'i seems to have held that an act of will can be understood only if it is associated with "The Will," writ large, as an immediate object of knowledge, whose "place" must be (in) the heart. In contrast, Abd al-Jabbar declares that such matters do not provide objects of immediate knowledge. We only come to form views about knowledge and/or will—what they *are*—on a secondary level. Our experience of states such as believing and willing/wanting, on the other hand, is immediate. Moreover, such experience is universal. But this means that we cannot hypothesize that we must know (or have formed an opinion of) what the will is *beforehand*, which we then come to understand by experiencing ourselves in the state of willing. Quite the contrary: we come to form opinions about such matters *after the fact*.

Admittedly, and like other psychological conditions, the state of willing that we experience obtains by virtue of some specific cause (*ma'na*). For Abd al-Jabbar, it is evidently a *ma'na* of the kind that Mu'ammar posited— that is, a function. He denies that the state itself is something concrete with a specific location. Reluctantly, he concedes that one might deem it a personal experience. The *ma'na*, in turn, would be whatever it is that prompts one to make the utterance in question in a particular context.

In recent years (relatively speaking), philosophers of language have raised the objection, based on the need they perceive for considering ordinary usage, that overly formal treatment of statements—that is, along the lines of academic logic—represents a problem. An entire body of literature exists discussing the *performative* use of language. We should note that here, well before the twentieth and twenty-first centuries, we can observe how due attention was paid to the different roles statements may have. Significantly, this view also concerns *constatives*—that is, acts of language that take into account the importance of specific contexts for conveying information.[4] What implications does this fact hold? In the main, it means looking at language as it bears on psychology and human experience (instead of viewing it as the gateway to formal logic and, in a further step, to abstract truth). It aims for a theory of knowledge about the world by way of investigating discourse; *speech*, not syllogism, offers the means for decoding meanings.

Thus, even though he did not take issue with the Matta-Alfarabi model directly, but only sought to defend free will, Abd al-Jabbar laid the foundations for an epistemological theory that uses language in a manner totally opposite to the way proposed by logicians of the Matta-Alfarabi school: knowledge is not "produced" by deducing true propositions through syllogistic reasoning; rather, it is generated inferentially through beliefs about the world, by means of methodical discourse enlisting natural language. The key is to understand what knowing something to be true means, rather than focusing on whether a proposition is true.

Finally, if knowledge should be understood in terms of belief—that is, being in the state of thinking that something is the case—we can understand why al-Ghazali considered *self-knowledge* to number among the items that can be known in immediate fashion, along with the principles of logic. Even more importantly, perhaps, we can understand why Avicenna—and later Persian philosophers, too—considered self-knowledge a matter as direct as our knowledge of Being and God. These aspects of philosophical tradition warrant independent examination and discussion. Before turning our attention to them, it is advisable to step back and take a bird's eye view of the overall Islamic "milieu" in which Abd al-Jabbar worked.

13

Expanding the View

At this juncture, we should expand our view and take in the larger picture in which our story of reason is unfolding. We do not know much about the life of Abd al-Jabbar. Born in Asadabad (Iran/Afghanistan), he started his study of the Qur'an and *hadith* early in life, then moved on to pursue *fiqh* and *kalam* under major scholars in Basra and Baghdad. According to one account, he was married and had a child, but not much else is known about his family life. We also know that he was contacted by a wazir at the Buyid court in Rayy, near present-day Teheran; this friend was a former student and colleague who had studied with him under the same teacher in Baghdad. He arranged for Abd al-Jabbar to be appointed high judge for the region. Henceforth, his fortunes and fame grew—quite considerably, it seems. He lived a long and illustrious life (apart from a brief spell after his friend died and the ruler changed; Abd al-Jabbar was briefly incarcerated and had to pay an enormous sum as part of the terms of his release). He passed away quietly at the fairly advanced age of eighty (1025).

Under the Buyids—a secessionist Shi'ite dynasty that effectively ruled western Iran for over a century under the caliphate of the Abbasids (which by then existed more in name than in fact)—the Mu'tazilite Abd al-Jabbar had free rein to teach his theories. But only a few years after his death, the political climate began to change. First, internal rivalries prompted the last Buyid prince to call for help from the neighboring dynasty; the army that arrived more or less assumed political control. A few years later, the Buyids finally fell to the Sunni Seljuk dynasty; the new rulers banished Mu'tazilite teachings, burned their books, and imposed what they claimed was an un-corrupted version of Islam on the population.

Our friend from previous chapters, the impoverished and unkempt Tawhidi, met Abd al-Jabbar in Rayy. He found nothing in him to like and provided the first (unfavorable) report about his character. (Later accounts, which were partisan in their own right, offer a different picture.) Tawhidi considered Abd al-Jabbar intellectually pompous and a religious sham; presumably, he thought him an impostor because of the high station he enjoyed at court and on account of his ostentatious (and expensive) attire.[1] Abd al-Jabbar had become extremely wealthy for a public servant, and he was not known to be generous in distributing his wealth to the poor—as a pious religious scholar was expected to do. Tawhidi hardly had enough money for a single garment. As someone who thought himself equal in learning, he likely felt jealous of his contemporary's position at court. Let us recall that his own sponsorship by a wazir proved both hard to obtain and short-lived. (Tawhidi's bitterness about his station and the "hypocriti-cal" intellectual environment surrounding him was so pronounced that he ordered all his books to be burnt after his death. Fortunately, some of them survived).

Already during the Abbasid caliphate, the Muslim Empire began to fracture. At about the same time that Abd al-Jabbar was prospering under the Buyids, in the western provinces of Iran, another intellectual fig-ure—arguably, an even greater one—was pursuing his studies, teachings, and writings in the eastern provinces: Ibn Sina, or Avicenna (980–1037). Avicenna lived and worked first under the Sunni Samanid dynasty; in the wake of Muslim conquests, their rule had spread from Persia to central Asia, all the way from Isfahan in the west to Kabul and the outreaches of Kashmir in the east.

Avicenna was born in Bukhara, the cultural and political capital, in present-day Uzbekistan.[2] Unlike Abd al-Jabbar, he led a life of constant wandering. From the outset, his existence was marked by insecurity and instability: he provided medical services to the Buyid rulers, but his rela-tions with them were often troubled because they were a matter of duty. Avicenna was required to accompany the prince or his general on battle expeditions; during the final one, he fell so ill that he decided not to treat himself any more. His relations with the princes proved so uncertain that he went into hiding for many years to avoid their demands; at one point, he was actually incarcerated for this reason. Also unlike Abd al-Jabbar, Avicenna seems to have shared his wealth, settled his debts, and freed his two slaves before he died.

It seems Avicenna first settled in Rayy in or around 1025—at about the same time that Abd al-Jabbar died. The last two Buyid princes, who were brothers, had already begun fighting over the succession under the regency of their mother, when her husband died. Until this point, Avicenna's travels do not seem to have taken him to Rayy. All the same, it is hard to believe he was unaware of Abd al-Jabbar or his teachings. He too had started his scholarly career by studying the Qur'an and *hadith*, but his inquisitive mind had led him to medicine. In the course of his studies, Avicenna delved into the Greek heritage; at the time, Bukhara equaled Baghdad for its open and cultured life. One anecdote holds that he first studied mathematics from an Indian grocer![3] Additionally, Avicenna acquainted himself with other religious disciplines, including jurisprudence and *kalam*.

Even if Avicenna did not visit Rayy before Abd al-Jabbar's death, he had already left his native region, which had fallen under strict Ghaznavid (Turkic) Sunni rule. He was seeking refuge and stability in regions governed by the Buyids, where Abd al-Jabbar's intellectual prominence spread far and wide. It is highly unlikely, therefore, that he was unfamiliar with the judge's teachings, and it comes as no surprise that Avicenna's philosophy constitutes a radical break—in its view of language, logic and metaphysics— with the so-called Aristotelian/neo-Platonist tradition. The treatment of statements—the building-blocks of logic—stands closer to the model proposed by Abd al-Jabbar than to that of Alfarabi. Avicenna's theory of formal knowledge—that knowledge represents a construct and does not faithfully mirror what really *is*—certainly does not correspond to the ways early Muslim philosophers conceived their philosophical project.

Avicenna's worldview was much broader in scope than that of early Muslim philosophers, simply by virtue of the time that had passed and the self-confidence that emerged following the initial reception of Greek intellectual heritage. Avicenna could also draw on a broader range of practical and theoretical experience. He was an independently minded "philosophical nomad," and his treatment of philosophy must have been informed by broader reading and activity. At any rate, he knew enough not to look down on *kalam*, as Alfarabi had done (and, later, Averroes and Maimonides would do). Instead, he took such views seriously and allowed himself to be guided only by his own intellectual inclinations.

Despite questions of common interest—e.g., language, free will, knowledge, the nature of God in contrast to the nature of the world, and so on—the intellectual focus of Abd al-Jabbar and Avicenna differed. The former turned to matters within Islam itself, such as the imamate (in effect, a political topic strongly rooted in the origins of the discipline of speculative discourse) and the ways Islam compares, as a religious body of thought, with other systems and religions.[4] Avicenna turned to matters within philosophy—logic and metaphysics—the sciences, and medicine. This divergence, in turn, reflects the difference between speculative discourse and philosophy as rational pursuits within the milieu of Islam as a whole.

But what is this "milieu"? From the beginning, it branched out from political groupings in Mecca—systems of thought scholars developed or "endorsed" as an extension of, and in reaction to, competing affiliations and alliances. By the period in question—the eleventh century—the Islamic world had become a mosaic of geo-religious territories, whose shapes and sizes changed along the lines of provincial rivalries and borders; here, scholars had to "find their place." Abd al-Jabbar's view fitted well with the rule of the Buyids in western Iran, where Isma'iliyya and Imamiyah forms of Shi'a, prospered, as did Mu'tazilism. Had he lived four or five years longer, he would have had to face the Sunni takeover by the Ghaznavid forces from the east (where Avicenna had been until he left after the Samanids fell to this Turkic movement). Reportedly, Mu'tazilite works and similar books of speculative discourse and philosophy were burned; Shi'ite scholars of all kinds (Qaramitah, Batiniyyah, etc.) were stoned, exiled, or imprisoned, and strict Sunni ideology was imposed.

Avicenna, on the other hand, seems to have been of a totally different temperament—which meant that he had to live "on the run." Although he wanted and needed patronage, he turned it down rather than submit to authority (in Bukhara, when the Samanid dynasty fell)—or he could not bring himself to secure a position in the political establishment as occurred in Rayy. Today, scholars debate whether he was Shi'ite and, if so, which sect of Shi'ism he adopted, or what legal tradition he belonged to; however, this is only because we feel more comfortable seeing him through predetermined categories—just as we feel more comfortable drawing sharp distinctions between the traditions of philosophy and *kalam*, or between Hellenic heritage and native thought. It is true the Samanids—under whose dynasty Avicenna was born and lived in his early years—were Sunni, yet their roots went back to a rich, Zoroastrian culture that dated from the Sassanid Empire. In contrast, the Buyids were Shiʿite, and the population under their rule belonged to one sect of Shiʿism or another (Ismaʾiliyyah, Twelvers, etc.). Moreover, Avicenna received his religious education from members of different sects. But for all that, he was "too big" to have been a follower of any particular sect, and the same holds for political association with any one faction. His "Islam" and way of thinking did not yield to petty affiliations. Precisely for this reason, he found it hard to "fit in."

Like another resident of Rayy almost a hundred years earlier—the famous al-Razi (a humanist practitioner of medicine and theorist whose philosophical doctrine on the Five Principles was viewed as non-Islamic)— Avicenna studied Galen and Hippocrates.[5] At the same time, however, he relied on his own medical practice and the natural human tendency to *infer* conclusions from observations. Consequently, he was aware of the tentative nature of the conclusions he drew and the limitations and inherent rigidity of the Aristotelian mode of deductive reasoning. This, more than anything, else explains Avicenna's approach to the nature of knowledge.

Indeed, our understanding of the figures here is limited by our tendency to see them through the lens of predetermined categories. As a result, one "insists" on seeing Avicenna as, for instance, a Twelver Shiʿite, an Ismaʾili, a neo-Platonist, or a hybrid concoction of Aristotle and Plotinus; in the process, one fails to see the person himself.[6] Such bias also leads to an exaggerated search for the Greek origins of Arabic terms in *kalam* or philosophy, and it obscures how the terms (when they exist) function in Arabic context. Scholars make the mistake, for example, of reading the Avicennian system of God's relation to the world as a "corrupt" or "distorted" version of Plotinus's *Enneads*, when, instead, they might appreciate it in terms of the author's own faith in Islam (informed, of course, by countless sources—Greek, Arabic, Persian, Sanskrit, etc.).

Thanks to Muslim expansion and political development, the Islamic milieu had become a rich and wide-ranging cultural space by the eleventh century. If we broaden our view a little, we can witness the incredible variety of ways that reason found expression and flourished. Traveling west to Umayyad Spain, we can meet with the polymath Ibn Hazm (994–1064), who was born in Cordoba, and explore the case he made for a literal reading of the Qur'an. In Fatimid Cairo, we might encounter Ibn al-Haytham, or al-Hazen (965–1040), who was born in Basra when it formed part of the Buyid dynasty, and ask him about his objections to Ptolemy or the formulas he introduced to mathematics. Traveling east, toward the Persian heartland and Central Asia—as far as India—we might encounter the polyglot al-Biruni (973–1048); he was born in modern-day Uzbekistan and died in what is now Afghanistan, yet his travels took him elsewhere, too—for example, to Bukhara, where he met Avicenna. We could ask him if he was satisfied with the answer Avicenna gave him about the possibility of other worlds—that if such worlds exist, they must be different in nature from this one. (Avicenna's theory of possible worlds set him apart from many, if not all, philosophers of the period; it merits comparison to ideas proposed by Leibniz.)[7] Most of these figures did not lead very stable lives, either. Al-Biruni was hauled off by Ghazni rulers from Rayy to serve in the eastern provinces. (He made the most of the adventure by acquainting himself with the sciences in India and producing the most thorough compendium to date of the region's cultural and geographic features.) Ibn Hazm—even though he hailed from the political aristocracy—wound up in jail more than once because he was suspected of political conspiracy. Ibn al-Haytham feigned madness and endured incarceration in Cairo for ten years rather than reveal that he was unable to devise a method of regulating the floods of the Nile; during this time, he completed his groundbreaking work on optics.

Returning to Arabia's Fertile Crescent and al-Ma'arra in northern Syria, we could meet with the blind philosopher-poet al-Ma'arri (973–1058), who held that all religions and prophets are false; according to some scholars, his *Epistle of Forgiveness* is echoed in Dante's *Divine Comedy*. In Nishapur, Iran, we could converse with the ingenious poet/scientist/philosopher Omar Khayyam (b. 1048) and learn how to reconstruct Euclid's theorem of parallels; we could hear him teach Avicenna's *Healing* to his students, or ask whether it is true that he designed an experiment for al-Ghazali to demonstrate how the earth is a sphere—perhaps even rotating around its axis.

Such was the Islamic milieu: a vast cultural space alive with the wisdom of ancient civilizations, creeds, and systems of thought, containing a plethora of nations and ethnicities with their own histories and traditions, divided geographically by petty political rivalries, but held together by the

Arabic language of the Qur'an and its messenger Muhammad. Had it not been for the Prophet, not only would there have been no Islam—reason, rooted in efforts to understand and explain this faith, would not have flourished, either. From the outset—and certainly later, too—reason entertained a complex relationship with politics. Whether different schools of thought were promoted, merely tolerated, or repressed by different political regimes, brilliant scholars could be found almost everywhere; but for all that, they were invariably subject to the political climates in which they lived.

This held equally for philosophers and practitioners of speculative discourse. We have already seen how Mu'tazilite fortunes rose and fell because of political circumstances. Likewise, one of the main reasons cited for the spread of the Ash'ari school of speculative discourse (and Islamic orthodoxy) is the support Saladdin offered it in the twelfth century. After unseating the Shi'ite Fatimids in Cairo, his Ayyubid Dynasty ruled Egypt and (greater) Syria. Here, the paths of religious scholars and philosophers diverged. Members of the former group could hold government posts and use their position to disseminate their theories. Philosophers, on the other hand, generally lacked the qualifications (and interest) to become part of the official system. There were, of course, exceptions, such as Averroes. But the general rule was that *nonreligious* scholars did not and could not be influential as *public intellectuals*—that is, effectively shape public opinion. Unlike religious scholars, they were not situated, much less empowered, to have their word heard by the general public.[8]

The cause was not the obscurity of their doctrines—the atomism advanced by the Ash'arites, or their discourse about the divine, was not less opaque than the theories of the philosophers. Though brilliant, the philosophers remained marginal, at best. Their feats in pure science were generally acclaimed at the time, and they still are now. However, the same does not hold for their philosophical doctrines, which were either shunned or mocked. Alfarabi (872–950)—with one eye on Socrates, and the other on the political climate in which he lived—may have seen that coming, and his writings in political philosophy are well worth studying for this reason.

14

An Interlude

Caliph, Imam, and Philosopher-King

Before moving on to Alfarabi and his school of thought—which effectively formalized, with negative consequences in the long term, the estrangement of philosophical pursuits from the traditional disciplines—we should take another bird's eye view of the fractured political landscape. Our attention turns to the ramifications of one of the earliest, unresolved controversies in Islam: the role of the caliph. As noted, disputations among scholars and political conflict began with the passing of the Prophet, and much of it centered on the question of political succession. We have already discussed some of the more theoretical claims made by linguists, jurists, theologians or religious scholars, and, in passing, philosophers. One way or another, varying approaches connected to people's and schools' understanding of their religion: how Muslims should live, and who or what has the final authority to determine the guidelines.

Muhammad's death immediately gave rise to the question—which continued to be debated long afterwards—about the precise role of his successor. While he lived, the Prophet had been both "the spokesperson" of the religion—its messenger—as well as a political ruler. When he died, it was hard but not impossible to decide on someone who would perform the second role; it proved impossible to decide whether anyone could perform the first. Supporters of his nephew, Ali, believed (and continue to believe) that the Prophet's "divinity" had somehow been transferred to the younger man. Following Ali's murder, and later that of his sons, supporters of this view (Shi'ites) continued to believe in an ideal Islamic order governed by a ruler (imam) to whom, one way or another, divinely established authority had passed.

But what about the other followers of the Prophet—those for whom choosing a successor was more a matter of pragmatic considerations? Initially, perhaps, they—the Sunnis—did not view the question as too much of a problem; after all, one major consideration could be easily met: the successor had to be a close associate of the Prophet—and would have been therefore sufficiently acquainted with his message, both in word and in spirit. However, as time passed and "practical" considerations came to involve power politics more than religion, both the call, and the need, for distinguishing between the two aspects of authority became more compelling: whatever the source from which political leaders derived their legitimacy, it was clearly not religiosity or religious scholarship; consequently, religious authority—now identified with pious scholars (jurists)—came to constitute a separate domain. It was a matter of those to whom the faithful looked for religious guidance. Over time, four major religious scholars (jurists)—some of whom, as we have noted, stood at odds with political authority—came to hold sway over the major legal schools in the Sunni community.

Thus, caliphates and imamates evolved as separate religious political systems or orders. In the former, religious and political authorities were seen as *necessarily* distinct. The Prophet may be succeeded by a political ruler, but this ruler never provides a point of religious reference. Following the first four caliphs (all of whom were close companions to the prophet), only one other caliph (Umar b. Abd al-Aziz, who ruled from 717–720) is considered by Sunnis to have come anywhere close enough to being *like* the Prophet in terms of religiosity to count as "rightly guided" (*al-rashidun*). By necessity, therefore, religious guidance was reserved for pious scholars acquainted with the Qur'an (God's Word), *hadith* (the Prophet's sayings), and the *sunna* (how the Prophet and his companions conducted themselves). On these three foundations, they defined what it was right for Muslims to believe and do. The task of the political ruler was to provide the general conditions (justice, security, prosperity) to ensure that Muslims will hold, and practice, these beliefs. In theory, the distinction still holds that politics and religion represent two distinct registers; religious scholars are supposed to formulate, independently, what is right for Muslims to believe and do. In practice, however, innovative judicial deliberation has all but ceased;

consequently, past judgments on ethical conduct have become more and more stratified, and politics has failed to *ensure* that modern Muslims can live their lives without being encumbered by archaic codes of conduct.

For Shi'ites, on the other hand, the separation between politics and religion is not a normal condition. The rightful imam represents a necessary figure within the Muslim community and the state. However, disagreement has long prevailed about *who* such an imam might be—how to identify him—and how to carry on with political life without sure signs of his presence. Over time, different sects have evolved. As occurred in Sunni political history, rulers or dynasties came to exercise power through standard political manipulations.

As we will see in the next chapter, Alfarabi and likeminded philosophers had an entirely different take on the matter: ideally, a political community would be ruled by a philosopher-king, uniting theoretical and practical wisdom in one. Reflecting on actual political circumstances, Alfarabi concluded that religious scholars and jurists belong to a lesser intellectual stratum than philosophers—essentially, because their "knowledge" of the world derives from faith and they employ an inferior methodology, inference, whereas philosophers proceed scientifically, making deductions from verified truths. In fact, Alfarabi's metaphysical truths were no more solid than those of his religious counterparts, nor was their logical methodology inferior. All the same, his dismissive attitude led to a divide between the two registers—the religious and the "scientific"—which prevented what might have been a healthy conversation with lasting, positive impact on Muslim life and identity. Jurists, after all, had long served to effect political change in practical terms. Political philosophers had every reason to reach out to them to develop a common language through which to ensure their social input. Essentially, jurists *deliberated* amongst themselves on Islam's code of ethics, in light of whatever exigencies arose. Because moral matters represented an essential concern for political philosophers, this highly developed field (see Chapter 9) might have provided the opportunity for exercising influence. But when Alfarabi disparaged the role of jurists, it widened the gulf (which is still pronounced, even now) between religion and secularism. A healthy separation between religion and politics among Sunnis would have been far better served if, right from the beginning, a common language had been forged between philosophers and jurists to address the needs of Muslim society. Today—whether in the Sunni or Shi'ite world—a common language promoting a harmonious relationship between religious identity and civic life remains sorely lacking.

The other impediment to a common language remains the virtual petrification of Islam's legal codex. It must be newly invigorated to take centuries of human development into account. Today, jurists and religious scholars need to break new ground to align the corpus of law with new realities. The focus need not—indeed, should not—be on what people believe, but what the right things for a Muslim to do are—how to conduct one's own life and live with others.

The moral life of the Muslim—what is, after all, flagged as being the first item on the list of law's purpose—would be best served, now as in the past, by a focus on practical issues. In the venture to revitalize Islamic law, the input of philosophers should be extremely useful. Unfortunately, because this venture started off on the wrong foot long ago, it is a major challenge to include philosophers in today's vital deliberations.

Philosophy and Politics

It is arguable that Alfarabi remained close to the philosophical heritage as it passed from Athens and Alexandria to Edessa and Nusaybin before finally reaching him in Baghdad. At any rate, this holds for the fields of logic, physics, and metaphysics. Even so, he read the philosophical corpus from his own perspective; whether he meant to do so or not, he ran together Plotinus and Aristotle and posited points of continuity between Plato and Aristotle where none existed. Whatever value we attach to these matters, however, where he broke new ground was in the field of political theory. This should not come as a surprise, given the political milieu where he lived and its contrast to ancient Athens. Both Plato's *Republic* and Aristotle's *Politics* took the city as the framework for political theory. For Alfarabi, on the other hand, the context was a vast, multiethnic, religious empire divided along internal fault lines; here, the lingua franca was not even the philosopher's mother tongue.

Alfarabi distinguishes between *umma* (nation), *milla* (religious community, or polity), and *falsafa* (philosophy). A nation is a community occupying a specific geographical space where a specific language has evolved. Its sounds correspond to the physiognomic features of its inhabitants, which are determined by geographic space. Alfarabi's *Book of Letters* traces the evolution of language from a set of basic sounds that are taken up and agreed on, which indicate specific meanings among speakers. They serve the purpose of basic communication about necessary transactions. Eventually, the process leads much further—as it were, to the pinnacle of language-use: demonstrative reasoning. Simple and single utterances evolve as speakers multiply, gradually yielding a "system." The two dimensions, language and the meanings speakers attach to utterances, combine and permit more complex operations—for example, connecting an utterance with a signification other than the one it first had, or conveying meaning through different forms of utterance. Significations evolve as social transactions become more elaborate, people multiply, and the society develops intellectually—proceeding from simple, particular observations to complex, abstract ideas. In this phase, Alfarabi focuses on how the world of linguistic operations relates to speakers, that is, how significations involve the ways speakers view matters, not how things really *are*. In this framework, common speech (the medium of knowledge for *kalam*, as we have seen) has a limited reach. It does not offer a "storehouse" where truths about the world can be found.

Relying on the Aristotelian categorization of types of language, Alfarabi considers interactive speech to be fundamental: informing, asking, responding, ordering, declaring, and so on.[1] Next comes oratory (rhetoric), which broadens the scope of language; similes and utterances that are not literal now stand in for initial meanings. This development paves the way for the third level, poetry: the scope of signification expands; at the same time, order, balance, and vocal harmony are also sought. Eventually, the two arts—oratory and poetry—are perfected, and the ablest practitioners occupy a distinguished position in the community. They are arbiters of the language—experts responsible for "fine tuning"—who import what is necessary for the system to develop fully and correct defective elements. In addition, orators and poets fulfill the community's need for oral recording and recounting historical events, whether from their own nation or another one. When optimally practiced, oratory and poetry proceed along the lines of syllogistic/deductive reasoning (whereby, it bears repeating, statements merely reflect speakers' observations and do not express truths that are certain). The next stage of sociolinguistic development is writing: poetry and oratory can no longer encompass events and ideas in their entirety, which now prove impossible to memorize completely. Once writing is instituted, *rules* must be introduced, eventually yielding a grammar that can be taught to, and learned by, individuals from other nations.[2] By extrapolation, the rules of grammar are generically different from the rules of logic: the former describe speech habits, whereas the latter—as we will see—are formulations concerning the world of ideas, where "real truths" are found.

At this point, five paradigmatic "arts" have developed: oratory, poetry, mnemonics, grammar, and writing. *Ordinary* language is still bounded by speakers' beliefs, and its reach is limited by appearances. When the process is complete and practical skills exist corresponding to the stage of trans-actional evolution the nation has achieved, the desire arises to investigate what lies behind the world of appearances. The study of nature and math-ematical orders begins, as does the art of argumentation: thinkers seek to articulate claims about the world (beyond observation) that are irrefut-able. Sophistical and dialectical skills evolve; at first, they are confused with one another—the lines between them are not clearly drawn. When the art of dialectics is perfected, it offers the best method—even though it still falls short of epistemological certainty (i.e., it may help to disqualify arguments, but it cannot prove them). By this time, the natural and math-ematical sciences have also been refined; these advancements finally make it clear what methods to use in order to arrive at certain knowledge—demonstrations that yield certain truths. The difference between science and dialectics is now evident: demonstrative proofs (in philosophy) can only be acquired by means of the method employed in science. (Of course, we should note that the "scientific method" Alfarabi had in mind meant deductive syllogisms exclusively; it was neither inferential or empirical, as it is also commonly taken to be today.)

At this stage of social evolution, attention turns to human affairs and associations, whose foundations lie in personal choices and individual will. The dialectical method assures that knowledge about such matters *nearly* achieves certainty. This is the stage, Alfarabi contends, that philoso-phy had reached by the time of Plato. The next and final stage in this pro-cess of sociolinguistic evolution occurred with Aristotle. Here, theoretical and general philosophy reached completion. With the art of demonstra-tive reasoning in hand, nothing of general import remained that would need further inquiry or investigation. From this point on, it has been a matter of learning and teaching alone (which must, of course, be tailored to the natural abilities of individuals). Teaching and learning occur either by means of the demonstrative method ("scientific language"), in which real truths about the world are revealed, or by means of dialectics, rhetoric (oratory), or poetry (all of which represent "ordinary" language). Rhetoric and poetry are best suited for the general public: imagistic similitudes and examples guide the masses down the right path in civil affairs by enabling them to picture theoretical truths about the world they do not have the intellectual capacity to know by studying philosophy on their own.[3]

Alfarabi framed the story of philosophy in terms of both Greek and Arab histories. In either case, the traditions of oratory, poetry, and dialectics precede philosophy. At the same time, he identifies a language-based definition of the nation (*umma*), which allows him to distinguish between the various nations that have adopted the religion of Islam. In this context, the question—natural for his milieu and essential for our understanding of him—arises: what about religion (the *milla*) as an overarching system of beliefs and values?

After intellectual evolution reaches its zenith, culminating in the attainment of certain knowledge with Aristotle—Alfarabi tells us—the need arises for *a lawgiver*. His role is to teach the public theoretical matters that have been verified through demonstrative reasoning, as well as practical matters that can be inferred by reasoning. The art of lawgiving involves making the populace imagine theoretical matters that they are unable to conceptualize as they truly are, as well as inferring specific political actions to be undertaken for the attainment of the proper end of human associations: happiness. (Significantly, Alfarabi parts with Aristotle on this point, affirming the Platonic goal in lieu of "the good life.") This final objective—which is only to be achieved within an overall order bridging the here-and-now and the afterlife—is truth, which the philosopher who has attained full knowledge identifies. As a lawgiver, such a man would set the guidelines and give the right instructions to make the community realize its most virtuous state. Once laws in these two areas have been laid down, the only remaining task would be to supplement them with measures for persuading, teaching, and guiding the public on how to achieve happiness.

In this context, *milla* stands for the final stage of organization in social evolution. *Milla* is the word Alfarabi uses for "religion." As he employs the term, it may refer to Islam or to another organizational system governing life in community. It has three features: lawgiving, a system of belief, and rules of conduct. A *milla* that proceeds from true philosophy would come closest to being a *virtuous* association. In fact, however, different kinds of *millas* clearly exist (reflecting, to a certain extent, the kinds of kingship Aristotle mentions in his *Politics*). Once a *milla* is established and the initial stage of the lawgiver has been passed, the need arises for two "sciences" or disciplines: *fiqh* (jurisprudence) and *kalam* (speculative discourse). The first articulates judgments in specific instances based on precedents established by the lawgiver. The second is for those who wish to emulate the lawgiver by making claims in theoretical and practical matters—or parties seeking to defend the general doctrines of the *milla* against those who mean to criticize or undermine it.

Alfarabi's hierarchy is clear: philosophy stands at the pinnacle of human effort. Ideally, *milla*, as a system of beliefs and prescriptions, would reflect and serve the ends defined by philosophy, whereas *umma* (nation) is defined by geo-linguistic borders. Having presented an ideal version of intellectual evolution in human communities, Alfarabi now describes other cases. Examples include religion that develops without a fully mature philosophical method, instances where a religion is transferred from one nation to another, and cases where a religion meets with philosophy imported from another nation. *This is the case*, he observes, *for the Arabs.*[4] As such, due care must be given to employing the right terms in translation in order to avoid ambiguity—even when it means taking over foreign vocabulary instead of using apparent cognates. (Having been told that philosophy has reached its zenith with Aristotle, we are left wondering about the nature of Islam's *milla*).

. . .

In all but the best-case scenario, philosophy and philosophers need to lie low and protect themselves against the *milla's* intellectual/religious establishment (jurists and discourse practitioners) and the general public. The religious system of one nation—possessing imagery and similitudes derived from true philosophy—may be transferred to another nation, and the community may come to believe that such allegories are the theoretical truths themselves; for all that, if the true philosophy is transferred, too, it may not be accepted—indeed, it may be fought against. Not only will philosophers not be enthroned: they must be careful and able to show how their truths are not inconsistent with what the public believes. Public attitudes potentially represent a source of great harm for them.

Did Alfarabi believe that Islam—which existed before Arabs encountered philosophy—had developed from a *milla* (e.g., Christianity) that itself proceeded from true philosophy? This would seem to be consistent with the story he tells. Significantly, however, he does not say.

When Alfarabi explains the general truths of philosophy, he presents a system of emanation proceeding from the First Cause.[5] Indeed, his *Book of the Political Regime* declares that this First Cause ought to be considered the God of Creation! Furthermore, the (ideal) first ruler—that is, the lawgiver— is *the* individual who has received revelation through the emanationist process of intellection; in reality, he is the king discussed by "the ancients." The virtuous community, Alfarabi affirms in his *Book of the Milla*, is practically one with true philosophy. In other words, we are led to conclude that only the lawgiver who has attained the insights of true philosophy can lay the foundations for *virtuous religion* (or human association).

Significantly, the sociolinguistic process of evolution leading to the arrival of such a lawgiver is altogether *natural*. In *Book of the Milla*, Alfarabi declares that the virtuous first ruler obtains the truths of philosophy by way of *revelation* and observes that he has already shown what this expression means in his treatment of the theoretical sciences; unmistakably, he is referring to the theory of emanation. Of course, it is conceivable Alfarabi saw the Prophet of Islam as the true lawgiver. However, he does not say so. Likewise, it is conceivable that he believed that the Islamic state has come closest to realizing the ideal, philosophical polity. But again, he did not say so. The most he says about where Islam fits in the picture is when he tells us that the introduction of philosophy *may follow* the establishment of a *milla* which itself is already based on a true philosophy—as in the case of the Arabs! The *milla's* beliefs *may* correspond to original philosophic truths; he does not say that they do, however.

Clearly, a philosopher with such views, who lived in an Islamic milieu with an established system of beliefs in similitudes (however much they authentically reflected the truths of philosophy), would have a hard time professing the way he thought. He could not realistically hope to acquire a prominent political position in the community—much less to be enthroned as "king," as per Plato's *Republic*. Perhaps the best a philosopher can hope for in such a climate, Alfarabi tells us, is that a ruler will "understand" or "sympathize" with him and offer a certain degree of protection allowing him to pursue his studies in seclusion. Indeed, Sayf al-Din al-Hamadani—the ruler of Damascus at the time—seems to have done just that, letting Alfarabi roam through the fields of the city toward the end of this life, recording his thoughts. The fact that early biographies hardly mention him until about a hundred years after his death reflects the isolated life he felt obligated to lead.

In keeping with various *imamate* views of Islam—which hold that knowledge of divine truth passed on from Ali, the Prophet's cousin and son-in-law, to select leaders over different generations—some theories contend that Alfarabi considered the *milla* in which he lived originally to have been virtuous, but to have grown degenerate by his time. That said, his writings do not corroborate such a view. A more likely hypothesis is that the optimal evolution of the *milla* he had in mind had originated among the Greeks, that it was followed by Christianity as a body of beliefs and prescriptions reflecting this true philosophy, and that it finally passed on to the Arabs in the form of Islam. Philosophy would then have followed. Such speculation, however—even if it is consistent with the theoretical and chronological history Alfarabi provides us—remains unverifiable.

Alfarabi lay low. He did not articulate his views on the human condition explicitly, nor did he disseminate them. In this, he differed from two of his contemporaries. One of them did not meet a happy end by most accounts.[6] The other was Abu Bakr al-Razi (d. 925), who lived in Rayy. Although he later achieved fame as a humanist expert of medicine,[7] al-Razi ruffled some feathers while alive. Both Alfarabi and Avicenna rebuked him for meddling in philosophy in the first place—the latter says he should have just stuck to his field of expertise! Al-Razi seems to have attracted criticism on two fronts. Professional philosophers took exception to his presumptuousness and denied that he was a "genuine" philosopher because of his seemingly "normal" style of life. (Al-Razi defended himself in an essay entitled *The Life of the Philosopher*, where he contends that even Socrates, especially toward the end, led a "regular" life—as opposed to an ascetic one.) The other claim, which was more serious, held that his theory replaced the one, true God to whom all existence can be ascribed with five fundamental principles that account for the existence of the world; such a perspective obviously differs from Islam and derives from older, Persian systems of thought. Al-Razi attracted wide attention—and therefore criticism—for his views, whereas his contemporary Alfarabi managed to avoid criticism entirely.[8] However, al-Razi probably "escaped" physical harm at the hands of his community because he had no pretensions to politics, and the public role he exercised was in the medical profession. At any rate, he was "non-Socratic" about his "heretical" theory. While enough evidence exists to show he held those views, he was not known for advertising them or using them to question and unsettle the religious beliefs of his contemporaries.

Alfarabi's conception of the optimal community concerns, first, an organized effort to attain human happiness in a world where no borders divide the here-and-now and the hereafter, and, second, the role of the philosopher in light of the sociolinguistic stages of social evolution which lead to fulfillment of this objective. These are eminently valid considerations in many political circumstances, including those of the present day. Many a vision for resolving turbulent human affairs have foundered by advocating rational objectives that clash with public perceptions. The troubling question arises, then, how the philosopher should decide whether intervention in public life will prove helpful or harmful—and whether it is incumbent on him or her to speak up instead of remaining silent.[9]

Many years after Alfarabi, a philosopher in Spain by the name of Ibn Tufayl (d. 1125) wrote a famous philosophical allegory, *Hayy ben Yaqzan*. The story centers on three figures. The first, Hayy, is an Adam-like autodidact who lives alone on an island; despite his isolation, he manages to attain the general truths of theoretical philosophy. The other two personages, Absal and Salaman, are young men living in a religious community during a relatively advanced stage of cultural evolution. Neither is satisfied with prevailing values and beliefs. Absal chooses the solitary life to do some soul searching; he retires to a faraway island he believes to be empty, where he encounters Hayy; from him, he learns that the beliefs in his community reflect the truths of theoretical philosophy (albeit imperfectly). Happy that he has found the answers to his doubts and concerns, he persuades Hayy to come back with him and share the truths that confirm their beliefs, thereby doing away with any doubts or worries that anyone may have.

Upon returning, Absal finds that Salaman had chosen the path of politics as a way to deal with his concerns, and has become the ruler. Salaman welcomes his old friend, and he and the community extend hospitality to the traveler's strange companion. They genuinely wish to hear what he has to say, as Absal urges. It is not long, however, before the futility of the exercise becomes clear. The community comes to take offense at what the stranger says. Salaman and Absal realize it was all a big mistake, for it proves impossible for the masses to digest the philosophical truths they are told. The allegory ends with Hayy and Absal deciding to leave and returning to their solitary island: they realize that the paths of philosophy and politics cannot cross.

The Philosophers' "Frenzy"

Both Alfarabi and al-Razi escaped harm. The first did so by lying low, and the second by keeping his beliefs to himself and appearing in the public eye only as a medical practitioner—an eminently respectable profession. However, a fate like the bloody and tragic end of Hypatia at the hands of Christians—and Ja'd and Jahm (and others, too) at the hands of Muslims—befell another figure of the period. The Persian Al-Hallaj (858–922), grandson of a Zoroastrian cotton-caner, met his end in Baghdad on the orders of Caliph al-Muqtadir; this probably occurred around the same time that Alfarabi gave up teaching philosophy there and left for Cairo (before finally settling in Syria). Al-Hallaj committed the "sin" of exposing his religious views and trying to convince members of the community to adopt them. He may also have been involved in political agitation against the caliph. Neither the famous poet al-Mutanabbi (915–965), who claimed to be a prophet early in his career, nor the equally acclaimed poet al-Ma'arri (973–1058)—who professed complete atheism—met such a fate. Nor, in the same period, did Ibn Rawandi (827–911), even though he was an avowed atheist and the son of a Jewish convert; like al-Razi, he was mocked by Alfarabi (among others).

The case of al-Hallaj was different. After some eleven years of imprisonment in a Baghdad jail, during which he was interrogated about his heretical views, he is said to have been executed in the same way that early dissidents had been killed: first, his limbs were cut off, then his head; finally, his disarticulated body was thrown into the flames. Ostensibly, he received this treatment because of his views concerning pilgrimage to Mecca:

should one seek God, he had asked, at a physical location or within one-self? In fact, however, it was other shocking declarations he had made that brought the charges. Al-Hallaj claimed to be one with God—indeed, to *be* God. This statement is not to be dismissed as the hallucination of a lunatic (although he might well have been considered one by many around him). The speaker was a Sufi. Thus, his declaration was based partly on some kind of pantheism, and partly on the psychological state of a man who has internalized such belief.[1] Whereas Alfarabi was circumspect in present-ing his theory, and al-Razi was guarded presenting his—neither party pre-sumed to be a "spokesman" for Islam; al-Hallaj made the bold claim that he had grasped the essence of revealed religion. Therefore, he counted as a threat to the community's system of beliefs and the established (political) order. The danger he posed followed from being a religious "activist"—a dissenter from within.

Matters seem to have changed by the time al-Ghazali wrote his fa-mous *Incoherence of the Philosophers* two hundred years later. Many scholars consider this work to represent a definitive turning point in intellectual his-tory; in a sense, it pronounces the death of Islamic philosophy in the "east-ern" provinces (Iraq, Syria, etc.). Al-Ghazali was born in Tous, Iran, in 1058; early in his career, in Nishapur, he received instruction from the well-known Ash'arite *kalam* practitioner Juwayni (1028–1085). Al-Ghazali quickly gained prominence as a scholar in his own right and held positions at the foremost academies of the time (the *Nizamiyyah*) in Isfahan and Baghdad.

This author's reason for taking on the works of the philosophers was the "looseness" he saw spreading in the community. People were abandon-ing established beliefs and practices; in so doing, they embraced the "rub-bish" of earlier philosophers such as Alfarabi and Avicenna. Those at the forefront of the trend, al-Ghazali declared, are not genuine rationalists; instead, they are imitators who possess no greater insight than Christians, Jews, or members of Muslim sects who simply observe what they have been brought up with; they have not employed proper reasoning to arrive at their beliefs. Al-Ghazali, then, cast a new light on Alfarabi, Avicenna, and philosophy as a whole. Philosophers no longer counted as harmless, marginal figures pursuing their projects in an ivory tower or out in the remote countryside. Rather, they were emblematic of a dangerous social movement on the rise—one that was turning away from Islam and flying the banner of rationalism to challenge tradition. Worse still, al-Ghazali contended, such positions derived from a speculative edifice made up of nonsensical and indefensible views.[2]

As we saw in earlier chapters, speculative discourse was a rationalist movement initially prompted by the Qur'an which aimed to understand the world as an integral whole. Reason, not tradition, should supply the tool of investigation. Later, philosophy was added as the method of inquiry and thought to guarantee epistemic certainty. But these supposedly rationalist theories and claims about God and the world conflicted with revelatory tradition and, al-Ghazali felt, threatened it. In his polemic against the philosophers (which includes his criticism of various discursive claims, whether Mu'tazilite or Ash'arite), al-Ghazali sought to rehabilitate the revelatory tradition. He did so basically by rational means—including the philosophers' own logical distinctions and syllogistic reasoning—although he often included polemical and derogatory language when referring to individuals and their theories. He aimed to show that reason falls far short of revealing reality (as philosophers contend): one must rely on the revelation guaranteed by tradition. On more than one occasion, al-Ghazali stresses that his project is not to present what he believes is the right answer; instead, he says, he wishes to lay bare the faulty reasoning of the philosophers, thereby "demolishing" the pillars of anti-traditionalist social trends.

Al-Ghazali's main argument is that philosophy's metaphysical claims (concerning the nature of God and His relation to the world)—while presented as solid proofs on par with the proofs of mathematics and geometry—are hypothetical; they lack the logical rigor of the exact sciences. Let us recall that Alfarabi's evolutionary model presented demonstrative reasoning as having reached completion immediately after the perfection of the mathematical sciences. In other words, Alfarabi proposed a metaphysical model for the real nature of God's relation with the world. Al-Ghazali argues that this model, though *pretending* to be a philosophical articulation of religious truths, is in fact totally different from—indeed, contrary to—what it claims to be: the ambiguous terms it uses (e.g., "creator," "cause," and "unicity") camouflage heresy. In effect, al-Ghazali argues, such philosophers are nothing but impostors.[3]

Al-Ghazali does not, for the main, take issue with the philosophers' method of syllogistic reasoning. At one point, he describes it simply as part of a mode of thinking for which other terms already exist—for example, "discourse," "dialectics," or simply "reasoning." What he takes issue with, instead, are the philosophers' metaphysical claims. These include the question about the eternity of the world and what it means to declare God its cause, the nature of God's knowledge (especially, His knowledge of particulars), and the question of resurrection and the afterlife. If Muslims took the philosophers' claims seriously—which, evidently, was the case to some extent—it would mean no longer finding it necessary to practice one's faith or display proper concern about the future (i.e., worry about Heaven and Hell).

Al-Ghazali felt he had to counteract the growing influence of philosophers on young political activists; the destabilizing power of the latter was on the rise. In the conclusion to his book, after addressing and critiquing twenty different claims (some of them shared by discourse practitioners), he asks two questions: should these philosophers be considered apostate? If so, should they be put to death? Although he does not answer the second question, his positive answer to the first (specifically, in reference to their views of eternality, resurrection, and divine knowledge) intimates a threat. Given the author's religious prominence, budding philosophers must have taken the matter very seriously.

But what was this so-called "philosophers' model" of reality al-Ghazali considered hypothetical and indemonstrable, which he viewed with contempt and described as nonsense? Closely following Alfarabi's account, al-Ghazali outlines his rivals' ideas: the universe is a spatially and temporally infinite sphere, beyond which nothing exists—not even a void. The (Aristotelian) Unmoved Mover, as the (Plotinian) Self-Contemplating Intellect, emanates an order of heavenly intellects, souls, and bodies in descending concentric orbits; the first, fixed orbit, is associated with the "First Intellect" and consists of the unmoving stars; the others are each associated with one of the (Ptolemaic) planets: Saturn, Jupiter, Mars, Sun, Venus, Mercury, and Moon; the latter, the lowest heavenly body, is associated with the "Active Intellect" and has the sublunary world as its domain. Through self-contemplation, the Unmoved Mover "radiates" the existence of the first—and highest—intellect, which, as it intuits and knows itself, beams forth a (universal) soul whose orbit lies in the highest, fixed stars; at the same time, its intellection of its own cause (viz., the Unmoved Mover) radiates downward and brings about the second intellect.

The process continues: the "radiated intellect" intellects its own cause, in turn radiating the intellect next in line; this then intellects itself and produces the soul (*anima*) associated with its respective planetary orbit among heavenly bodies. The "mechanical" structure is actually a living organism. Pure forms and matter permeate the picture: the souls governing the stars are like our own souls, which control our bodies. Emanation proceeds at each level as the intellect contemplates its source and radiates another intellect; hereby, it contemplates itself radiating the soul associated with a constellation of bodies in movement (i.e., stars); finally, this process reaches the lunar orbit, governing a concave structure that contains the materials constituting the sublunary world (fire, air, water, and earth). Here, the second-to-last heavenly intellect radiates the Active Intellect, whose intellection of its source—and itself—irradiates the material intellects and souls in the sublunary world of human beings; at this last stage, the multiplicity of forms and matter follows from the countless rotation of the spheres and the interaction of the stars.[4]

This "top-down," Plotinian model has, as a corollary, a process of ascension which leads from the bottom up and promises the intellectual perfection and happiness of human beings. The multitudinous forms in the world of sensible objects act, through the Active Intellect, as potential "rungs" for the human mind. They can be abstracted from the particular matter they invest through an act of union between the intellect and the intelligible (i.e., the knower and the known). The process is both horizontal (covering the physical world) and vertical (ascending the ladder of higher and higher genera). Ultimately, it leads to union with the immediate source of *intelligibilia* itself: Active Intellect. Through communion with the Active Intellect, perfect knowledge and ultimate happiness are achieved. However, total "extraction" from the sensible world is required at this stage: not only must the intellect draw away from the intelligibles of the material world; the human intellect must also pull itself out of its existing material form (body). Herein lies the true paradise for the philosopher—and, evidently, afterlife for the rest of us! The model has no room for a vision of bodily resurrection, a beginning of the world, or its end. Indeed, there is no distinction (generic, spatial or temporal) between God and the world: God *is part* of the world—an "internally estranged" mover or cause—not "outside" of it as an all-knowing Creator.

Al-Ghazali did not take issue with all aspects of this model (such as the number or arrangement of the orbiting spheres), and he refrained from passing judgment on parts that are hypothetical and cannot be confirmed or disconfirmed by reason alone (such as the necessary and unitary nature of God). On the other hand, he did try to show that the "proofs" philosophers used to support their claims were invalid (such as the proof that there can only be one Being that is inherently necessary—a controversial thesis, as we shall see). More important, he sought to demonstrate that some were worse than invalid: they amounted to heresy. Al-Ghazali made both Alfarabi and Avicenna the targets of his polemic (as well as the Mu'tazilites insofar as the model reflects some of their doctrines, too). However, he was aware that the two philosophers also differed on basic issues—for example, God's knowledge of particulars (which Avicenna affirmed, but Alfarabi did not) and the role of the intellect (a thesis that Avicenna rejected). The model follows Alfarabi more than Avicenna, who had other ideas about the nature of necessity (moral, logical, and physical) in the world. On the whole, however, al-Ghazali lumps the two philosophers together, presumably because the audience he wished to convince thought they formed a pair.[5]

It is difficult not to sympathize with al-Ghazali's indignation: religion asks us to believe matters that, if we use our reason alone, we may well consider unbelievable. In this matter at least, religion is clear: it calls on us to have faith. Philosophers, on the other hand, try to convince us that inherently unbelievable matters can in fact be explained and even proved by the "science" of reasoning; however, in applying their science, they replace one set of "unbelievables" with another, which they suppose to represent the real truth (rather than a second- or third-hand imitation of it).

For instance, philosophers cannot prove that the unitary nature of the First Cause and multiplicity is inconsistent with the claim it spontaneously generates. They explain how multiplicity proceeds by postulating a series of emanations: the first is a single intellect, from which—through two separate acts of intellection—multiplicity unfolds. One argument for the claim that the First Intellect performs these two separate acts is that it exists in the mode of possibility—that is, it is not self-caused and therefore necessary of itself; because it is not necessary of itself, by definition it is not necessarily of a single nature. But, al-Ghazali asks, is the First Intellect's possible nature the same "thing" as itself—is it the same as its very existence? Or is it something else? If it is the same, then no multiplicity may proceed from it (as holds for the First Cause vis-à-vis its own nature, which is necessary). If it is different, then why not also claim that the First Cause also harbors multiplicity?

Here, too, being-in-existence is not the same thing as being-necessary-for-existence. The nature of necessity differs from the nature of existence; likewise, the nature of possibility is different, too. If one were to respond to this hypothetical question by affirming that the meaning of necessary existence is existence itself, one could claim that the meaning of possible existence is also existence itself.[6] Both claims would be equally hypothetical and indemonstrable. Indeed, al-Ghazali argues, the logic of the model implies the absurd conclusion that the entire world (not just the First Cause-First Intellect relation) consists of a series of linear, causal connections: the existence of each entity is explained by a single, other one, and each entity explains just the existence of only one other entity.

Al-Ghazali goes through the philosophers' arguments—those in support of "heretical" positions on the world's eternity, knowledge, and the afterlife, as well as those claiming to prove what already stands as an article of faith. One by one, they are shown to be either refutable or unverifiable. Neither do they form part of what counts as "immediate" or "necessary" knowledge, nor can they be "proven" as valid conclusions of verifiable syllogisms. Ultimately, they are just conjectures. (Al-Ghazali would say, for example, that no logical difference holds between believing that God created everything all at once, and claiming that the existence of things in the world may be explained by mediation in a series.) The arguments and counter-arguments are intellectually vigorous and challenging. Averroes (1126–1198) later took them up in his *Incoherence of Incoherence*.[7] Contemporary scholars came to consider causality the hallmark of al-Ghazali's philosophy, which he denied[8]: his position went against the view, commonly held by philosophers, that the entire structure of the universe amounts to a mechanistically determined network of necessary causal relations.

Herein lies a seeming paradox: compared to the indigenous literature of *kalam*, which prized free will and responsibility, the philosophical model imported from Greece (at least as al-Ghazali viewed it) was rigidly deterministic and permeated with fatalism! Al-Ghazali was a Muslim scholar brought up with, and well versed in, speculative discourse; hence, his dim view of this way of viewing the world is understandable. Significantly, even though his Ash'arite background was "atomistic"—a general feature of his brand of *kalam* (only some Mu'tazilites held this position)—he did not critique the philosophers' view of causality on the basis of occasionalism, that is, by arguing that happenstance collisions of, and divisions between, atoms account for phenomena. Instead, he understood God's will to override all else. Inasmuch as any two given things are distinct, one cannot be said to have brought the other into existence. This axiom—when applied to (supposed) relations of cause and effect in the world—implies that such relations are *coincidental* rather than *causal*.[9] For any two events, whereby *A* is taken as a natural cause for *B*, the truth holds that, so long as *A* and *B* are different from one another, anything at all (and not just *B*) could in fact follow *A*. Our "confidence" that *B*—and only *B*—will occur is given to us by the grace of God alone. On account of this grace, we discount the possibility of any number of infinite things occurring after *A*, and we develop the habit of expecting that only *B* will occur. Al-Ghazali's choice of expressions to describe "coincidentality" (i.e., our habit of expecting a particular thing to happen in connection with the occurrence of something else—whether simultaneously or afterward, *'adat, bi'littifaq*, or *bi'liqtiran* [by habit, by coincidence, by association]) has prompted many scholars to remark similarities between his theory and that of David Hume (who also reduced causality to a natural intellectual habit). Besides reducing what we consider consequences to matters of habit, al-Ghazali also wishes to emphasize that God's own "bringing about" of so-called consequences also represents a "habitual" rather than a necessary procedure.

Al-Ghazali's argument for "coincidentality" (that if two things are different, the one cannot cause the other) does not stand on solid ground. Indeed, on this basis one might argue that God cannot be the cause of the world—which is certainly not a conclusion he would have welcomed. A more sophisticated argument would have been—and as Avicenna proposed (from whom al-Ghazali likely borrowed the idea)—that, when there are any two objects, *A* and *B*, which are *possible* in themselves (i.e., they could be anything at all), *A*, in itself and *as such*, is neither a cause for, nor is it caused by, *B*. An important corollary of this argument (which al-Ghazali also employs) explains miracles described in the Qur'an: Abraham is what he is, and fire is what it is, and both are such that Abraham can be placed in fire without burning.

To be sure, al-Ghazali's "attack" produced the desired effect. From this point on, Baghdad, Basra, and surrounding areas produced few major philosophers. Let us also recall that Mu'tazilites had begun to lose ground to the Ash'arites after Saladin established the Ayyubid Dynasty in Cairo. Basically, the space within which rationalism prevailed had shrunk; the fields of speculative discourse and jurisprudence tended to be religiously conformist—instead of embracing "unconventional" philosophy or the freely roaming investigations pursued by the early Mu'tazilites.

Even though room for rationalism grew smaller, however, a curious thing happened. About a century later, al-Ghazali's own works were attacked by the preeminent Sunni legal scholar, Ibn Taymiyyah (1263–1328). Philosophy's "crown jewel"—the logical system that even al-Ghazali had declared scientifically indispensable—faced a challenge by another system of logic as brilliant as it was devastating. As we will see in the next chapter, Ibn Taymiyyah's critique effectively tore down philosophy's rational defenses; thereby, it claimed logical reasoning for the Muslim school of jurisprudence alone. Ever since, one might claim, reason in the Muslim world has been stripped of both metaphysics and logic; from this point on, it has stood captive to religion.

But Ibn Taymiyyah came some hundred and fifty years later. In the meanwhile, philosophy developed in the East along different lines, which one might describe as "experiential." It included the so-called "orientalism" or "illuminationism" of Suhrawardi (which was inspired by Avicenna) and the "Sufism" of Ibn 'Arabi, Ibn Sab'in, and, later, Mir Damad. Finally—at around the same time Descartes was sowing the seeds of modern European philosophy—came the "primacy of being" elaborated by Mulla Sadra. But like speculative discourse, traditional (Farabian) philosophy still had adherents; its most prominent representatives in the West were perhaps Ibn Bajjah (Avempace [1035–1139]) and Ibn Rushd (Averroes [1126–1198]). The latter's contemporary Maimonides (1135–1204) is credited with having conferred the title of "Second Master" on Alfarabi. Like Alfarabi, both Averroes and Maimonides looked down on *kalam*, which they deemed an inferior form of rational inquiry.

Averroes, more than anyone else, came to represent Aristotelianism in the Latin West. Initially, he was welcomed as the embodiment of progressive rationalism hailing from ancient Greece. Later, he was viewed with less sympathy and thought to be hostile to religion. Finally, he met with antipathy, when Aristotelianism came to count as an obstacle to scientific progress rather than a means of advancement. By the end, Averroes had fallen so far in Western eyes that, instead of the many deferential references one finds in Aquinas, only one footnote mentioning him occurs in Leibniz's discussion of metaphysics in *Monadology*.

Before continuing our story, a short reminder of the bigger historical picture may be in order. Even as al-Ghazali was writing—and right up to the period in which Ibn Taymiyyah lived—two major political upheavals were raging in the Islamic world. To the East, a giant Eurasian empire—the Mongols—was taking shape; eventually, it expanded westward into Muslim territories until Baghdad, the cultural capital of Islam and the Abbassid caliphate, was taken over and destroyed in 1258. In the West, the Crusades had begun. In 1099, barely twelve years after al-Ghazali died, the second earth-shaking event occurred when Jerusalem fell into captivity after a massive bloodbath. As pressure came from both ends, as well as from within the Islamic world itself, the pieces started to break apart; different dynasties divided by sect and ethnicity vied for dominance: Seljuk, Abbasid, Ayyubid, Hamdanid, Ghazvanid, and others—including, in Persia, the Ismaili sect led by Hasan al-Sabbah (d. 1124).

Hasan al-Sabbah founded the legendary Assassin fortress of Alamut. This impregnable stronghold became the retreat of the philosopher Tusi (1201–1274). Tusi—a politically enigmatic figure but a brilliant scientist— had studied in Nishapur and known the Sufi poet Farid al-'Attar; at one point, he fled the Mongolian army advancing on the Sunni capital of Baghdad, where he was based, and carried with him as many books as he could from the city library—the largest the world had known until then— just before it was burned to the ground. But when Alamut was finally taken over, he joined ranks with the Mongolian invader Hulago Khan, who brought him to Maragha to establish an observatory there. Tusi, Farid al-Din 'Attar,[10] Ibn 'Arabi (with whose son-in-law Tusi corresponded), and Omar Khayyam are representative figures of the new philosophical trajectory adopted in the Muslim East after the "defeat" of Farabian and traditional logic. This orientation combined science (rigid demonstrative syllogisms) with poetry (imagination); it was sufficiently sure of its mastery of the Aristotelian logical system of philosophy to liberate itself from its hold and open new windows onto the world.

Back to Wine and Logic

Let us recall the example of wine that al-Ghazali used in his work on jurisprudence when seeking to reconcile logic and the transmitted tradition.[1] In order to reach the conclusion that wine is prohibited, he observed, one must combine the Prophet's prohibition of intoxicants with a demonstrated truth: that wine is an intoxicant. Putting one and one together, we can deduce that wine is forbidden. For this reason, al-Ghazali maintained, legalists need syllogistic logic to arrive at a conclusion just as much as philosophers need the received tradition to complete their syllogism. (Assuming, of course, they desire to do so in the first place.)

The choice of this example must have reflected a reality of concern to legal scholars of the time. Ibn Taymiyyah makes extensive use of it when explaining the limitations of *syllogistic* reasoning as compared to *analogical* reasoning—the methods of philosophers and legal scholars respectively. Toward the beginning of this study, we encountered the immoderate bibulousness of early Muslim rulers.[2] The habit of consuming wine—or, at any rate, the desire to do so—must have still existed much later, since Ibn Taymiyyah decided to use this specific example, too. Throughout *The Response to the Logicians*, he discusses the concern of people who wish to know whether wine made from *grapes* is also prohibited—as opposed to wine made from other ingredients (specifically, *dates*, which were employed when the Prophet issued his prohibition).

According to Ibn Taymiyyah, the Prophet's declaration that intoxicants are prohibited is clear, and the received tradition considered the statement authentic. In making this declaration, the Prophet meant *all* intoxicants. We do not need to investigate each intoxicant—or each kind of intoxicant—to determine whether it, or the class it belongs to, is forbidden. As long as we are told something is an intoxicant, we can immediately conclude that it is prohibited. No syllogism is required, Ibn Taymiyyah maintains. *Proving* that wine is prohibited by syllogism—as al-Ghazali proposes—invites trouble, for this means one has to prove, to begin with, the truth of the *statement* that wine is an intoxicant (or, even more precisely, that it intoxicates). To establish its truth, one would have to examine each and every instance of wine. Clearly, the task is impossible, for it involves all the wine that exists, all the wine that has ever been consumed, and all the wine that ever will be made. Induction—the obvious means by which we formulate, on the basis of examples, a statement that is supposed to be universally true—does not offer a reliable means for guaranteeing the statement's truth. (At any rate, one assumes Ibn Taymiyyah would have thought—this would be a self-defeating exercise insofar as one would have to consume what he argues one is forbidden to taste).

Ibn Taymiyyah is not arguing here against the *form* of syllogism. He is simply pointing out the inductive limitation of its components—in particular, the reliability of the universal statement it employs. To use the statement as part of a syllogism, we need to make a general statement with confidence. How do we achieve such confidence? Ibn Taymiyyah observes that we must employ analogy. This operation is different from induction: it is not an additive procedure whereby the quantity of objects sharing the same feature leads us to conclude that all of them have the property in question; rather, the procedure involves understanding *why* one object has a particular feature, which then allows us to conclude that another item has it, too. Clearly, answering the question *why* something possesses a property is not just more comprehensive than noting that it has it; it also provides a foundation for generalization: *any* object which has this property must be submitted to the same considerations and judged similarly. In the case of intoxicants, this means we should look for the reason for prohibition. Whatever the reason is, finding it in any intoxicant (or, for that matter, in any substance at all) will automatically *justify* the judgment that prompted date wine to be prohibited in the first place.[3] Otherwise, Ibn Taymiyyah observes, we face the task of either inspecting each object of a *finite* set singly to verify that it is an intoxicant, or we must content ourselves with a generalization extending to objects infinite in number, in which case our determination will remain indefinite (and have to be reconfirmed with each new instance).[4]

This might all sound like common sense, but it is important to realize that the Aristotelian model of syllogistic reading permits a conclusion to be drawn only when a general (or universal) statement—about *all* members of a set—provides one of the premises. Therefore, while one may accept that (deductive) syllogistic reasoning offers a proper form of reasoning, one has to remember that, in the final analysis, it still depends on some form of induction; and if this is to provide us with a reliable general statement, it is better achieved through analogical reasoning, the method by which we determine *why* a statement we take to be true is true in the first place. In brief: Aristotle's vaunted system of syllogistic logic does not provide a self-sufficient method for achieving certainty. Ibn Taymiyyah's observation about universal *empirical* statements may not seem controversial (especially among scientists and logicians in our own times). For instance, if one were to make a general statement about the characteristics of wood or water, it is clear that—embedded in this generalization—one must make an inference from particular observations (however many one considers to warrant a generalization). By highlighting the *inferential* basis for a deductive argument, Ibn Taymiyyah is simply calling attention to the argument's weakness, or, alternately, the fact that deductive logic depends on induction for (theoretical) reliability.

Ibn Taymiyyah's point goes deeper, however, for the induction we require has a more solid foundation when the analogical approach is used. Nor is this all. Let us recall (as in, say, Alfarabi's model) that philosophers claim there are general forms or ideas subsisting in the natural world, which *themselves* warrant the truth of our statements about them. While we may first become aware of the impressions we receive from, let's say, observing different bits of wood, we can make a true, universal statement about the general form of *wood* (which underlies our impressions) only through intellection. According to this view, a universal statement does not prove verifiable through numerical calculation (e.g., by drawing on the rules of probability theory), but by grasping a universal or general idea mentally.

Ibn Taymiyyah takes this doctrine about general ideas head on. For a general idea to qualify as true for innumerable objects in particular, certain characteristics or features must be deemed essential. A ready-to-hand Aristotelian example that philosophers would use in this context is "Man is rational animal." (Arabic would use the term *al-insan*—"human being"). They would claim that both rationality and "animality" represent essential features that *constitute* what being human is. Man has other characteristics, to be sure—for instance, being a biped, having the ability to laugh, and any number of other qualities. Even when taken together, however, they do not constitute what man is: they do not identify human *essence*. We are still able to conceive the idea of "man" if we disregard all these other qualities, but we cannot do so if we abstract from rationality (*differentia*) and animality (*genus*).

Ibn Taymiyyah rejects the claim that *forms* or general ideas are somehow "out there" in the world, merely awaiting intellectual discovery; he also rejects the further claim that some of these forms (e.g., "rational," "animal") will be "found" to be joined as "essences" in other forms (e.g., "man"). He discusses the two sources that philosophers consider the gateway to knowledge: conception and judgment—the fact that we conceive simple ideas as a first step and then express relations between them by making statements. Ibn Taymiyyah observes that, based on the way philosophers say we come to conceive ideas, we are never in possession of single (unitary) concepts. For example, we cannot conceive the idea of "man" as presented by the philosophers except by conceiving two further ideas: rationality and animality; this, however, already amounts to conceiving a *relation* between ideas expressed by a proposition, statement, or judgment. The philosophers' distinction between two distinct phases (a sequence) when explaining how knowledge is achieved does not hold, then. However they may seek to present the matter (for example, by claiming that such a coalescence of three different ideas actually means conceiving a *single* idea—a matter of *definition* rather than a *judgment* expressed in a normal subject-object statement—it may still be argued that we are entertaining three different ideas instead of just one. Accordingly, the distinction that philosophers make between the two sources and phases of knowledge is not clear.

More important, such examples of inherent connections between ideas are questionable. We are simply *told* that "man" contains some elements that are essential and others that are not—specifically, "rational" and "animal." But how can one verify claims that exclude some qualities and include others? We simply *posit* some features of an idea as essential, but no natural or objective way exists to test our claims.

The examples at issue are definitions. Philosophers claim they represent the essences of different ideas or general forms. Ibn Taymiyyah does not dispute the utility of definitions. On the contrary, he affirms that they are helpful. However, he argues that we should treat them as we do names, insofar as they can be used for *distinguishing* between one idea and another. It is another matter entirely to claim that they identify an objective or natural essence. Indeed, the standard practice when we seek to explain an idea is simply to separate it from other ideas by means of features that (we think) set it apart. This—distinguishing one thing from another, as occurs through naming—is what defining means. It is not about using a theoretical microscope to discover essential features as opposed to non-essential ones—especially since the latter are associated with the idea at issue as much as the former.

In general, Ibn Taymiyyah is very critical of Avicenna; however, he acknowledges that his predecessor also critiqued the distinction between essential and accidental qualities of objects.[5] Indeed, Avicenna rejected the entire notion of essentiality and replaced it with causality, affirming that no two ideas are *essentially* interconnected.[6] By reducing definitions to tools for making distinctions (analogous to the function of proper names), Ibn Taymiyyah brings the general truths and abstractions of philosophers crashing down to earth: they involve the altogether straightforward matter of people's perceptions and the ways thoughts about them are expressed. Alfarabi grants them a special status, but they are no different than the ordinary language people use every day. Philosophers claim these statements should be employed to construct an edifice of knowledge. "Demoting" them to ordinary language draws a striking contrast between them and the transmitted tradition (the Qur'an and *hadith*), whose divine foundations prove much more solid. The "sayings" of this tradition do not come from ordinary people but God and His Prophet.

But what certainty can we have about basic principles of thought—that is, about the edifice of knowledge philosophers claim to have identified? Ibn Taymiyyah has already argued that *all* general statements (including basic principles of thought) are based on an empirical generalization. In each case, analogy—his preferred method for achieving certainty—proves more reliable than inference. This means that our certainty extends only as far as the analogy holds. However, even assuming that the analogy holds, it is something entirely different to claim—as the philosophers do—that this is what our actual edifice of knowledge is built on. Take, for instance, the basic principle of non-contradiction: that something cannot possess a certain quality and at the same time not possess it. This principle, Ibn Taymiyyah argues, does not serve the purpose the philosophers intend, namely, as a building block of knowledge. One does not come to infer (or come to know)—for example—that one's house is made of wood on the basis of the primary principle that houses are either made out of wood or not made out of wood. It might never occur to people who know that their house is made out of wood (on the basis of a particular observation) that it cannot both be made out of wood and not made out of wood. Positing primary principles as the elements that build up knowledge amounts to hypothesizing a virtual world. Knowledge is not obtained in this manner. Instead, people formulate general beliefs about the world around them on the basis of particular observations—some of which may be true, and others not—and construct what they know accordingly; at the same time, these beliefs vary from person to person and from circumstance to circumstance.

A common way to explain *a priori* synthetic statements—which Ibn Taymiyyah has in mind here—is to say that the truth of such statements is independent of the empirical context from which they have been drawn (unlike normal empirical statements). For instance, the empirical statement that wine intoxicates is true[7] so long as all kinds of wine actually do intoxicate. But if someone invented a nonintoxicating wine, the statement would cease to be true. In contrast, *a priori* truths are supposed to hold no matter what happens in the world. For example, the statement, "Either the house is made of wood or it is not made of wood," would be true even in a world where wood did not exist. Ibn Taymiyyah would not dispute the *truth* of such statements, but he would observe that they are irrelevant for the purposes at hand: even if true, they are not basic to our knowledge (i.e., factually "primary" or "immediate"). He probably would not deny the possibility of constructing a body of knowledge on the basis of such truths, but such an edifice would be a hypothetical construct, not a genuine representation of how we actually go about accumulating knowledge. Indeed, he would argue that such an edifice, constructed of universal statements, does not offer knowledge about the external world, but only how we think. "Out there" in the world, there are no universals or general ideas—only particular objects.

Ibn Taymiyyah does not deny that we can have certain knowledge. However, like most "traditional" scholars, he would identify *sense impressions* as the source of such knowledge. Certainly, they are not general principles of logic (which most of us do not even know about). Thus the certain knowledge we acquire concerns particulars in the observable world—which, of course, vary from place to place, and from person to person. It may also involve what we *hear about*, when we have confidence in the source from which we hear it (for instance, that so-and-so is the ruler of some country, even if we have never even been to that country, much less met the man in question). This, of course, fits well with the entire tradition of *sam'* and *tawatur* (that oral transmission of original Islamic sources, given meticulous verification, provides the best source of knowledge). Likewise, we can be certain about our immediate sensations and passions (such as feeling hunger or anger). But Ibn Taymiyyah adds yet another intuition as an object of certainty: one's moral sense (e.g., that doing a just act is good[8]). All in all, then, certain knowledge, for him, attaches to immediate experiences and particular sense impressions.

What, then, of general ideas and concepts? How do they relate to one another (for instance, the idea "man" and the idea "animal")? What relationships obtain between universal statements? Because they do not, in fact, exist in the external world, they offer "certainty" only about matters in our own minds. The ideas we have do not exist in the world but only within us; they are not objective, but subjective. Accordingly, their organization is subjective, and not a mirror of abstract relations between forms belonging to "higher reality." How we decide to organize our thoughts is a subjective rather than an objective matter. One category of mental relations stands apart: mathematics. To be sure, mathematical relations are mental and not given in the outside world, yet they are "thought-independent"—that is, they are not a function of how we decide to formulate them. In sum, Ibn Taymiyyah argues that logical principles, although true, are neither primary nor basic—and that mathematical truths, though necessary, are neither basic nor immediate objects of knowledge (for we know their instantiations prior to knowing their general principles).

Unlike al-Ghazali, Ibn Taymiyyah does not admit the logical apparatus of the philosophers and rejects their claim that knowledge can be achieved only by this means. Indeed, he faults al-Ghazali for having declared that the logical apparatus of philosophy is necessary for arriving at knowledge.[9] It is partly al-Ghazali's fault, he continues, that people—

including jurists—have fallen prey to the belief that the philosophers' claims about logic are true; in continuing to work on and with logic, they have gotten lost and ensnared in useless entanglements. It is not the case that people were—or are—unable to think without this apparatus, or that knowledge is impossible without it. In fact, it is so convoluted and involves so many unverified hypotheses and mistaken assumptions that one should simply do without it.

Although the arguments in Ibn Taymiyyah's *Response* are somewhat scattered and the text is full of repetitions and digressions, its force of argument is compelling. It begins by critiquing the claim that essences have an independent existence; it proceeds to contest the assertion that definitions reveal these essences, and then takes apart the distinction between conception and judgment (i.e., between singular terms and statements); finally, the work addresses various claims about syllogisms (including the position that two premises are both necessary and sufficient).

Ibn Taymiyyah dismantled the supports of the philosophical project in a way that had not occurred in the Islamic milieu previously. His ultimate critique of syllogistic reasoning along Aristotelian lines is made more plausible by the measured way he proceeds. Ibn Taymiyyah does not claim that one does not achieve certainty by this method; rather, he affirms that whatever certainty one may gain can also be reached by employing analogical reasoning; at any rate, syllogism implies analogical reasoning, which is therefore more fundamental.

Was Ibn Taymiyyah prompted by something more than observation to attach greater value to analogical syllogisms? Returning to our initial discussion of the role of jurists, we should recall that the latter focused on *particular* injunctions or specific behaviors. In addition, *particular* statements in the Qur'an (and the *hadith*)—even those that are general in nature such as about the benefit of honey—held certain truth for them. Therefore, they had no use for the general statements proposed as truths by philosophers or the conclusions they arrived at by deduction. However, it remained to be shown why, in particular, the deductive methodology of the philosophers was not full-proof. Thus, Ibn Taymiyyah needed to explain how al-Ghazali's "fudging" of the wine syllogism—for instance—supported his own argument.

Al-Ghazali's use of this example seems simple and innocuous. If intoxicants are forbidden and wine is an intoxicant, it follows that wine is forbidden. But there is more here than meets the eye. One of the premises comes from a *hadith*, and the other is (supposedly) a verifiable, empirical statement. The reason al-Ghazali draws on a *hadith* in this connection is very likely the absence of a conclusive prohibition of alcohol in the Qur'an. (At one point, the faithful are exhorted to *avoid* intoxicants because they are the wiles of Satan; another passage enjoins them not to approach prayers *while intoxicated*.) To complicate matters further for jurists, it so happens that the wine people consumed in the early days, when the Prophet still lived, was (mostly) distilled from dates (*khamr*); wine distilled from grapes (*nabidh*) became common only later. While the *hadith* explicitly mentions prohibition and intoxicants (*musker*, or that which makes one drunk), none of the three accepted sources actually records an explicit prohibition of wine (*nabidh*) in particular. Furthermore—and this may be the crux of the issue—the two sayings of the prophet do not in fact fit into the standard form of the syllogism having the required conclusion: one of the sayings holds that intoxicants (in general) are forbidden—that *A*'s are *B*'s; while the other holds that intoxicants are *khamr* (date wine)—that *A*'s are *C*'s. Together, these two premises do not produce the required conclusion *C*'s are *A*'s. What al-Ghazali does is exchange subject and predicate in the statement "intoxicants are date wine" to help him arrive at the conclusion, "date wine (*khamr*) is forbidden." Ibn Taymiyyah rejects such an operation, declaring that the Prophet did not have to resort to syllogism to make his point; nor, by extension, do Muslims need a syllogism to understand and abide by the prohibition. There is also a practical reason he refuses syllogism: the fact that, in this case, the prohibition would hold only for date wine. When he lived and wrote, this was not the issue: the question was whether wine made from grapes is prohibited. The most serious problem, however, is having to reverse the Prophet's saying—exchanging subject and predicate. Without such a rearrangement—a conscious 'tinkering' with the prophet's saying—the syllogism does not work at all: as already noted, to say all *A*'s are *B*'s, and all *A*'s are *C*'s—the sentence-*forms* of the two *hadiths*—would not lead to the required connection between *B*'s and *C*'s (that date wine, or wine in general, is prohibited)!

Such deliberations on how to "produce" or pronounce a new judgment in Islamic law based on a prophetic saying or a Qur'anic verse stood behind the jurists' emphasis on analogical reasoning. For example, it is now commonly accepted that smoking breaks one's fast, whereas earlier, no one had any idea that such a habit existed. How is it possible even to consider producing a judgment if not by trying to determine the original reasoning behind the proscription of eating food and then applying it to inhaling smoke? Here, instead of "climbing down" the deductive ladder of a normal syllogism, one seeks the reason why consuming food—or intoxicants such as date wine—was declared forbidden; inasmuch as this reason applies to smoke and grape wine, it is warranted to infer that tobacco and wine are prohibited.[10] Taking this approach, one treats date wine as a point of departure (the initial "fact"), grape wine as a branch or a derivative offshoot (the item under consideration, to be judged), and intoxication (which would play the role of the middle term in a normal syllogism) as the *'illah* (reason) or *daleel 'illah* (sign or indication of the reason) why the judgment holds for wine.

Ibn Taymiyyah's reasoning is sound. Thinking analogically is far more natural and common than syllogistic reasoning in everyday life. Thus, if we believe that driving a car in the wrong direction is dangerous, we are likely to infer the same of bicycling. The analogical inference here is not "vertical"—whether unilaterally inductive (one more piece of wood), or deductive (from a universal to a particular); instead, it is "horizontal" or *lateral* (passing from cars to bicycles). The term *daleel* that Ibn Taymiyyah employs is the same word discourse practitioners used to explain how new knowledge is acquired[11]: one must look for the specific "lead" that warrants making an inference. Mu'tazilites contended that this approach would yield "belief-with-certainty" (i.e., belief that the matter stands as a fact). Ash'arites held that it yielded belief alone.[12] Al-Ghazali, we recall, sought to understand the Mu'tazilite *daleel* as the middle term of a syllogism. Ibn Taymiyyah's method of analogical inference squares with the Mu'tazilite project, as they were interested in how to infer one proposition from another without relying on induction or deduction.

Needless to say, analogical reasoning was not a new discovery. Logicians were well aware of its existence. However, they held that it could only produce conclusions that are uncertain—in contrast to conclusions deduced by syllogistic means. Ibn Taymiyyah thought otherwise, and he argued that the issue of certainty or uncertainty has less to do with the form of a syllogism than with its content. Sure knowledge produces sure conclusions, whatever the method employed—whereas tentative premises produce only tentative conclusions. Presumably, normal syllogisms containing principles of thought and mathematical truths produce conclusions that are certain, while those containing generalizations about other matters prove less certain. In the case of analogical reasoning, certainty about one item (and the reasoning behind it) warrants certainty in the conclusion inferred. Above all, the most certain items of knowledge and premises we use—which, therefore, must underlie all our further claims, whether made by syllogism or analogy—are those that have reached us, via reliable methods of transmission, from the Prophet.

Ibn Taymiyyah's *Response* deprived philosophers of the main weapon in their arsenal. In presenting his arguments, he "appropriated" logic for religion. This was no mean feat. If—as we argued at the very beginning of our study—the Qur'an gave rise to a veritable tidal wave of rational inquiry, the paradigm established by al-Ghazali and Ibn Taymiyyah reached as far as reason went and subsumed it under religion, eliminating the need for further, "independent" thinking. Why go off on one's own and try to construct a so-called rational view of the world based on logical principles if one already possesses the elements assuring certain knowledge?

It is impossible to exaggerate Ibn Taymiyyah's influence on the Sunni Muslim world, still today—especially if we bear in mind how his thinking connects with Ibn Hanbal's school of jurisprudence and the fact that it represents the undisputed spiritual source of the Wahabi movement (whose adherents founded modern Saudi Arabia). While it is not primarily Taymiyyah's logical work that is studied—his demolition of logic is both celebrated and taken for granted—his extensive legal scholarship has come to be the hallmark of modern Sunni Islam.[13] In effect, he directed the intellectual compass of the Sunni world toward the transmitted corpus of the Qur'an and *hadith*. Reason was granted a restricted role: by way of analogy, it could extract further knowledge from tradition (ideally, in the hands of jurists). This, together with the "petrification" of the transmitted corpus in a language that spoken Arabic has grown away from more and more, has contributed significantly to the stalled intellectual progress of the Arab Muslim world, as we will see.[14]

Given the status Ibn Taymiyyah enjoys among Sunnis, there is one very important (and redeeming) aspect of his thought that should not be overlooked. He unambiguously affirms that moral intuitions are universal[15]—that is, they are not limited to, or determined by, the cultures or habits of one nation more than another. Therefore, in the modern world, where liberal orientations tend to allow for different moral standards, Ibn Taymiyyah actually provides a strong case for arguing, say, in favor of gender equality in Saudi Arabia, or for the use of equal standards at international tribunals such as the United Nations.

In this context, it is also worth noting the somewhat puzzling fact that he based his argument on a passage by Avicenna. Here, the latter asks us to imagine which of our beliefs we would not question, even if we found ourselves detached from our particular circumstances. Avicenna wants us to conclude that we would not find our moral intuitions to be independently reliable, but we would still be committed to the certain truths of logical principles. Ibn Taymiyyah rejects this conclusion and claims that however much we might detach ourselves from contingent circumstances, we would remain committed to our moral intuitions—which are intuitions shared by all humankind. Al-Ghazali used the same thought-experiment in his criticism of the doctrine of natural morality, but without mention of its Avicennian origin, in his argument *against* the Mu'tazilites (see Chapter 9).

At any rate, it is interesting to look at the post-al-Ghazali philosophical landscape from Ibn Taymiyyah's perspective. After Avicenna, he mentions only two "Aristotelian" philosophers of note in Islam's "Eastern region": the Jewish convert Abu'l Barakat al-Baghdadi (1080–1165), who was critical of Avicenna's philosophy, and the Egyptian Afdal al-Din Al-Khunji (d. 1244), who admitted on his deathbed—according to Ibn Taymiyyah—that philosophy had taught him nothing. In the "Western region"—the Iberian Peninsula—Ibn Taymiyyah lists Avempace and Averroes.[16] He also mentions non-Aristotelian philosophers he describes as non-Muslim, but who were influenced by Avicenna in one way or another: Fakhr al-Din Razi (1149–1209), Suhrawardi (1155–1191), Ibn 'Arabi (1165–1240) Tusi (1201–1274), and Ibn Sab'in (1217–1269).

It is clear that of all Muslim philosophers, Avicenna stands out as the "main offender." Al-Kindi is simply derided for not putting a single sentence in proper Arabic together, and Alfarabi is acknowledged as the "second master"—so that he can then serve as a target for all the traditional arguments Ibn Taymiyyah can muster against philosophy (both logic and metaphysics). Unlike his predecessors, Ibn Taymiyyah says, Avicenna did not limit himself to the philosophical corpus of the Greeks; he also introduced elements "borrowed" from Mu'tazilite *kalam*—presumably, in order to make philosophy seem to be a legitimate Islamic pursuit.[17] Ibn Taymiyyah's charges against Avicenna go much deeper, then. Invoking Avicenna's autobiographical account of being brought up in an Isma'ili Shi'ite family, Ibn Taymiyyah links his predecessor with the founder of Alamut, Hasan al-Sabbah, and the Qaramitah sect responsible for stealing the black stone from al-Ka'ba! In this light, Avicenna is portrayed as a *batini*: someone who keeps his heretical beliefs concealed while pretending to be a Muslim.

Whether Ibn Taymiyyah actually believed the accusations he made or just invented them to tarnish Avicenna's image is not clear. By itself, the autobiographical reference Ibn Taymiyyah mentions does not offer much evidence. Moreover, when considered objectively, the fact that Avicenna appealed to a nonorthodox strain of religious scholars, mystics, and philosophers does not prove that he consciously set out to be their spokesman. It may just prove his independence of mind and intellectual confidence; after all—and unlike his predecessors—he had acquired such fluency in, and facility with, philosophy's subject matter that he broke new ground for inquiry and, in the process, *naturalized* it. There is no doubt he was an original thinker. For all that (or perhaps for this very reason), some later scholars took Ibn Taymiyyah's charges seriously and viewed Avicenna in ideological terms alone—as we will see in the next chapter.

18

Motion and Light

History and legend about the Alamut mountain fortress in the Day-lam region of Persia often run together. This holds especially for the early period, when it was occupied by Hasan al-Sabbah, from 1090 to 1124. The fortress remained under the rule of his Ismai'li successors until 1256, when it finally fell to Mongol forces; its valuable books and archives—said to contain the secret teachings and rites of this clandestine Shi'ite sect—were set ablaze. All that survived were some instruments probably used by the scientist, philosopher, and Avicenna commentator Tusi during the last twenty years of the fortress's existence. It is likely that Tusi himself rescued them when he joined ranks with the invaders.

The legends did not concern only the teachings of the secretive imamate sect. More than anything else, perhaps, they arose because of this group's uncanny ability to maintain discipline and carry out strikes against its principal enemy: the Sunni caliphate of Baghdad. The way Hasan took power in the fortress stands as a paradigm of the sect's methods, which were indirect and stealthy. Hasan had pretended to be a teacher and in-gratiated himself to the guards and surrounding community. When he finally gained enough followers and made his identity—and plans—known, the sitting ruler was unable to rally any support. Hasan rose to power without shedding any blood in battle. For all that, the elite "strike-force" (*fida'iyyin*) he set up had a reputation for never failing to hit targets. Often, its members managed to infiltrate, in disguise, the innermost chambers of the party they had been charged with assassinating. Everyone knew they placed no value on their own lives and would get the job done at any cost.

Everything beyond this is legend: there are tales that before they were sent out, Hasan would drug them and make them think they had seen paradise; this is where they hoped to return after carrying out their mission.

The Alamut fortress was just one of a series of fortified sites all over Persia where resistance to Sunni Seljuk rule flourished; the circumstance caused serious problems for the Abbassid caliphate in Baghdad. Mindful of this context, some scholars have read al-Ghazali's polemic against philosophy in general, and against Avicenna in particular, as an attack, commissioned by ruling interests, on Isma'ili and other subversive Shi'ite doctrines—as opposed to a genuine intellectual project. Al-Ghazali certainly offered a patently ideological polemic when he wrote a book to expose what he called the scandalous doctrines of the *batiniyyah*: Shi'ites who hide their heretical beliefs behind an innocent-seeming Islamic front. Indeed, we recall that Ibn Taymiyyah candidly referred to (what he claimed were) Avicenna's clandestine Isma'ili beliefs, based on Aristotelian doctrine but dressed up in false Islamic garb; this, he contended, distorted both Islamic articles of faith and Greek philosophy. We also recall that he disapproved of how al-Ghazali offered his critique: in effect, Ibn Taymiyyah held that al-Ghazali was responsible for allowing (Avicennian) philosophical discourse to penetrate Islam by making the study and use of Aristotelian logic seem legitimate.

Recently, the prominent Moroccan philosopher Muhammad Abed al-Jabiri (d. 2012) has argued for understanding the philosophical writings of al-Ghazali and the tradition he inaugurated within an essentially political framework. These works, he claims, represent the ideological counterpart to real battles waged by the ruling Seljuk caliphate in Baghdad and the Persian Shi'ites. In his introduction to Averroes's *Incoherence of Incoherence* (a response to al-Ghazali's critique of philosophy) and other works, as well, Jabiri portrays al-Ghazali as a polemicist simply out for "money and fame," working at the behest of Sunni rulers in Baghdad and seeking to help them combat mounting Ismai'li agitation. As Jabiri points out, it was a losing proposition in this particular region of the Muslim world: al-Ghazali only publicized Avicennian philosophy further. Of course, Jabiri does not mean that al-Ghazali meant to help it win more support, or even that it "won out"; rather, the polemics served to make philosophy set the terms for debate even among traditional Islamic scholars and, ultimately, facilitated the rise of the (misguided) illuminationist philosophies of Suhrawardi, Mir Damad, and Mulla Sadra.

Jabiri argues that al-Ghazali's real target for criticism was Avicenna rather than philosophy as such. But in targeting Avicenna, al-Ghazali entirely disregarded the real source of philosophy, Aristotle. Thereby, he confused Avicenna's readings of Aristotle with Aristotle's own positions. He wrongly assumed—and made the general public think—that his arguments were directed against philosophy, when in fact they were directed only against Avicenna's wrong-headed interpretations and innovations. On the one hand, this confused polemic weakened Aristotelian philosophy in the Muslim East—if it did not put an end to it altogether. On the other hand, and paradoxically, it further incorporated Avicennian philosophic discourse into the Islamic milieu, encouraging a new philosophical trajectory defined more by Avicenna than by Aristotle. Such assimilation concerned, above all, the need perceived by Sunni scholars—in the wake of al-Ghazali's (failed) polemic—to counter Avicenna's doctrines; this, however, only integrated them further into Islamic religious scholarship and discourse.

Ibn Taymiyyah had maintained that Avicenna incorporated Islamic discourse (e.g., the views of *kalam* scholars) into his version of philosophy. Now the opposite was occurring: his discourse was introduced, however unintentionally, into *kalam* literature! Ibn Khaldun, in his *Muqaddimah*, had discussed both philosophy and *kalam*, arguing that the latter had become contaminated, over time, by philosophical terminology and ideas. Drawing on one of his observations, Jabiri argues that so much Avicennian discourse entered *kalam* that the time came when it was no longer possible to distinguish *falsafa* from *kalam*. He notes, besides the works of al-Ghazali himself, two ostensibly orthodox critiques of Avicenna that contributed to the trend: *Battling with the Philosophers* by al-Shahrastani (1086–1153) and *Mabahith Mashriqiyyah* by Fakhr al-Din Razi (1149–1209) (who also wrote a critical commentary on Avicenna's *Al-Isharat wa'l Tanbihat*). Avicenna's doctrines had worked their way into the very thinking of his opponents. Indeed, Jabiri continues, this occurred to such an extent that the new version of *kalamic* philosophy that evolved in the works of later scholars came to determine the curriculum of study at the major Islamic universities of al-Azhar (Cairo), al-Zaytounah, and al-Qarawiyyin (Tunis)—and until the beginning of the twenty-first century, at that. (As if to confirm that Avicenna held insidious Isma'ili opinions, Jabiri points out that none other than Tusi—our "suspicious" friend from Alamut—rose to his defense against al-Shahrastani and al-Din Razi, authoring *Battling the Battle* in response to the first and as a critical assessment of the latter's critique of Avicenna's *Al-Isharat wa'l-Tanbihat*.)

In sum, Jabiri affirms that Avicenna's wayward innovations are to blame both for steering the course of philosophy in the eastern Muslim world toward illuminationist mysticism, and for facilitating the adoption of these errors by the orthodox (Ash'arite) scholarship of *kalam* elsewhere. These very developments, he argues, were already evident to Averroes when he took on the task of responding to al-Ghazali's *Incoherence*. Even at this early stage, he could tell how Aristotle's system would be taken apart, and the pieces put in service of different movements with their own agendas.

It is instructive to keep Jabiri's analysis in mind when considering Averroes's *Incoherence*—what the author saw as the main error of earlier philosophers (specifically, Alfarabi and Avicenna). In brief, they had adopted a Plotinian version of emanation theory and postulated a *First Cause* in lieu of Aristotle's "self-contained" theory, which posits a *final cause*. But for all that, it warrants notice that Jabiri (perhaps like Averroes himself) does not take a major difference between the two philosophers into account. Alfarabi treated the forms emanating from the First Cause as being fully instantiated and identifiable "entities" (Platonic forms, one might say), which ultimately come to reside in the particulars of the sensible world.[1] Avicenna, on the other hand, treated the emanations as immaterial, "supra-terrestrial" entities that are not inherently determinate (that is, he viewed them as non-Platonic forms); they are articulated first by the heavenly souls, and then by the human *self* (or soul) by means of its "imaginative faculty"; therefore, he maintained, their "essences" do not precede their existence (as we will see in more detail in the next chapter).

Notwithstanding this difference, the model of emanation they share was enough to justify Averroes's criticism. The point of departure is a hypothetical First Cause that radiates forms downward; eventually, through the active intellect governing the lowest sphere, the world inhabited by human beings receives its order. Avicenna conceived the First Cause as possessing will and knowledge; Alfarabi viewed it as simply being engaged in self-contemplation. Either way, the world's existence proceeds *from* this source. The model, however, stands entirely at odds with the Aristotelian view, in which the Unmoved Mover is an immaterial "intellect" that acts as a final cause, the sum-total of the highest genera of forms that initially subsist in the material world. As Aristotle saw it, the world proceeds *toward* this ultimate point, not *from* it.

There is no "hint" of divinity in the Aristotelian Unmoved Mover. In contrast, Avicenna's First Cause resembles, at very least, the God of Mu'tazilite discourse scholars. They, too, attributed knowledge and will to God, which they claimed were not distinct from His essence. In other words, Avicenna's understanding of the emanation model came very close to a theory that could easily have occurred in indigenous *kalam* literature, providing a philosophic interpretation for the Muslim doctrine of creation. Thus, while Aristotle's Unmoved Mover (the final cause) and the emanationist First Cause both explain *why* the world exists—through motion and change—they do so from diametrically opposed directions. In the final analysis, Aristotle's Unmoved Mover, even though it is an immaterial intellect, amounts to a mechanical device that heavenly bodies "seek" (which is what accounts for their circular motion). Human beings can discover it by abstracting from the observable world and gaining ever-higher realms. According to this conception, the universe is a self-regulating machine, whereas Avicenna's First Cause may be viewed as a "creator," even though it is co-eternal with the world; this approaches the orthodox concept of God, yet it distorts it, as well.

Although Averroes includes Alfarabi in his critique of the emanation model, Avicenna receives harsh treatment (in a text that presents itself as a refutation of al-Ghazali!). The reasoning is clear: as Ibn Taymiyyah had already objected, Avicenna succeeded in making philosophy *relevant*. Islam admitted philosophical examination. In light of how reason, inspired by the Qur'an, flourished early in Islam and brought forth efforts to understand its many implications in rational terms, Avicenna's project might be considered an advanced stage in (if not the highpoint of) the story of reason in Islam—a complement to the inspiration fueled by God's message, not its putative replacement. From an orthodox point of view, however, the idea of bringing reason—even if inspired—to bear on religion was and is anathema; and this has been the case from the very beginning, when speculative discourse first emerged.

There is no such thing as an Islamic philosopher, Ibn Taymiyyah declared, invoking an earlier, orthodox source whom he does not name. The notion was also anathema to Averroes, who held that philosophy (in its "unvarnished," Aristotelian form) and religion should never be mixed.

Unlike Ibn Taymiyyah, he considered both to be valid representations of the truth. But whereas Ibn Taymiyyah's reasoning is clear—philosophizing about religion undermines the latter's foundation—Averroes's position leaves one confused. What, from a philosophical point of view, is so sacrosanct about the Aristotelian model that it must remain untouched? Why did he prohibit "naturalizing" philosophy and trying to reconcile Aristotle and the Greek tradition with the Muslim world? Was it simply the fear of religious backlash? (At one point, he was temporarily deposed from office, and his books—along with other works of philosophy—burnt.) Were this the case, couldn't one argue that he—and not Avicenna—was closely guarding secrets and viewed philosophy as a "secret science," an "elite" pursuit not to be divulged to the "masses"?

In his introduction to *Incoherence*, Jabiri pinpoints the difference between Averroes and Avicenna. What bothered Averroes about Avicenna was the latter's "nonscientific" approach to philosophy. Specifically, Aristotle's mechanistic model—which Avicenna set aside—is presented as a rational rather than a mystical approach. However, the view admits debate: if one relies on reason alone, surely the model of self-regulation, which posits an ascending series of forms extending up to some supreme self-intellecting form, is neither better nor worse than the emanation model. It makes more sense, then, to view Averroes's concern in terms of the effort to make philosophy *public*—that is, relevant to the Muslim community. Alfarabi had not sought to do so. Nor, more important, had it been the aim of Averroes's own teachers, Avempace (Ibn Bajjah) and Ibn Tufayl. The former's *Governance of the Solitary* and the latter's allegorical tale *Hayy Ibn Yaqzan* show a clear preference for separating philosophy from politics—for reserving philosophy for an elite. Whatever one thinks of the matter, surely one must admire a philosopher who—believing that the affairs of his co-religionists and compatriots would benefit from his insights—tried to make this happen instead of hiding knowledge away. At the very least, judging that an innovation or new idea is bad because it does not fit with what the "first master" once declared hardly amounts to an endorsement of reason.

Avicenna is said to have held an array of "deviant" beliefs: for example, to have discounted the role of the intellect and replaced it with an immaterial soul that pre-exists and survives death; introducing an "imaginative faculty" supposed to facilitate seeing events in advance; "reading the stars" and performing magic; affirming that heavenly bodies are endowed with a soul or life, which suffuses the universe; conferring the power of will on the First Cause—and even affirming that it possesses knowledge of everything in the cosmos. He is supposed to have all but applied Muʿtazilite doctrine and innovations influenced by the Ismaʾilites to his philosophic model. Jabiri even qualifies Avicenna's doctrines as "hermetic" (an appellation deriving from the fact that Hermes, by the time of Islam, had acquired the reputation—based on syncretic Egyptian, Greek, and Zoroastrian religion—of presiding over mystical/magical pursuits and beliefs). Clearly, something more than emanation stood behind all the various innovations Avicenna had introduced: his unified theory of existence and the universe jarred with the received Aristotelian tradition, yet also sought to reconcile it with native ways of thinking. But what, exactly, did it entail?

As Jabiri points out, Avicenna indicated that his major work—*The Healing*—contains passages enabling the attentive reader to glean philosophical insights of his own. But Avicenna also intended to write a separate book (to be called *Eastern Philosophy*), which would spell out his views in contrast to those of Greek thinkers. He is known to have written a (no longer extant) treatise, *Al-Insaf*, which tried to set the record straight on acceptable and unacceptable tenets both in terms of his own philosophy and in relation to contemporary philosophy in Baghdad (where more Farabian views prevailed). However, it seems that ultimately he did not consider it necessary to write the work on Eastern philosophy. He left behind what might be regarded as a short introductory treatise, *The Logic of the Easterners*, but it contains nothing that one does not find in his major work on logic.[2] In light of this fact, scholars—including Jabiri have generally concluded that his mystical and allegorical writings, from later on, best describes his "Eastern" philosophical views.

Avicenna's use of the word "Eastern" (*mashreq*) may contain an etymological hint, as this is where the sun rises. Later, in the *Hikmat al-Ishraq* (*Wisdom of Illumination*) by Suhrawardi (1155–1191), the "East" (*mashreq*) is equated with "illumination" (*ishraq*); the theory of emanation derived from Plotinus finds expression in terms of *light*: the outflow from the Supreme Light of Lights (*nur al-anwar*). *Mashreq* and *ishraq* seem to be synonymous here. Is it possible that Avicenna himself had identified the process of emanation (of forms proceeding from the First Cause) as an outflow of (spiritual) *light*? If so, what is the significance in this particular context? After all, the notion of light is already implied in the image of emanation, which means the outward flow of *existentia*, even if a medium is not specified.

For Aristotle, as we have seen, motion on a circular model represents a self-sufficient, mechanical operation—almost an automated one, even if it is explained in terms of a fulcrum, at the center or apex, that acts as a point of attraction for the movement of immaterial heavenly bodies. Avicenna does not seem to have been content with this model. He insists on exploring the underlying reason for the distinction made between the apex (which does not move) and the rest (which does). Simply positing this distinction is not enough: it has to be shown *why* the one is immoveable while the others are moveable. Needless to say, he does not mean only to point out that, once such a generic distinction is made, we need to explain how the Mover animates other things. More fundamentally, the categorical distinction between moved and unmoved is not intrinsically coherent or self-explanatory. *This* is what requires explanation. Thus, his main concern does not involve the co-eternality of mover and moved, much less the "practical" issue of how to account for movement. Rather, a fundamental logical problem stands at issue: the fact that there is no basis for Aristotle's categorical distinction between two types of entities—an immovable mover (or movers), on the one hand, and movable ones, on the other. Positing the apex as a *final cause*—as the Aristotelian model proposes—does not resolve the problem. Such a theory might explain the mechanism behind one thing moving and another not doing so, but it does not explain why one thing is of one nature and the other is different in kind.

Besides the matter of accounting for a categorical distinction between what moves and what does not (either in terms of a first or final cause), Avicenna may have also considered how emanation could be viewed in terms of efficient causality—that is, how to understand emanation as a causal process. This would fall in line with the Muslim view that God causes (and knows) everything. Both the Aristotelian model and the emanation model posit some sort of area or space (however we conceive it—as logical or actual) in which higher forms subsist. Either they emanate from a First Cause or they are supreme genera abstracted from the material world. These higher forms are alternately conceived as a *plenum* interceding between the worlds of non-matter and matter (and therefore of motion); or, as per emanation theory, they are thought to act (by way of intellection) as mediators and provide the impulse for motion in this fashion. As Avicenna saw it, two items required explanation: how to account for the mover-moved distinction (thereby explaining the nature of higher forms, among other things); and how to view or explain the "overflow" that produces the "impulses" that bring motion about as *efficient causes*. Needless to say, they were both of particular concern to him as a Muslim.

Avicenna addressed these questions by offering a theory of motion that introduced a categorical distinction between an existent that is necessary of itself and one that is possible of itself but necessary by another.[3] In so doing, he proposed to explain the more fundamental matter of *why* the unmoved and moved are as they are; they differ because of their respective *natures*: the former is self-sufficient, and the latter requires a cause in order to be. This distinction does not undermine the hypothesis of contemporaneous eternality—which he also affirmed.

Avicenna's famous—and philosophically groundbreaking—distinction between categories of existents (what is necessary of itself, on the one hand, and what is only possible of itself yet the necessary consequence of something else, on the other)[4] offers a logical response to the otherwise unanswerable question: what accounts both for an "Unmoved Mover" (whether it represents a first or a final cause) and for the difference(s) between "it" and entities in motion. By its very nature, Avicenna submits, what is posited as an unmoved mover must be self-caused—an existent necessary of itself. This is what distinguishes it from other things that are not self-caused by nature—which need something outside themselves to come into existence. In other words, "Prime Mover" means that its very nature or essence is Being. This is not the case for everything else. (For Averroes, Avicenna thereby violated Aristotle's "sacrosanct science" most "grievously.")

But even if Avicenna provided the missing foundation for the (Aristotelian) mover-moved distinction, he must have still wondered how to "translate" this logical explanation into a (Plotinian) theory of emanation—that is, how to replace a mechanically rotating plenum with the existential outflow from the First Cause accounting for how motion is brought about. Surely he remarked that the term "emanation" (*fayd*) has no real content: it does not offer a substantial alternative to the readily comprehensible concept of mechanical motion it is supposed to replace. By what means does emanation occur, through what medium? Here, it is reasonable to suppose that Avicenna entertained the notion of a supralunary (perhaps a spiritual) light—in the strong sense of "illumination"; at any rate, such an idea later provided the point of departure for the illuminationist theory of Suhrawardi and others.

Avicenna does not seem to have committed his thoughts on the matter to writing, but we can imagine that he viewed emanation as a process through which the First Cause *radiates* (illuminates life into) the descending levels of existents. In this case, light provides the flowing medium that intercedes between pure form and matter, by which an existential outflow of causes (and therefore motion) proceeds—much in the same way, perhaps, that the Qur'anic verse (as it was understood by later writers) employs the metaphor of light from God to explain His relation to the world. Avicenna must have considered light, which possesses an ethereal nature—today, one would describe it as a particle/wave hybrid—as a possible medium for allowing efficient causes to produce their effects, thereby accounting for the outpouring of the various entities (i.e., bridging the gap between immaterial causes and the material world). Could it be that he had a *scientific* basis for proposing light in this context?

An interesting recent study on Ibn Tibbon[5]—a follower of Maimonides, who proposed to reconcile the philosophic view of the world's eternality with the biblical view of creation by distinguishing between its supralunary (heavenly) and sublunary (material) parts—presents the Jewish philosopher as having articulated two key principles. The first concerns the Avicennian hypothesis of earth and water; the other concerns light. To account for the dryness of parts of the earth within a theoretical framework affirming water to be the lighter element (which, it follows, should cover the earth in its entirety), Avicenna argued that earth is made to rise out of water through certain meteorological circumstances and physical events; cyclically, dry earth ascends, even though it is the heavier element. Averroes, who followed Aristotle's view that dry land had always existed, rejected Avicenna's "audacious" innovation, which affirmed that the earth (and everything on it) was periodically "reborn." However, Ibn Tibbon adopted Avicenna's thesis. It allowed him to reconcile philosophy with the biblical account of how the surface of the earth was covered with water at the time of "creation"; in addition, it permitted him to understand references to *light* as the medium that—because it is emitted by *luminous* heavenly bodies and *acts on water as a translucent element*—had (and has) the power to cause the reactions in water (and between various elements in the submerged earth) necessary for dry land to emerge. As chance would have it, a volcanic event (in the Reykjanes Ridge, Iceland, in 1211) "confirmed" Ibn Tibbon's view that a scientific explanation for the emergence of dry land from a water-covered earth is possible—and therefore the likely solution to an otherwise insoluble postulate concerning the relative weights of earth and water.

Rejecting Averroes's bland affirmation that dry land had always existed and adopting Avicenna's postulate, Ibn Tibbon took the further step of crediting light for the emergence of dry land. As far as we know, Avicenna himself had not gone that far—even though it is conceivable that he entertained the notion of a heavenly body transforming darkness into light when its translucent reflector, water, is immanent. At any rate, Ibn Tibbon, who explicitly drew on Avicenna's postulate to "explain" the eternality of the world, did not ascribe such a view to him.

As we have noted, the image of light would not have been an innovation in this context, for emanation already contains the idea of some kind of flow or radiance—an unspecified, ethereal "outpouring" of what then comes to constitute material bodies. Therefore, even if "Eastern" and "light" represent terms Avicenna found ready for use, his philosophy as a whole should be viewed in terms of the overall sum of innovations and interpretations it presents; on the basis of his extant works, it is easy to see how his model fitted logic, physics, and metaphysics to the perspective of emanation. Most important is what follows from his categorical distinction: rejecting the interpretation of relations between ideas along essentialist lines (as occurs in both the Aristotelian model and the emanation model) in favor of a causal understanding, which reserves the identity of essence and existence for the First Cause. (The next chapter will discuss this point in further detail.)

Unsurprisingly, the first of twenty questions Averroes addressed in *Incoherence* was this very problem: how the Unmoved Mover brings about movement. The task was difficult. While he wished to preserve the Aristotelian scheme for explaining how the world is arranged, he knew that the model had little, if anything, to do with the prevailing view of God's relation to the world in Islam. Moreover, while seeking to critique Avicenna's "theosophic" model (which at least attempts to give a philosophical portrait of God's relation to the world), Averroes wanted to uphold the orthodox view of Islam. Both this work and others wind up presenting a binary model—a theory of "double truth": it seems that what one eye beholds remains independent of the other![6] All the same—and somewhat curiously—Averroes seems to have wanted to concede *something* to the prevalent Muslim view that God had created the world; he did so by drawing on the concept (found in various versions in *kalam* and in Avicenna) of *discrete* eternality (*huduth*): the notion that the world is eternal and infinite but, at the same time, always manifested in new forms.[7]

As a "good" Aristotelian, Averroes believed that the motion-theory for explaining the world was more "scientifically respectable" than competing views—especially one that considered the relationship between the First Cause and the world simply to involve the distinction between existential categories, or, alternately, the Plotinian model claiming that *the soul* infuses the world, and that it effects motion in the same way that our minds determine our movements. Of course, from an orthodox, Sunni perspective, neither a theory based on light nor one based on motion would be acceptable, for both models challenge the canonical view that God created the world in time—that is, that the world is not infinite. Paradoxically, whereas Avicenna had presented his system as unitary and metaphysically complete—which represented an act of considerable daring in the intellectual and ideological milieu he lived in—it was Averroes who argued in favor of a binary model—"science" and faith—and warned that the doctrines (or arguments) of one should not be mixed with those of the other.

Averroes, then—and not Avicenna—put the brakes on rational inquiry. True, Avicenna's inquiries led him to views that may have seemed "irrational" to Averroes: that the creation is an eternal act of "Let there be light," as it were. However, this is simply a matter of opinion. It is certain that the Aristotelian/Averroistic model is not inherently more rational. What is more, it is difficult not to see Averroes's binary scheme as an affront to reason, for it prohibits inquiry into the very matters the Qur'an inspired Muslim thinkers to contemplate in the first place! Arguably (as we will see in short order), Avicenna's own philosophy also presupposes two levels of insight—the one corresponding to material reality and the other to the transcendental realm. However, this does not amount to two representations of truth in his eyes. Reality is one, and it can only be grasped transcendentally.

The Nature of Truth

Despite Ibn Taymiyyah's dismissive remark that Islam has no philosophers, Avicenna (his target) stood head and shoulders above all other Muslims who pretended to this title. Not only did Avicenna free himself from preset systems and styles; he also pursued reason until he arrived at its limits. Investing all his faith in the search for the truth, he expanded the realm of discovery into the vast domains of the imagination. Avicenna reflected on the Greek and Hellenistic traditions available to him, then gave free rein to his own powers of mind to see how they worked; along the way, he made adjustments and ultimately produced a system of his own. The system he devised did not address the issue of the Prime Mover/First Cause to the exclusion of all else: it dealt with every aspect of philosophy from the ground up. What is more, Avicenna accomplished all this in a flowing philosophical language free of the cumbersome phrasings associated with its early beginnings in Arabic.

If the *kalam* style seems homegrown and natural in contrast to translations and commentaries of Greek texts, Avicenna's philosophical idiom gives the same impression: it *naturalizes* philosophical Arabic (which also, perhaps, explains why he was accused of *kalamizing* philosophy). Let us recall the way Abd al-Jabbar viewed language: the meanings of statements are context-based. Abd al-Jabbar—and other discourse practitioners, too—held this view because of the importance they attached to natural language both as the frame for, and as the subject matter of, logical discourse. It followed, in their eyes, that abstract meanings represent nothing more than mental constructions that speakers come to form on the basis of experience; they do not indicate the independent existence of abstract entities in metaphysical space. In contrast, early Baghdad philosophers viewed language simply as a gateway to logic, that is, as a means to attain metaphysical insight and achieve knowledge of, and communion with, the order of abstract entities.

Avicenna shared the discourse practitioners' perspective on language; he considered the meanings of statements to be context-based rather than reflections of logical or metaphysical realities. Unlike discourse practitioners, however, he did not view language as the *frame* within which truth can be captured, nor did he think that it imposes a limit on philosophical inquiry. In other words, like the philosophers, he deemed formal logic necessary. Unlike them, however, he saw logic in the same light as language: the logical relations expressed in formal manner are constructs, not independent abstract entities existing in an ordered logical or metaphysical space.

When it was first introduced to Arab culture, philosophy defined truth as a linguistic statement reflecting an objective state of affairs in the world, an articulation of the relations that independent ideas or meanings entertain with one another. This understanding presupposes that abstract ideas or meanings have some kind of autonomous existence in logical or metaphysical space; here, they are interconnected in specific ways, and statements about them (ideally) capture this reality. The entire edifice of so-called genera, species, *differentia*, and particular or general accidents—the way the world is organized according to early logicians—stands on this mental foundation. As such, *man, animal,* and *rational* count as metaphysical entities connected by virtue of their respective essences, which determine where and how they are positioned in the ontological "scaffolding."

Avicenna, on the other hand, considered the elaborate edifice holding the world together to be merely a logical construct—just as he thought the meanings of words to be framed by speech contexts and to reflect our own mental habits rather than external reality. This position followed from his rejection of the theory that essences attach to ideas (or to objects in general), or that an assigned place in the scheme of reality guarantees the true nature of entities. Indeed, he went further still and claimed that—with the exception of the First Cause—everything that exists lacks any intrinsic quality requiring it to exist in the first place, let alone to exist in any specific way. The "reality grid," as it were, is constituted causally.

One of Avicenna's major innovations, then, was to set aside the classic distinction between existence and essence. Indeed, he maintained that essence is logically posterior to existence (as we will see in fuller detail). But if this is the case, what does it mean to come to know the connections that hold between ideas? Is it not necessary to extract the defining quality from the ideas-in-themselves to determine what fits together and what does not? What—to take up the language of al-Ghazali and others[1]—is the "middle term" that bridges two distinct concepts? Avicenna's answer is simple: the "Active Intellect" inspires (or causes) the imaginative faculty to make such connections. This medium prompts forms to come together, in both the material world and the world of mental reflection. Here lies another key innovation: according to Avicenna, reason does not perform self-sufficient operations mechanically; instead, it depends on the driving force of imagination.

The philosophy of the day recognized the statements used in syllogisms as the "building blocks" of logic and commonly identified two distinct sources of knowledge: conceptualization and judgment. The first accounts for the cognition of single ideas signified by singular terms, and the second involves (the act of) connecting one idea to another through predicative statements. For example—and like all logical treatises in use at religious universities until the end of the last century[2]—al-Ghazali's *Intentions of the Philosophers* followed this line of reasoning: our cognition of a single idea—say, "wood"—assures our access to the elements constituting the reality that surrounds us; once we have made the proper judgments about how they relate to one another (for example, by noting that wood burns), we may be certain of a secondary means of possessing knowledge. Combining true judgments enables further statements that also prove true.

But as Ibn Taymiyyah noted, cognizing an abstract idea, even if a singular term designates it, is hardly as straightforward as it might seem. For example, the claim that genus and *differentia* are essential constituents of the species—as in the statement, "Man is a rational animal"—means embedding the concepts of "rational" and "animal" in that of "man"; consequently, grasping the idea of "man" effectively amounts to cognizing two further ideas: "rational" and "animal." Ibn Taymiyyah issued a twofold challenge to the philosophers. Either such an example represents a definition rather than a statement (that is, it does not predicate one thing of another), in which case its truth is analytic and a matter of convention. Or it predicates something of something else, in which case the supposed cognition of a simple idea amounts to predicating one idea of another—that is, it is not the cognition of a simple idea at all! In the second case, the claim that single ideas are cognized proves groundless, since the process involves a relation between two ideas; what is more, there is no basis to hold that the relation between them is *essential*, since either idea may be conceived in relation to something else altogether (for example, "man" can be understood in relation to "biped," "rational," "angel," etc.).

The problem Ibn Taymiyyah identified has far-reaching implications. If two sources of knowledge exist—conceptualization and judgment—and the first source may be reduced either to convention or to nonbinding relations, then the conceptual apparatus as a whole begins to look arbitrary; at any rate, it does not offer building blocks for certain knowledge. But if this is so, what can guarantee certainty? Traditional philosophical treatises claim that we must begin with elementary principles: judgments that contain their truth within them or are otherwise determinate in self-evident fashion (for instance, the principle that two judgments contradicting each other cannot both be true: if one is true, then the other must be false). Equipped with such elementary principles and the single, cognizable ideas we relate to one another in the form of predicative judgments, we then proceed to organize our edifice of knowledge: differentiating and combining features of different ideas, recognizing which of them belong together and which do not, and finally weighing our judgments to produce statements that are (also) true. In this sense, we arrive at definitions (e.g., "man is a rational animal") *after* we have evaluated single ideas, not beforehand.

This approach might explain how we arrive at definitions, but it does not shed any light on how we cognize single concepts. Ibn Taymiyyah—who noted that even Avicenna acknowledged the validity of his argument—claimed that in the process of evaluating various aspects of our ideas, it is still a matter of judgment when we single out some as essential (e.g., "rational" apropos of "man"), and others as nonessential (say, "biped"). In other words, distinctions between ideas' essential and nonessential attributes or qualities are arbitrary. If this is so, then definitions represent matters of convention and do not express a truth that is "out there" in the world. As we have noted, Ibn Taymiyyah contended that given the absence of a solid, natural foundation for the truth of our knowledge-claims, religious statements have a much firmer basis: they are rooted in the words of the Prophet.

Ibn Taymiyyah rightly invoked Avicenna to back up his argument. However, he did not explore the full ramifications of Avicenna's radical thesis. Indeed, they have not received their due from scholars to this day (see following). Avicenna observes that when we claim to cognize a single idea, we actually cognize a set, or family, of concepts by virtue of the fact that our minds are entertaining an idea at all. Necessarily, mental objects are shaped along the lines of the categories through which we understand them. Likewise, declaring such an object part of a logical relation modifies it in terms of the categories allowing it to be treated as part of a logical statement. In other words, Avicenna meant that, as a mental phenomenon, a given idea necessarily occurs (or presents itself) to us as general or specific, diffuse or focused, abstract or embodied, and so on. But all these aspects are external to the original idea itself. What is more, when an idea comes to be posited as a component of a statement—that is, when we think of it in terms of its logical role—it acquires further, additional features, such as being a subject or a predicate, and so on.

The idea as a mental object being general or specific, or as a logical category being subject or predicate, or a term in a syllogism, and so on— these formulations represent aspects of an idea over and above just being itself: "predicate-hood" or "subject-hood" do not inhere in the idea of, say, "man." Consequently, we actually encounter four different levels of existence and meaning: the idea itself, the idea as it holds materially (as when we affirm that a given horse displays "horse-ness"), the idea as conceived by the mind, and, finally, the idea as posited in a logical relation. Strictly speaking, these four planes are not identical at all. Even as we categorize "man" as a *definiendum*, and "rational animal" as a *definiens*, we are not identifying or talking about the idea of "man" itself, but the *logical object* "man." After all, when we consider the idea of man in itself, we do not consider it a *definiendum*. Similarly, we do not consider it a subject, a predicate, a species, or anything of the kind. We only have access to—and by definition can only think or talk about—the idea insofar as it occurs in our minds or is posited as a logical object. Avicenna's major work already makes as much plain.

We should recall that the school of Alfarabi, following Aristotle, would posit that the idea of "man" somehow exists in, or for, all the human beings that have ever been or ever will be—such that, by means of our intellection of objects in the world (that is, the act of observing a sufficient number of them to recognize the essential feature they share), we arrive at a pure conception. Plato had claimed that ideas in their pristine state subsist in an immaterial plenum, and that all earthly manifestations are "shadowy" or imperfect. He and Aristotle did not disagree that such a plenum exists. However, they differed on whether it represents the final stage in an intellectual ladder or the cosmic starting point for a process descending into the world of matter. Either way, the plenum amounts to a self-organized hierarchy: an array of ideas with self-sufficient being in and as themselves, organized in relation to one another. Each idea has features connecting it, whether by essence or otherwise, to another idea: this is the reality we eventually come to see and know, and this reality is what enables us to identify the objects in the world around us.

On the other hand, Avicenna's explanation of what pure ideas are—an explanation as striking as it was unprecedented—does away with the plenum as a hierarchy, including all that goes by the name of *mahiyyat* (essences). We must not forget (as many scholars who have written about Avicenna seem to have done) that these, too, are "ideas" or "forms"—as when we say that the essence of *man* is to be both *rational* and *animal*. Avicenna's formulation of what an idea is by itself makes each term out to be *unconnected* with anything else. As he viewed matters, then, the classical distinction between essence and existence—whereby "Man is a rational animal" somehow subsists in a metaphysical plenum before it enters the real world—simply falls apart. Instead, in such a metaphysical plenum—which he deems merely hypothetical—only ideas-in-themselves subsist; they are all wholly separate from everything else, including the idea of *existence*.

Accordingly, whatever connections come to hold between them are not so by virtue of anything that any one of them possesses in itself. Without such connections in a hypothetical plenum of ideas, all one can possibly explain about the connections we discern, whether in the spiritual or the physical world, is *causality*. If two inherently unrelated ideas are "found" to be connected, it must be due to an exterior cause. Of course, ideas are only ever "found" in this way—the metaphysical plenum is hypothetical, after all—thus, the fact that they are in *this* state, that is, their *existence together* in such a state, confers "priority" to them. "Essence" does not come first: one idea does not provide the essence of another idea until both have come to exist in a specific relation; they do so because one is "made" to stand in relation with the other—not because it inherently entertains a relationship with the other idea. Indeed, Avicenna's outright criticism of Platonic Forms must be seen in this light—as a criticism, that is, of the supposed existence of that naturally ordered metaphysical plenum, where what we take to be an essence of something has a nature predisposing it to be an essence of that thing: its "predisposition"—Avicenna would claim—is simply *to come to exist* as an essence *or not* of *anything*.

Avicenna goes further still: even as we come to consider ideas as ideas-in-themselves, we will perforce find ourselves looking at them as something else, namely, our own objects of thought. More generally, what we in fact encounter are mental or logical objects, not ideas *in themselves*. Naturally, then, one wonders: what *is* the idea on its own terms? Avicenna develops the logical implications by affirming that we do not really know anything beyond the fact that ideas are what they are—that each of them is self-identical. In itself, "horse-ness" is just "horse-ness." We cannot say or think anything beyond what the idea already is, because as soon as we do so, we have "clothed" it with something else (be it material, mental, or logical) which is not intrinsic to it. Even if we wish to ascribe singularity to "horse-ness"—that is, affirm that it is *one thing* and one thing only—we must introduce a new idea (namely, "singularity"). To consider an idea as a *single* idea means considering two distinct ideas (here, horseness and singularity): neither one inheres in the other. They are connected causally—through our mediation—and not because of something belonging to either one.[3]

That said, Avicenna did not claim that hierarchies (whether in the immaterial or material worlds) do not exist. His point is that the "glue" holding things together stems from causality, not essentiality; it is not the case that one is tied to another by nature, or by virtue of some higher, independent logic. Rather, they enter relations through a universal process of causation (logically) initiated by the First Cause, whose nature is *necessary existence*: its (or *His*) essence is existence, pure and simple. In turn, they are reflected in the different ways the world around us takes form, whereby objects (whether as ideas that come to be related with one another, as manifested in matter, in the mind, or as logical entities) are as they are, not because their essences determine them to be so, but because they are causally determined to be as they are. Stripped of essential natures that tie one thing to another, the "reality grid" appears as one logically possible world; other connections between its parts are conceivable (at least in theory). Of course, Avicenna wished to advance the claim that this world, while only possible in logical terms, has a necessary cause: the Creator stands behind it. In this light what we call "essences"—insofar as these are ideas themselves—are either *posterior* to existence or simultaneous with it: they are essences *insofar as* they are actualized, not prior to achieving this state.[4]

Avicenna's thesis might seem to imply a kind of (intellectual) estrangement from the world. His "demotion" of the intellect—a key element of the Farabian system, where it ascends levels of abstraction until
it achieves final (comm)union with Active Intellect—appears consistent
with the way he separates objects of intellection (and logical discourse)
from the ideas themselves. Likewise, Avicenna interprets sensory knowledge primarily to be that of sensory data (the impressions we receive), not
knowledge of (material) objects *per se*. He makes this position even clearer
in his *Al-Ta'liqat*, where he places Aristotle's *primary substances*—which
provide the components of reality and, therefore, of the knowledge we
have—at a remove from our cognitive faculties: just as ideas are shrouded
by features determined by the modalities our minds posit, what we take to
be primary substances are "hidden" behind the data or impressions reaching our sensory faculties.

But if the intellect does not provide the medium for gaining knowledge of reality in its purest form, what does? One might suspect the answer
to be "nothing at all"—that, by definition, the barrier separating our impressions from reality cannot be crossed, and we must reconcile ourselves
to the fact that our knowledge has reached a dead end. This rationalist line
of thinking was advanced—much later (and in Europe)—by Immanuel
Kant, when he distinguished between *noumena* and *phenomena*: the first
are inaccessible and therefore best left alone. Avicenna did not choose this
option. Instead of the intellect, he declared the soul—or self—the subject
of knowledge, and the imaginative faculty the instrument of cognition.
Imagination—which he placed alongside the psycho-physical faculties
previous theories had recognized in human beings—allows the self/soul to
be "illuminated" by the idea relevant to the object at hand. A mental form
results, which has not been extracted or abstracted from the object itself
(as per the Aristotelian or Farabian model); instead it is emanated from
"above"—from the plenum of immaterial forms—as a kind of inspiration.
For Avicenna, "Active Intellect" provides the medium through which separate forms come to be causally connected with one another, whether in
physical matter or in the mind. Once it has occurred in the mind, or as a
logical object, a given idea comes to be associated with other ideas and un-
dergoes further definition or categorization.[5]

Indeed, Avicenna explains prophecy (or the holy [*qudsi*] faculty of
insight) as the ability of an exceptionally sensitive imaginative faculty to

"pick up" or "grasp" causal connections between ideas or forms radiated by the Active Intellect. The entire edifice of human knowledge—including what we regard as rational—is grounded in inspiration (or, at very least, activated by imagination). This view does away with what might otherwise seem to be a generic difference between "rational" and "transrational" knowledge. No Kantian "dead end" occurs. Instead, the imagination steps in to complete the edifice of knowledge. (The only exception Avicenna makes concerns "mathematical objects," i.e., numbers; these, he contends, are intrinsically or organically interrelated in their purest form.)

According to Avicenna, then, we do not have immediate sensory or cognitive access to the world as it is; we only encounter representations. This is why the theory of the intellect is ultimately of no use to him. But for all that, his theory does not mean we are detached from reality. At the "end of the tunnel," as it were, there is a light linking us (our souls/selves) with the plenum of forms, which offers the "glimpses" that occur when we cognize ideas and, in turn, relate them to one another. Such knowledge is transcendental. It offers a way to break free from the cognitive apparatus determining—and limiting—what we see of reality. In theory, it offers the means to see the ideas-in-themselves extending along a grid of causality, all the way to infinity. Ultimately, a complete vision of reality can only come about if we free ourselves from the matter where our souls "reside," acquiring a nature like that of the pure forms—and capable, for this reason, of beholding them.

Taken to its logical conclusion, Avicenna's transcendental thesis looks like an introduction to a mystical philosophy. His philosophy uses reason to define the limits of reason; in so doing, it reveals a way to transcend it. The transcendental part compensates for what might otherwise appear to be a skeptical philosophy: ultimately, the estrangement from the world that follows from the gulf between what *is* and our contingent cognition may be overcome. In his allegorical writings, Avicenna uses the term *'irfan* to refer to transcendental knowledge of the truth (replacing the more common term *ma'rifah*). These works feature metaphors of light, the East, and Sufi grades (or stations) of knowledge. But at the same time, the causal order they posit replaces the natural order proclaimed by Aristotle: the world is not put together in chaotic or arbitrary fashion. Detailed and strict, the causal grid is optimally arranged. Thus, after discounting traditional sources of knowledge—conception

and judgment—as lacking a solid foundation, Avicenna's system proposes a wholly different, but equally secure, framework: self-knowledge
and knowledge of God.

Where knowledge of God is concerned, ideas of existence and necessity are immediate—that is, primary. (This view resembles Kant's proposition that space and time are objects of immediate intuition and underlie all
claims to knowledge.) As such, the idea of God—the sole Being of pure necessity—provides an object of immediate intuition. We cannot understand
transient phenomena (i.e., anything in the world of possibility we inhabit)
if we do not measure them against what is permanent (necessity). Self-
knowledge also provides an object of immediate intuition, for it would stand
firm even if one tried (in a thought experiment) to deny all that one knows
about oneself.[6] Here, Avicenna's point resembles the one he makes about
pure ideas: in and of themselves, each idea is just what it is, and everything
associated with it is external to its true nature. (Some scholars have misread
Avicenna's views on this matter as arguments—as attempts to demonstrate
the existence of God, or the soul. However, he does not seek to "prove"
either one: both are objects of immediate intuition; therefore, they afford
the very conditions for all claims of knowledge we can possibly make.[7])

Avicenna's allegorical writings—*Al-Isharat wa'l Tanbihat* (The Epistle
of the Bird) and *Hayy Bin Yaqzan* (The Epistle on Love)—are sometimes
considered to represent a philosophical about-face. This view is mistaken.
A close reading of his major work, *The Healing*, already provides rational
justification for what he says later on. Avicenna did not change his position, nor did his philosophy unfold in two stages. First, he outlines what
reason comprises, indicating both its scope and its limits. Second, he employs imagistic language that allegorically portrays both the domain of
reason and what lies beyond it. The matter does not admit representation
any other way: although logical language can explain reason, it becomes
an obstacle as soon as the sphere of reason ends, blocking exploration of
what lies beyond.

Let us recall that Alfarabi understood language to have evolved until
it reached a pinnacle: systemization as syllogistic or demonstrative reasoning. For him, poetic language represented an early stage of evolution; beyond syllogistic discourse, there is nothing more, or new, to learn. Relying
on Aristotle, Alfarabi also affirmed that the development of the *deductive*
methodology of the mathematical sciences in particular has given us all the

tools necessary to attain knowledge. In contrast, Avicenna effectively declares that we must move in a full circle and return to poetry, metaphors, and allegory in order to grasp reality fully. Indeed, even the mathematical tools Aristotle/Alfarabi present as the paradigm for deducing certainties about the world are fueled by imagination. In other words, we must break free from the chains in which logical language and the intellect bind us. The authority of reason—as the poet Bashar found out at the very beginning of our story, and as the Mu'tazilites learned when they began to exercise reason freely in the attempt to translate the inspiration fired by the Qur'an—can easily change from a medium for liberating the mind into a chain restricting further progress.

Curiously, it was none other than Ibn Tufayl—the famed author of *Hayy Bin Yaqzan*—who secured a position for Averroes (Avicenna's principal critic) as his successor at the court of Cordoba. Avicenna was the first to tell the story of Hayy, the autodidact, Absal, the seeker of truth, and Salaman, the representative of political authority. Ibn Tufayl's "version" also presents a terrain of knowledge beyond what language is able to grasp. He adds a further dimension of allegory, describing how achieving such knowledge is like a blind man suddenly gaining sight: there is nothing that was not known beforehand, but now it is discerned more clearly, with a higher faculty.

Perhaps this is also how Ibn Tufayl understood Avicenna: his forebear had identified the truth, but only imperfectly; now, it was a matter of cultivating the imagination to see it fully. (The process involves "taste," or direct epistemic experience, as some representatives of Sufi tradition would put it.) In this light, Avicenna may be considered to have paved the way—and based on the authority of reason, at that—for a rationally justified mystical tradition. Alternately, Avicenna might have been aiming his sights much higher. His *Hayy* explores the cosmos just as much as it explores human epistemology (to which Ibn Tufay restricted his version of the allegory). Arguably, Avicenna's account reaches further and covers a region of reality beyond what is circumscribed by reason. If this is so, the emphasis does not fall on seeing the same reality through different eyes; rather, it involves seeing further stretches or expanses of it—dimensions that, in theory, can only be seen from an immortal perspective. Like the desert poets of old, Avicenna must have been fascinated by the sky and the stars—and, given the revelations in the Qur'an, by a reality one can grasp fully only after death. His *Hayy* is an allegorical journey into that uncharted world, as are his *Epistle of the Bird* and *Epistle on Love*. The Ptolemaic model—a finite series of concentric planetary orbits culminating in the fixed stars—must have seemed too confining to hold the mysteries of the universe, and so he described another vision.

The journey in the *Divine Comedy* begins with Virgil guiding Dante through Hell and Purgatory. Beatrice, embodying the light of reason, leads the poet as his cosmic journey moves upward, through the Ptolemaic planets. At each stage, Dante learns the cause responsible for each feature of human existence, as well as the (mis)fortunes of those who stand under the influence of the heavenly body in question. But at the highest point, Beatrice leaves Dante: his vision of holy splendor must be his own, without the mediation of another (reason). As the poet beholds the beatific vision, glowing with love, his soul fuses with it, and his individual will and desire become one with the divine. Now, Dante gains mystical insight: the mechanical and spiritual motions of the universe are energized by the Love that is God.

Avicenna, on the other hand, has only one guide: Hayy. The sage is ancient, yet his physical features appear youthful. His city, he tells his charge, lies in the environs of Alquds—"the Holy." This name, which is the same as that of earthly Jerusalem, has a special significance. Some scholars have argued that it refers to a celestial or mystical habitation. It is more probable, however, that the name was chosen because of the earthly city's role as the Prophet's gateway to the presence of divinity in Islam. This is key to understanding Avicenna's allegory (as well as the place of Jerusalem in Islam). In both Mecca and Medina, the Prophet's "connection" with the divine occurred through the revelation transmitted via the angel Gabriel, who *descended* to earth. However, when Muhammad sought out the divine presence himself (significantly, this is the only "miracle" in his story other than the revelation of the Qur'an), tradition holds that he journeyed to Jerusalem. The Prophet ascended to the heavens from Jerusalem, not from Mecca or Medina. The symbolism is clear: God can find us wherever we may be, but for us to reach Him, the "gateway" is Jerusalem. To achieve "transrational" knowledge, one must turn to Jerusalem. (As we have noted, Avicenna uses the expression "the holy" to refer to prophetic insight: a highly sharpened or refined imaginative faculty capable of receiving inspiration.)

Fittingly, Hayy tells Avicenna he has the "profession" of traveler. He journeys all over the world, and he knows its most distant corners. In the Sufi tradition, "traveler" means one who constantly seeks the path leading to God. Avicenna asks his guide to tell him about the faraway regions he has visited. Hayy begins by explaining how the voyager must first learn to control two basic kinds of passion: impulses such as desire, greed, and gluttony—on the one hand—and tendencies toward irascibility and violence, on the other. But one must also cultivate the ability to steer one's imaginative faculty—knowing what to dispel as fiction, and what to recognize as truth; this faculty can prove either deceptive or revelatory. When one has done so, it is possible to catch glimpses of the distant land, but one's vision is only intermittently clear. In order to reach it once and for all, one must shed one's material form entirely. (Alternately, one must rid oneself of natural desires and passions—the self, as the later poet Farid al-Din 'Attar describes it in his masterpiece, *Conference of the Birds*.)

Hayy describes the regions of the world only after telling Avicenna that a traveler must drink from the Spring of Life to be able to make such a journey. A special elixir allows one to walk on water or even fly up steep mountains. (This calls to mind the ascetic Rabi'ah, from the early days of Islam.[8]) The world, Hayy continues, is divided into three regions: the land to the West (which stands closest to where Avicenna is presently located), the land at the center of the earth, and the land to the East. There follows a detailed description of arid deserts, salty seas, mountains and cliffs, kings and queens, and armies and beasts: all the terrains and beings one might expect in a phantasmagoric tale.

The differences described between the Western and Eastern regions suggest, in addition to physical space—containing all the states of social and physical existence (the Earth[9] and skies above: planets, constellations, and stars)—another psychological or immaterial expanse that includes all the aspects of the human mind: the passions, senses, soul, and so on. Accordingly, the journey in the Western region seems to be a physical voyage outward that takes stock of the material world both above and below—as in the natural sciences. Conversely, the journey in the Eastern region looks like voyage inward, through the labyrinths of the human psyche, eventually leading to a vision of God: the source of illumination who, like the sun, veils Himself in His own light and cannot be directly seen. In the Eastern region, the Qaf mountain must be ascended; this is possibly an allusion to the Qur'anic *surah* of the same name explaining how the earth is held in place by invisible anchors, which declares that the truth can only be beheld at death, when one's sight becomes as "sharp as iron."

This mystical mountain finds mention later in the Sufi tradition—for example, in Farid al-Din 'Attar's *Conference*, mentioned earlier, which describes, stage by stage, an arduous journey undertaken by a flock of birds seeking the presence of "the king of the universe." The *Conference* contains elements both from Avicenna's *Epistle of the Birds* (the need to free oneself even from earthly knowledge), as well as from his *Epistle on Love* (love is the force that moves the world). A hoopoe guides the voyagers. Along the way, the birds express second thoughts, and each in turn contrives one excuse or another to abandon the long and trying search for the truth. The hoopoe—who presents himself as the only party capable of delivering the birds from misery and then, at the middle of the narrative, is confirmed in this role by unanimous suffrage—employs the art of persuasion throughout, weaving beguiling tales to make the flock stay the course.

It is possible to recast Avicenna's allegorical narratives in a more straightforward manner—identifying the symbols they contain and what they stand for, or proposing a point-for-point interpretation. However, the best way to approach them—and to benefit from what they offer—is probably to read them directly, gleaning whatever occurs to one's imaginative faculty in so doing. When contemplating a painting, even a viewer knowledgeable in aesthetic theory bases his or her appreciation on a direct "encounter." The same holds for "mystical" allegories and transcendental poems—from Attar to Rumi, the master of the form.

Fardajan and Beyond

With Avicenna, our story of reason in Islam seems to have arrived at a crossroads. How should we understand this decisive juncture? Scholars still debate the matter—as they did from the very start.[1] One way to view it—and perhaps this was Avicenna's own perspective—is to consider it the point where imagination, which is what inspires rational thinking in the first place, must continue the journey of discovery on its own. Now, the pursuit of knowledge in its pure and original sense—the fully free and unhindered search for the truth—must transcend both reason (as traditionally conceived) and science, too. Without denying the value of these pursuits, Avicenna—who continued to practice analytical philosophy and applied himself to scientific subjects (including astronomy)—evidently concluded that another field of inquiry remained uncharted. Its exploration required the cultivation and full exercise of a faculty that, having served reason, had to be freed from it and allowed to operate on its own.

From Avicenna's standpoint, once this terrain has been entered, normal categories for understanding and explaining what exists no longer suffice. That said, he did not turn into a "mystic," as is sometimes claimed, nor did he reject the value of scientific pursuits. Indeed, just as a transcendental orientation in Islamic philosophy (which included forms of mysticism) is attributed to his influence, some of his closest followers and admirers are known for their scientific endeavors. Examples include Tusi (d. 1274) and Omar Khayyam (d. 1131). With Avicenna, two complementary spheres of inquiry met, then: reason and science, which flourished in the Western region, and the pursuit of transcendental (or transrational) knowledge, in the Eastern region. Hayy—the luminary of pure form—tells Avicenna that he stands closest to the first and seeks to guide him to the second. These two facets of reality complement each other. They are not two versions of the same reality (as Ibn Tufayl claimed in reference to epistemic states, and Averroes maintained in the context of religion and philosophy).

The distinction between "necessary" and "possible" is crucial for understanding Avicenna's position. Reality consists both of how the physical world is organized and the ways that our own mental and logical categories are put together to understand it. However tempted we may be to think so, no natural correspondence exists between them. Our thoughts about the constitution of objects—taken singly, together, or in relation to one another—need not correspond to how they really are. Indeed, each and every part of the physical world (and everything that occurs to the mind, too) could be anything—like a stem cell, we might say today. It is possible-in-itself, and everything that *is*—including correspondences between what exists and how we see it—fits together by virtue of an external cause. This "causality grid" underlies reality. An image borrowed from Leibniz may serve to illustrate the matter.[2] What there is and how we categorize it may be likened to two different clocks. If they keep the same time, this does not occur through some natural mirroring of the truth; instead, it happens by virtue of an external agent—an outside "hand." For Avicenna as for Leibniz, it is the hand of Providence: Being that is necessary-in-itself, self-sufficient. For Avicenna, insight is achieved on a lonesome path. The journey happens within, and it involves giving free rein to imagination and a process of self-purification. As in Dante's *Divine Comedy*, the vision one beholds ultimately proves a matter of personal experience.

According to the report of his faithful companion and biographer al-Juzjani, Avicenna wrote his *Hayy* over the course of five years, when incarcerated at the fortress of Fardajan. There can be no doubt that the work inspired Ibn Tufayl to write his own *Hayy*. By some ruse of history, the latter book found its way to Europe as early as 1671 in Latin translation, under the title *Philosophus Autodidactus*. It appeared in English in 1708, and later in German and other languages, as well. Reports hold that it influenced and inspired many European writers and philosophers of the period.[3] Although Avicenna's *Hayy* did not appear in Europe for another two hundred years, philosophers, mystics, and poets in the Eastern region of the Muslim world read it attentively. In Andalusia, its admirers included

Ibn Tufayl, Ibn 'Arabi, and Ibn Sab'in; in Persia, it was read by Tusi, Omar Khayyam, Suhrawardi, Farid al-Din 'Attar, Hafiz, Jami, and Mir Damad; eventually, it informed the thinking of the school of Isfahan and Mulla Sadra. A further reader of note is the Jewish scholar Ibn Zayla, whose commentary was printed in the first European edition (in French) at the end of the nineteenth century.

If the figures mentioned here share any conspicuous feature, it is the fact that they all pronounced a transcendental imperative. In some cases, this imperative entailed Sufi theories of self-renunciation: the soul dissolving into God through ascetic practices. In other instances, it led to poetry. On the other side of the proverbial coin, it inspired analytical philosophy in keeping with tradition and pure science (mathematics, physics, astronomy, medicine, and related fields). In this context, it is worth noting that—counter to what Jabiri alleged about his interest in magic and the stars—Avicenna authored a work explicitly discouraging astrological pursuits; he did not do so because he did not believe that the cosmos does not influence human affairs, but because he did not think it possible to determine this influence through scientifically verifiable methods.

In his Fardajan allegory and his allusion to the story of Salaman and Absal in *Al-Isharat*, Avicenna challenged readers to "solve the puzzle of symbols" on their own. The challenge was met in different ways. Tusi read and reread everything he could to determine where the original story might have come from. After some twenty years, he identified two sources. Both versions feature the conflict between bodily and spiritual inclinations (as in the allegorical tale of Ibn Tufayl). In each instance, different types of adventure express the theme. In the first, Absal appears as a fair lady: both a source of love and its object. (When Avicenna alludes to this tale—very briefly—he presents Salaman as the reader's "self," and Absal as the level of wisdom or understanding—*'irfan*—that has been attained.) The second is a translation from the Greek made by Hunayn Ibn Ishaq that is curiously reminiscent of the biblical tale of Solomon and Absalom; here, the latter is portrayed as having "gone off"—or having been "sent away"—from the city (Jerusalem) and becoming involved in military expeditions (against, or on behalf of, Solomon).

Other versions were written, as well. One features the theme of sexual seduction; here, the woman plays the role of Pharaoh's wife, as in the story of Joseph; Absal is her "victim." In all of them, however, the themes of unity and separation recur—occasionally with explicit reference to kinship and political conflict (as in the case of Solomon and Absalom). The outstanding work among them is an allegorical tale composed in lyrical form, *Salaman and Absal* (later translated by Edward Fitzgerald—who also brought Omar Khayyam's *Ruba'iyyat* to the attention of the Western world in 1904). The Sufi poet Jami (d. 1492) portrays Absal as a beautiful woman; she nurses Salaman, who has been generated spiritually, and, once he has reached an "appropriate" age, seduces him. Salaman and Absal melt in love and lust. A fire consumes them, and only Salaman is left—a pure soul, but now forlorn and bereft. He must (re)awaken to what is real and perfect in love: the Ruler of the World. At the end, the poet offers the keys to the symbolism: the Shah, the Sage, Salaman, Absal, the desert to which the lovers elope, the paradise island where they sojourn, the fire into which they leap, and Zuhrah, the unsurpassable beauty and object of real love.

For Avicenna, "the East" represents a region where the imagination provides both a spiritual map and a practical guide for how the human soul may best live in the world. "The West," on the other hand—even if he described it in imaginative terms, too—stands for the natural world: the earth and its place in the cosmos. East and West complement each other, but the whole is best seen from the East.

21

The Cosmos

If the Qur'an shook pre-existing mental and perceptual categories by calling on believers to consider natural phenomena as signs to understand what the world *is*, this call resounded most fully when it came to comprehending the physical structure surrounding the earth. How do the skies and earth "fit together"? Prior to Islam, poets, philosophers, and scientists had long contemplated stellar phenomena and sought to explain them. Understanding this structure meant understanding the "bigger picture" and grasping the ultimate mystery of existence itself.

Observation data and theories about phenomena abounded in different cultures—Babylonian, Indian, Greek, and others. By the time that Muslims began to look into these matters, two general scholarly perspectives stood at the ready: Aristotelian and Plotinian. The first underscored the world's mechanistic, perfectly circular, and earth-centered structure, and the second identified a purposive, spiritual dimension infusing it. In addition to those two approaches, Muslims had come into possession of the *mathematical* Ptolemaic model. It is important to appreciate that these three paradigms—physics-as-part-of-science (Aristotle), spiritual infusion (the *Enneads* of Plotinus), and the astronomical model (Ptolemy)—were viewed as all belonging to a single order. The world, after all, is one, and whatever it comprises is subject to the same laws, be they human actions, vegetative cycles, the behavior of the elements, the movements of the stars, or anything else. Surely—in whatever combination, and whatever the details—they must all fit together or reflect each other. Investigation of each field naturally required its own tools and approaches, as did the study of the stars. At the time, the exploration of stellar phenomena essentially meant charting their positions and movements: extrapolating trajectories and patterns through time, and accounting for them with precise figures and equations. In other words, it meant applied mathematics.

Interestingly, for our purposes here, the means employed in such endeavors were primarily *inferential*, a matter of hypothesizing patterns—and not the deductive (Aristotelian) methodology Alfarabi hailed as the "ultimate" tool for reasoning. Still, this kind of mathematics seeks precision, too. If anything, it represents a unique "application" of reason (equations expressing positions, directions, and velocities) drawing on the imagination (hypothesis), and translating the results into a system by means of technical language (model).

For nearly two whole millennia prior to Islam, the total number of heavenly bodies surrounding the earth was thought not to exceed the 1,022 stars, in forty-eight constellations, that Ptolemy finally catalogued. Even so, the world seemed large enough—almost too vast to be fully comprehended. In the introductory parts of *Almagest*, Ptolemy had considered and rejected the notion that the earth, at the center of the universe, could be anything but stationary—as he noted, animals and other things would be flying off its surface if it were "falling." From this perspective, he contended, the surrounding cosmos extends in wider and wider concentric spheres, and each of them (beginning with the moon) rotates around the earth. Five of the "bodies" whose movements may be observed with the naked eye—Mercury, Venus, Mars, Jupiter, and Saturn—display a peculiar pattern: although they follow an orbital rotation around earth, they seem to do so in retrograde fashion, as if sliding back across the sky before continuing their journey. The sun was thought to occupy a place between Venus and Mars, and a final ring of fixed stars completed the picture. The "seven skies," then, are the orbits of these heavenly bodies (the planets, plus the sun and moon), each of which is associated with a certain number of glittering stars; the rest of the glittering stars were thought to be fixed ("pasted") to the global surface encompassing the whole.

For Aristotle—as for most astronomers who came before him, whether Greek or not—all the orbs were homocentric with respect to the earth. This was largely a theoretical assumption, based partly on mankind's *actual* point of observation and partly on aesthetic notions of clean lines. Ptolemy's theoretical assumptions about the earth-centered world were

Aristotelian, but his observations (and data) showed orbital motions to be somewhat more complicated. Accordingly, he constructed a mathematical model to explain them. Aristotle's model of perfect orbits did not quite fit the facts. A particular challenge was how to account for the vast array of movements, including those of the "wandering planets" (i.e., those that displayed a retrograde motion). On the basis of the already-existing concept of circularity (the sphericity of the earth, and of planetary motions around it), concrete data, and new calculations, Ptolemy hypothesized a unique off-earth observation point—the equant—from where to make his "clockwork" calculations of planetary motions. The mathematics just didn't work to have that observation point be on earth itself, or at its center.

In the abstract, hypothesizing such a point made very good sense. A layman, today, understands that a satellite image can provide a more precise picture of a river flowing along uncharted territory than an earth-bound perspective. Ptolemy's equant was similar, but it applied to the sweep of stars around earth, offering a bird's-eye view of the entire cosmos, as it were. His innovation concerned a territory that he assumed could not be mapped out by other means.

Yet ingenious as the model was, and despite equations reflecting the positions and velocities of "wandering stars," it meant that the earth's position had to be shifted from the exact center of a perfectly concentric system, which now received the designation "eccentric." The eccentric occupied a position equidistant from the earth and the equant. Both the equant and the eccentric are *virtual* or *mathematical* points rather than physical or real ones. Positing a mathematical observation point to replace an actual location on earth must have seemed (and, in fact, came to be viewed over time) as a dubious contrivance. Why, if the cosmic system is geocentric, can't the earth provide the center for calculations? For Muslim astronomers—and later, too—it seemed odd to locate the earth in such an incongruous fashion. A distinction was called for, if only in theory, between the *physical* reality of the world as it had been conceived since Aristotle and the *mathematical* model that astronomy now presented.

Still, postulating such a point surely encouraged further conjecture—especially when new observations called for a better hypothesis. Perhaps the point should be located elsewhere. Perhaps the very fact that a further hypothesis proved necessary meant that more accurate measuring techniques should be developed. Whatever the case, the mere distinction between map and model can only have emboldened mathematician-astronomers to introduce changes in a way they might not have done otherwise—had they believed that they held a faithful mirror image of the universe in their hands.

Indeed, efforts to account for this discontinuity likely stood behind the suggestion that astronomy, though included as part of the corpus of Aristotelian physics, should be separated from kindred fields—that it be granted a different title: *al-hay'a*, literally, "form" or "shape." This nomenclature, which started as early as the mid-ninth century[1] and gained currency among philosophers from Avicenna on, encouraged scientists to "try out" different mathematical solutions to account for observations and make "adjustments"; after all, the "map" was still tentative and required verification. Work in this field—possibly the most important and mysterious science inasmuch as it set out to determine the structure enveloping the world we live in—sought to refine the Ptolemaic model to approximate reality, if not to reflect it. As astronomers collected new data, compiling tables and making more and more precise observations of stellar motions, they introduced new equations and conceived new geometric patterns to describe the velocities and directions of various heavenly bodies more accurately. They were encouraged to do so by knowing that what they were working with was still a model. Ideally, the earth's position would serve as the basis for calculations, and a single formula would account for the motions of heavenly bodies near and far.

Ptolemy's model presented a picture that did not yet do so; he thought the retrograde orbital patterns of the outer planets required equations and formulas different from those accounting for the motions of the inner planets (Mercury and Venus). The significance of challenging such a view by a Muslim astronomer would be evident later.[2] Granted, this was just a model. Even so, astronomers would have reasonably wondered why the point of measurement was not the earth itself, whether all the measurements were precise, why a *single* formula did not account for all the motions of heavenly bodies and, indeed, whether the earth's real position was not, in fact, the actual center of the world. Although Ptolemy was able to solve a pre-existing dilemma facing astronomers concerning the location and velocity of planets (the "wanderers"), his postulate of the equant must have left astronomers wondering whether more precise measurements and better equations would not yield a model that was "truer to form." In other words, astronomers working with this model wished that orbital motions could be explained by an earth-centered model that did not need an equant hypothesis.

Neither Avicenna nor Averroes (who had an Aristotelian sensibility) was persuaded by the Ptolemaic postulate. The renowned scientist and mathematician Ibn al-Haytham also had already expressed his doubts about many of Ptolemy's postulates and calculations in his *Shukuk 'ala Batlimos* (*Aporias*), stressing that the "model" was more hypothetical than real. Other Muslim astronomers, such as al-Bitruji (d. 1204) from Andalusia, drew up models locating the earth at the center. Obviously, the efforts came to naught. All the same, these examples show that the virtual off-center position of the earth in Ptolemy's model prompted concern, as did the position and function of the equant. Later, Ibn Shatir (d. 1375), who belonged to what one might call an "Eastern" school of thought (as follows), dispensed with many of Ptolemy's postulates when making calculations (including equants and eccentrics) and demonstrated that the earth does not in fact lie at the center of the world. Ibn Shatir partly worked as the "time keeper" at the Damascus Mosque, where he had to provide exact times for the five prayers of Muslims; his "bible" for scientific calculation comprised empirical observations and tests, rather than any preconceived or pre-modelled equations provided in the Ptolemaic system. But advanced as it was, and though far more accurate in reflecting orbital motions, his own model was still geocentric (a "classical" worldview). As it turns out, Ibn Shatir's models and measurements were later mirrored in Copernicus's work, sparking speculations about whether he had not been working on a heliocentric model of his own.

Be that as it may, Ptolemy's equant allowed him to account for what, in mathematical terminology, is called the uniform *angular* speed of a planet along an orbit (the *deferent*) around the eccentric. This was then matched to epicyclical motion of the planet around its own center to account for retrograde motion—deviation from uniformity—and explain why its "speed" seemed to vary. Introducing the equant resolved a longstanding dilemma concerning the determination of planets' location, direction, and velocity. As noted, Ptolemy's recourse to equants and epicycles was motivated partly by his belief that it was impossible to provide a single account or model for all the planetary motions from earth: while he thought a central circular model would do for the outer planets, the same did not apply to the inner ones.

Such engagement with Ptolemaic mathematics—and movement away from strict adherence to primarily Aristotelian postulates about the world—is what allowed astronomers in Islam to make technical advances that laid the groundwork for ultimately discarding an earth-centered model altogether and developing a heliocentric model—that is, what is known as the "Copernican revolution." That said, it is important to emphasize that this groundwork did not necessarily serve an explicit *purpose*; the point was not to show that the sun, instead of the earth, occupies the center of the cosmos. Indeed, the very opposite may well have been the case: mathematical adjustments to the Ptolemaic model were only meant to make more sense of actual observations and uphold the view of the earth's centrality. It just so happens that they were what was needed to construct the Copernican model!

There is much speculation, today, whether Copernican heliocentrism was somehow anticipated by Muslim astronomy. However, the matters at issue lack explication in precise terms. A "heliocentric" view of the world was not an entirely new concept—Muslim scholars were aware that such a view had already been presented in earlier Indian and Greek civilizations. Especially after Baghdad fell to the Mongols in 1258 and major astronomical research moved further east, the notion seems to have received serious discussion; in the thirteenth and fifteenth centuries, some scholars at observatories commissioned by the Mongolian rulers (Hulago Khan and Ulugh Beg) are known to have tried to find mathematical support for this model. However, it remains unclear whether they sought simply to correct and refine the Ptolemaic model (based on a geocentric worldview), or embark on a heliocentric project. Numbers count, too: although *some* of the astronomers of the time are known to have been inching toward heliocentrism in their calculations—or at least to have been *experimenting* with the mathematics for such a view—the majority must have simply been hard at work trying to refine and correct the prevalent Ptolemaic model.

As later became clear in the Christian West, a heliocentric view of the world was never just a mathematical concept. Serious reflection required a radical transformation in one's mode of thinking—not only in philosophical terms (inasmuch as Aristotelian postulates were "dumped"), but also in religious ones: such a view meant entertaining a radically decentered view of the universe. It is important to note, however, that this would not have seemed scandalous in the Islamic world. As we have seen in previous chapters, post-Avicennian philosophy already dispensed with some of the underlying tenets of Aristotelian philosophy. Indeed, it is not surprising, then, that some of the earliest philosophers/astronomers who considered a heliocentric world were of an Avicennian rather than an Aristotelian bent of mind (see following). What is more, it merits consideration that, in contrast to the Christian context, nothing in the Islamic codex would have presented a *religious* obstacle to adopting a heliocentric (or other) worldview. Nothing in the Qur'an states that earth lies "at the center of the world." Additionally, the Qur'an indicates that everything in the world—including the earth—is somehow suspended in space by invisible "anchors"; one passage even intimates that our planet (specifically, mountains that seem to stand firm) sweeps along like clouds in the sky. Other passages about the earth—significantly, *not* the universe as a whole—refer to how God may level it at will. Most striking for Muslim astronomers, perhaps, was the reference to *seven* skies. An astronomer pondering these verses would surely have been open to considering all kinds of models, and would have been willing to discard the Ptolemaic geocentric worldview altogether.

Even adding up these two circumstances (religious and philosophical), however, does not mean that Muslim astronomers were bent on proving a specifically heliocentric view. Willingness to consider a non-geocentric world does not automatically mean endorsing a heliocentric vision. It simply indicates openness for imagining and studying different options. The efforts and innovations of the post-Mongolian scholars at Maragha and Samarkand mentioned earlier should probably be viewed in this light. Still, it was such mathematics and modeling that ultimately prepared a "paradigm shift." Previous hypotheses and equations had to be seen and shown to be inconclusive or wrong, as well as unnecessarily cumbersome. It was along these lines, away from the rigid Aristotelian structure, that Muslim astronomers slowly approached and prepared for what was to become the revolution associated with Copernicus.

Some fundamentals of the classic worldview were not accepted at face value. The "stationary" quality of the earth—a Ptolemaic postulate argued for in the introduction to *Almagest*—had already been questioned by Nasir el-Din Tusi (our friend from Alamut), as well as by al-Qushji (d. 1474), who also challenged the Ptolemaic notion that the model for the outer planets does not apply to inner ones. Even the earth's centrality in this classical formula was "disproven" by the Syrian Ibn Shatir, when he demonstrated how orbital motions of the planets could be explained away from Ptolemy's models.

For many Muslims scholars—as for the fathers of the Christian Church (and, later, the scholastics of medieval Europe)—a geocentric, Aristotelian understanding of the world was a "given." However, it was not given for Muslim scholars in every sense of the word: it had already been adjusted to accommodate different theoretical outlooks. For example, it was more natural for them to give this worldview a Plotinian interpretation, or even an "occasionalist" one centered on a First Cause, than to accept the Aristotelian model wholesale, much less understand it in purely mechanistic or essentialist terms. While Muslim scholars of various stripes uniformly accepted a First Cause and an order of perfectly circular orbits all constituting a single reality, they differed on whether the "grid" that constitutes it comprises pieces that are inherently interconnected, or whether each of these parts—whether in the mind or in the external world—connects with others by virtue of an extrinsic cause. Coming from the tradition of speculative discourse, "atomists" disagreed with "Aristotelian" philosophers who held that matter is infinitely divisible. For the former, the order apparent in the universe must not be mistaken for intrinsic causal chains. God constantly acts upon this order; thus, it could also be otherwise. At the same time, philosophers such as Avicenna (whom Tusi defended against critics) also held that causal chains are not intrinsic, even though they are causally necessary inasmuch as they are, and were, brought about *ab initio*. From either perspective, the order that exists amounts only to one possibility among others—it is not the rigid Aristotelian scheme reflected necessarily in a given set of equations.

One could review different areas of knowledge (e.g., physics, morality, law, etc.) and show that Muslim scholars did not consider their knowledge claims to be certain; at any rate, they did not hold their objects of knowledge to be intrinsically as they saw them. Arguably, such an attitude toward astronomy encouraged open-mindedness for the science that reached them.[3] However, as scientists pursuing definitive and precise answers by working on the specific mathematical model they had, Muslim astronomers more likely wished to *depict* the Ptolemaic order of the structure enveloping the world accurately, since it did not quite *mirror* what it was supposed to explain. Furthermore, although they were well aware of theoretical speculation concerning the nonmechanical nature of the physical world, they did not view such speculation as the first item of business.

. . .

Ever since Ibn Shatir's works came to light at the middle of the past century, there has been increasing conjecture whether the mathematical advances made in Muslim astronomy were informed by a purposive search for a heliocentric model in one way or another—or if they *directly* influenced the "Copernican revolution." At this point, however, the matter remains largely speculative. Much depends on unearthing more manuscripts from the period. In any case, it is well known that many of the aforementioned ideas and findings "filtered" into the West; Copernicus himself even mentions some of them (e.g., perhaps the most comprehensive "handbook" of the works at the Maragha Observatory, the *Zij-i likhani*—a compendium of models and tables first translated into Greek by Gregory Choniades, who had come from Byzantium to study at the observatory). But two of the most important mathematical innovations by Muslim astronomers—which historians often contend that Copernicus used (the so-called Tusi couple and the 'Urdi *Lemma*)—find no mention, even though it is quite likely that he "borrowed" them. A third *proof*—concerning Qushji's Mercury model—is another, perhaps even more striking example.

. . .

Historically, official Muslim interest in astronomy began in the Abbassid era of al-Ma'mun. From this point on, observatories were constructed to enable the study and verification of Ptolemaic astronomy, as outlined in the *Almagest*. The practice was aided by the algebraic and geometrical equations found in Euclid's *Elements* (which date from much earlier—around 300 B.C.) and later Greek commentaries. But these equations and proofs were not accepted wholesale. Muslim mathematicians made adjustments, uncovered mistakes, and contributed new equations and proofs—as occurred in all of the inherited sciences, from paleontology to medicine. In this context, one should not omit Muslim mathematicians' invention of trigonometry—accounting for angular and other measurements in spherical shapes. In astronomy too, and right from the beginning, Muslim scholars reflected on natural anomalies they encountered—deviations or new features—and sought to provide more exact measurements and accounts for motions occurring in the sky.

As an Abbassid center, Baghdad remained a major learning hub until its fall and destruction by the Mongols in 1258. But as previously mentioned, Baghdad's political control over the eastern provinces was already curtailed by offshoot Shi'ite regimes, including that of the Isma'ili imamates holding out at Alamut and other castles along the valley. The famous scholar and astronomer Nasir el-Din Tusi is said to have moved to Alamut in anticipation of the Mongolian invasion of Muslim territory, with a full caravan load of books and instruments from Baghdad. In the hundred-odd years since its takeover by Hasan al-Sabbah, Alamut had boasted its own library. Scholars would visit, sometimes to review the sect's clandestine literature (all of which was set aflame in 1256, when the Mongols finally took over the fortress and destroyed it).

History, however, has curious twists. Hulago Khan, grandson of the Mongolian Empire's founder Genghis Khan—whose army had swept across eastern Muslim provinces and massacred populations wholesale—made a decision that proved critical in the history of astronomy: he would bring Tusi out of Alamut and take him back further east; then, he would ask him to specify an appropriate location to build an observatory, to design it, and to direct its activities. In consequence, Maragha (in the East Azerbaijan province) came to be the most advanced center for astronomical research to date; by far the most important innovations in astronomy occurred here.

The polymath Tusi, whose philosophical leanings were more Avicennian than Aristotelian, also excelled in an executive capacity. His center attracted scholars from near and far—including China. One of the first men he recruited, when the project was still in the design stage, was the Syrian engineer Mu'ayyad al-Din al-'Urdi (d. 1266)—known to posterity for introducing and proving the so-called 'Urdi *Lemma*. (This equation is found in Copernicus's works; later, Kepler would ask how Copernicus managed to draw on a formula whose proof he did not offer.) Visitors included European astronomers, who took back ideas and translations to enrich study in their own lands.

Needless to say, all of this required financial support. It is to Hulago Khan's credit that the observatory prospered for as long as he did. The institution started to decline after his death—but not before providing a model for Ulugh Beg (a mathematician in his own right), who commissioned an observatory on an even grander scale in Samarkand, in 1428. Here and, later, in Damascus and Istanbul (where al-Qushji received a teaching position after his tenure in Samarkand), the "Maragha project" survived as a distinct, "Eastern" school of thought. One of the earliest features of this project was the "Tusi couple." In the course of subsequent events, Copernicus used this revolutionary concept to shift the focus of the orbital system to the sun. Tusi had had something else in mind: he simply wanted to find a new method to do what Ptolemy had tried to accomplish with the equant.

Tusi's stroke of genius was to devise a different way to make the calculations Ptolemy's imperfect model required. It involved introducing a second circle, in addition to the one already mapped out for each planet's orbit. By this means, he showed how a given planet could be "seen" to run through its epicycle at varying speeds while maintaining a uniform circular motion around the earth—in other words, how uniform circular motion resolves into linear motion. To this end, two circles are posited, one with half of the other's diameter, touching at a tangent and rotating in opposite directions; the smaller, inner circle rotates at half the speed of the larger one. As soon as rotation begins, the tangential point (i.e., the planet) proceeds in a straight line until it reaches the circumference of the larger circle at the opposite end. Besides its aesthetically beautiful "geometry," Tusi's postulate rendered *the unique observation point* for calculating planetary motions redundant: the necessary calculations could be made from *any point*.

Although Tusi himself did not make a further step—for example, taking *the sun* as that "any point"—it was now possible for someone else to do so. His student Shirazi already discussed the possibility. Tusi's colleague, al-'Urdi, refined the notion of this couple through his *Lemma*, showing that the point in question for the outer planets lies *at* half the distance from the equant point posited for the planetary epicycle. Later, Ibn Shatir—and then, finally, al-Qushji, who demonstrated that the inner planets (his proof concerns Mercury, specifically) fit a model that does away with equants and epicenters altogether—it became even more "natural" to take such steps.) When Copernicus shifted the focus of planetary rotation to the sun, he already possessed the mathematical tools necessary to do so. Even so, the change he proposed—as someone living in a culture steeped in Christian theology—required a revolutionary leap of imagination.

.   .   .

Two final observations about astronomy's progress in Islam should be made. To hold its ground, any scientific theory must both account for observed facts and enable predictions about them to be made. Up to the sixteenth century, the Ptolemaic model fulfilled both requirements, more or less. Along the way, adjustments proved necessary, but as a whole the theory remained intact. As Thomas Kuhn observes in a study that now counts as a classic in the history of science, every field of research reaches a point when the number of adjustments requires a new theory altogether. The replacement of the geocentric, Ptolemaic model by the heliocentric, Copernican/Galilean model exemplifies just such a paradigm shift.

.   .   .

The second item concerns *imagination*, the faculty Avicenna granted the primary role in his theory of knowledge. Mathematics, it may be argued, is *the* paradigm of an imaginative science. From the very beginning, philosophers have asked about the ontological status of its "objects" and "tools": numbers. Philosophers in Islam did so, too—just how precisely numbers connect with each other, and what their hypothetical nature means. Representing equations by means of geometric figures (or *vice versa*) can facilitate understanding, but the practice enlists the imagination above all. Even though many physical sciences (including astronomy) employ physical observation to obtain data for numerical calculations, the mathematical approach stands apart inasmuch as equations—even though empirically-based and inferential—propose exact universal rules or conclusions. The mathematical ability to capture general truth exactly, by hypothetical means, is precisely what makes it an *imaginative* science: it produces *models*.

To arrive at his model, Ptolemy had to envision points and figures: deferents, eccentrics, epicycles, and equants. Such constructs allowed him to provide equations that accounted for observations and enabled predictions. Significantly, he did not discover the points and figures by way of a demonstrative syllogism (or even inferentially—by using some probability theory or another). Ultimately, it seems, inspiration played a dominant role—the "jump" from observation to hypothesis. According to a modern school of thought associated with Karl Popper, the decisive factor for science is a hypothesis's falsifiability; inferential conclusions of a universal nature are not verifiable. Needless to say, this distinction between falsifiability and verifiability was not current in the times of Ptolemy (or Islam). A theorem's accuracy was considered in terms of observation and predictive ability. The premises it drew on could be accepted for as long as these conditions were satisfied. The theorem itself did not have an observable, physical component.

. . .

It is hardly surprising, in a scientific culture of this kind, that philosophers (or astronomers acting in a philosophical capacity) performed an analogous but different move when they hypothesized the existence of an immaterial, or spiritual, framework for the structure of reality. For the most part, it occurred to them naturally enough—given their faith as Muslims and the ready availability of Plotinian theory to identify a "spiritual anchor" for their model. It would have been self-evident that a Prime Mover accounts for why everything exists in the first place and why prevailing "mechanics" are as they are. Indeed, the existence of a nonphysical ordering point must have seemed far more real than mathematical hypotheses. The Plotinian model, then—which associates the planets and stars with an immaterial spirit suffusing and animating the entire system—must have made intuitive sense (even though, as we will see in the next chapter, alternatives were proposed). In other words, *imagining* would have played an important role in the mental process they undertook to achieve knowledge.

While we stand light years away from culture as it existed then, we remain familiar with the affinity between imagining and knowing. We should bear in mind that today—when heliocentric cosmology has proven inadequate for explaining new observations—we are being called on again to exercise our imaginations, to picture how our ever-expanding galaxy derives energy from black holes within it, which are created by the collapse of stars, and revolves around them. The same holds for other galaxies, too—all of which presumably orbit black holes, as well. In turn, the whole likely revolves around a central black hole, which grows larger and larger as smaller black holes merge with each other. The result is a "Big Nothing"; some of its features we can identify with inferometers, but the void itself is invisible by definition, because its gravitational force prevents any light from escaping. In brief, we are being asked to imagine a Big Nothing either as the Prime Mover or the Final Cause behind the order we see!

. . .

The Maraghah Observatory operated for some fifty years before it fell into disuse and ruin. As noted, an even more impressive observatory following its model was constructed in Samarkand by Ulugh Bey in the fifteenth century. By then, however, the real advances in astronomical research had shifted to Europe. By the mid-sixteenth century, Tycho Brahe was able to demolish, once and for all, the classical Aristotelian notion of a "final" outer sphere containing "everything."[4] Kepler did away with circular orbits. Less than fifty years later, at the beginning of the seventeenth century, the telescope was introduced in the Netherlands. This inaugurated a new era of astronomical observation. Galileo, of course, was the first to develop and use the new instrument. He demonstrated, empirically, that the cosmos was not as people had thought it to be since time immemorial.

Cosmic Lights

It is interesting to consider what the "Sheikh of Illumination," Shahab al-Din Suhrawardi (1155–1191), would have made of the colorful and magical aurora, had he been given the chance to visit either the North or South Pole. Suhrawardi was born in a village near Maraghah, and his travels did not take him beyond Iran and Arabia; he was killed—possibly executed for his heretical views—in Aleppo at the young age of thirty-six. Had he seen these celestial phenomena (or even been told of them), he would probably have thought they proved his thesis that light, as a substance, constitutes all that exists—especially since they occur simultaneously at the two opposite ends of the globe. Had he lived longer still, he would certainly have appreciated the modern theory that matter itself is a form of energy (as expressed by the famous formula, $E=mc^2$): the "Big Bang" releases photons that eventually come to form everything in the universe. However, his theory remained wholly speculative. If Avicenna had wondered whether light is what explains motion—and, therefore, whether emanation plays the role of Aristotle's final cause—Suhrawardi stated as much. His delightfully original *Wisdom of Illumination* explores the consequences.

This work is one of a kind. It begins with a brief but highly astute logical analysis of quantified universal statements and the Aristotelian syllogistic figures they represent; but for the absence of variable notation (which was not introduced until our own times), this part could easily be thought to belong to a modern textbook of logic. However, it ends like the prayer book of an ancient esoteric sect, with a series of entreaties to God, the source of cosmic lights—and therefore of all that exists. Between these two points, Suhrawardi replaces the received categories of physics with a system of his own, eliminating traditional distinctions between the four elements, matter and form, and substance and accident. His vision presents a foundational "light grid" extending throughout the universe; this structure underlies and constitutes anything and everything, including our very souls.

Suhrawardi's "doctrine of lights" departed from prevailing conceptions just as stunningly as, later, Leibniz's notion of monads—which replaced what we see and know of the world (including ourselves) by spiritual corpuscles diffused throughout the universe, constituting what (we consider) solid matter. Whereas Leibniz's monads are *alive* (in a sense), Suhrawardi's lights are divided into those that are "light-sensitive," and therefore alive, and others that are not. Leibniz saw no need to refer to any predecessors in support of his doctrine. In contrast, Suhrawardi listed a veritable host: the Pre-Socratics, Plato, Indian thinkers, and, above all, representatives of ancient Persian tradition. These references were meant to bolster his project of "deconstructing" the peripatetic philosophical tradition (i.e., Aristotelianism). Nominally, Suhrawardi retains the Plotinian hierarchy of planets and stars extending from an outermost sphere down to the moon and earth. In effect, however, he takes apart this model of intellects, souls, and matter by affirming that a "light of lights" structures and animates the universe. As he sees it, emanation (*fayd*) *is* illumination, pure and simple.

Suhrawardi did not shy away from presenting his model as just that: a model. From the outset, he tells the reader that, just as astronomers construct their theories on the basis of what they have observed, his view follows from what he has seen (and what has been seen by others sharing the same facility of *in*sight). The difference is that what he has observed includes phenomena in a world invisible to most people. Inasmuch as one endeavors to discern the bigger picture, one stands apart from those who content themselves with the framework of what is ordinarily observed. We should note, in this context, that Suhrawadi's "insight" does not refer to mental vision as opposed to physical optics. The matter is crucial inasmuch as it involves what the nature of perception and the perceived *is*. Although the world is constituted by what he calls "bodies" and "forms," he means that what exists—chiefly, what is endowed with *life*—can see and/or is "seeable." Suhrawardi denies that there is *being* as such—a general state or condition accounting for what exists.[1] Like other abstract terms such as "color" or "substance," "being" refers to a mental notion—not to a state or condition in the external world. The world is made up of particular existents, but none of them is "there" because *being* constitutes it. Indeed, no such thing exists in the external world at all. What, then, accounts for, or determines, what exists? Suhrawardi's answer is *light*. Sight is its instrument, as it were, and it has two aspects: from an active perspective, seeing, and, from a passive one, being seen.

From this vantage point, Suhrawardi claims that what *he* sees (and what other sages have seen throughout history) in the so-called world of the spirits actually *exists*. This prompts a question: is there no difference of substance between what inhabits the "two worlds"? Does seeing what exists in this world not depend on the fact that it possesses physical being (as opposed to what belongs to the other world and is "spectral" in nature)? Suhrawardi provides an ingenious response by rejecting the two principal conceptions of vision that prevailed in his day: the Greek view that light proceeds from the eye, and the notion that objects reflect light onto the eye (espoused by al-Hazen/Ibn al-Haytham[2]). Suhrawardi proposes a process that may be translated as "fronting" (*muqabalah*): vision is simply a matter of seer and seen facing one another, each in the other's presence.

This postulate eliminates the need to speak of light being reflected on to, or off of, things—which presupposes independent physical existence (and makes spectral objects harder to explain). Even so, one might ask, surely seeing involves an image that somehow is registered on the retina? The shape one sees must correspond to the form of an object in the outside world. Suhrawardi argues this is not the case.[3] To illustrate his point, he employs the example of mirrors. What we see in mirrors does not exist in three-dimensional, physical space. We should picture our relationship to objects in the same way: what we identify as existing in the "real world," *relative to the light* infusing it, only possesses the kind of existence that images in mirrors have; it, too, is spectral. As far as our perception is concerned, there is no fundamental difference between what we take to be spirits and what inhabits our world. In other words, the "fronting" model means that the images formed in our eyes under (what we consider) normal conditions do not represent all that stands before us. To put the matter in the terms of modern scientific discourse: the innumerable quantity of data, or "bytes" striking our senses at any given point far exceeds the relatively limited number of them that we actually process.

Was Suhrawardi proposing the thesis later associated with Bishop Berkeley—that to be is to be seen (*esse est percipi*)? Certainly, he held that light originating from a primary source—God—suffuses the universe and constitutes the objects within it. To exist as a defined entity is either to perceive and be perceivable, or simply to be perceivable. But Suhrawardi thought there was something more in the universe than what has appearance: dead bodies. The latter neither perceive nor are they perceivable. Suhrawardi's word for them is "darkness." These dark "things" are not forms themselves; that is, they possess no features that might lend definition to anything else. Suhrawardi employs two crucial terms in this context: "that which appears" (*al-zahir*) and "that which is invisible and indefinite" (*al-ghaseq*); the second term does not occur in the philosophical tradition before him. Bodies can belong to one category or to the other.

To understand what he possibly had in mind in postulating this negative plenum, we might draw an analogy to what physicists now call "dark matter": the hypothetical stuff held to exist because of a gravitational effect observed on visible matter, but which neither emits nor reflects light itself. Suhrawardi's hypothesis invites this comparison because the living bodies he identifies either emit light or both emit and reflect it. Dead bodies, in contrast, are not photosensitive. At the same time, however, such "dark" and therefore "unperceivable" matter must be distinguished from the spectral world—which contains living bodies that only a special power of insight can discern. For Suhrawardi, the living (or light-reactant) world encompasses far more than what we normally see, yet it is smaller than the world at large (which also contains the dark plenum).

Still, it seems unclear why Suhrawardi hypothesizes these dark and dead bodies, all of which represent nothing but undefined quantities (and therefore prove indistinguishable both *per se* and from each another). The most likely explanation is that, inasmuch he did not believe in a vacuum, he held that the world must be "filled out" with far more matter than is visible—in analogy to the outermost sphere where the most distant stars are situated. Accordingly, he would have thought it necessary to postulate such a plenum to complement the visible (apparent) world. As such, this realm of contrast plays the same role as dark matter today (which makes it possible to account for gravitational phenomena affecting visible matter). For all that, Suhrawardi did not provide an explanation.

The whole world—living and dead—originates with the *light of lights.* This spiritual power suffuses the universe; with intensity that declines as its essence spreads from the source, it endows "apparent" bodies with the ability to react and perceive or, if they occupy a lower position, simply to react. The process practically qualifies as organic: the light animating the forms of the world differs in grade, but not in kind (or quantity), from the point of origin. Suhrawardi opposed his thesis to the prevailing Plotinian view that multiplicity (i.e., intellects and bodies) proceeds from unity (the First Cause); unlike *emanation*, which occurs step-by-step, *illumination* happens all at once. By Suhrawardi's account, light is not itself a body. Therefore its profusion does not involve the movement of particles decreasing in number, activity, or power.[4] (All the same, the model does call Plotinus's "world-soul" to mind, especially insofar as Suhrawardi, like Avicenna before him, granted primacy to spiritual faculties instead of intellectual ones.)

If being (that is, living) means being "photosensitive," then the ontological distinction between the possible and the necessary—one of Avicenna's central theses, meant to explain the gulf between God and the rest of the world—no longer proves relevant: both the source and the recipients of light constitute an integral, simultaneous whole, and no modal category is required to distinguish the "being" of the one from the "being" of the other. Suhrawardi discusses possibility as a mental notion among others, like color. (Significantly, he does not treat necessity.) A given body is not possible per se (that is, no possibility is instantiated in it), nor does anything categorized as possible prove necessary because it comes into being through an external cause. Once a body has been categorized as something possible, that is simply how it continues to be. Otherwise, Suhrawardi observes, we would have to admit the absurd conclusion that if something possible can become necessary, it can also become impossible! But at the same time, he still affirms the presence of causal relations, which he explains in terms of light.

In analogy to matter—described as possible but without the potential to be different from what it is—"dark matter" is not dead; rather, it does not have the potential to become sensitive to light. The symmetry is not complete, however: light-sensitive bodies may turn dark because darkness is the absence (or withdrawal) of light. The world's constitution is as follows (note the primacy attached to the notion of "thing"): either a thing is a light in itself, or it is not; that which is a light per se is either simply and purely light, or it is a form for something other than itself (an accident); whatever is not a light in itself is either something requiring no place in order to exist (in which case it is undefined (*ghaseq*) substance), or it is a form for something other than itself: dark form. In this view, bodies, including the planets, either are dark and undefined or they are defined by light, which provides form. Suhrawardi affirms that there is no need to define "light itself," as nothing simpler or more elementary exists into which it might be broken down. There is nothing more apparent or visible than clarity, and light is what is clearest; it requires no further explanation.[5]

Undefined bodies and their obscure forms constitute "dark" or "dead" matter. This plenum of invisible and indeterminate entities is destined to remain as it is. In contrast, visible and defined bodies are constituted (or instantiated) by a form of light that makes them appear as we know them. At the same time, they may be constituted by another category of light that exists both in itself and for itself (i.e., not for something else). What is this higher kind of light? It is *living*, but, even more important, it exists *for itself*, as self-consciousness possessing manifest self-identity. Suhrawardi explains the matter as follows: a being that is aware (or conscious) of itself is not indefinite (*ghaseq*), for its *self* appears to it; nor is any form of light a light for itself inasmuch as it appertains to something other than itself. Therefore, the higher category must be light pure and simple, something one cannot point at. When explaining the immaterial identity of human beings, Suhrawardi uses language he might seem to have taken from Descartes: "were you to examine the matter, you would not find what it is that makes you who you are—except a thing that is conscious of itself, which is your 'I-ness.'"

Of course, Suhrawardi was not advancing an original claim when he said that souls are self-conscious, immaterial entities, and that identity is constituted on this basis.[6] His originality derives from how he understood the element of light: souls are lights in and for themselves, and consciousness simply consists in the perceptibility of this light—whether it concerns oneself or other objects. It is no wonder, then, that he proposes that spiritual or spectral beings may *be seen* every bit as much as what we take to exist physically. The material and the immaterial stand on par with each other; in either case, their visibility represents a function of the *seer*.

In introducing the *Wisdom of Illumination*, Suhrawardi identifies different categories of knowledge in terms of possession and seeking. He calls them "research" and "godliness," respectively. The first refers to the approach common among contemporary scientists and philosophers. The second refers to the path of the Sufis—that is, a quest for divinity within that also manifests itself as outward conduct. Suhrawardi declares that his book is written for those who combine both approaches; it is not intended for parties seeking only to attain conventional knowledge. The reader must already have beheld a divine flash of light and now consider such experience second nature. Suhrawardi mentions other works he has written, which present and critique peripatetic theories, only in passing. *Wisdom of Illumination*, he declares, takes aim for something higher; colleagues and followers have long asked him to reveal some of his real teachings; finally, he has undertaken the task.

The introductory observations on logic are brief but insightful. Suhrawardi's view of what conventional philosophers "revere" so highly is evident in the considerable space he devotes to treating fallacies; this part of logic, he declares, deserves attention. For him, logic is primarily a defensive skill—good for guarding against mistakes in arguments. It does not provide a method for attaining knowledge or finding the truth (as Alfarabi, among others, had maintained). Indeed, most philosophical discussion of syllogisms—the figures and rules governing them—is of no substance whatsoever. Viewed properly, all of this, along with what has come to be known as "propositional logic," can be reduced to simple rules. Two observations Suhrawardi makes in this context are key: on the one hand, we should understand all syllogistic propositions to be necessary (i.e., even statements whose truths are merely possible may be reformulated as matters of necessity); on the other, we may reformulate quantified existential statements (i.e., those modified by the word "some") in universal terms (modified by the word "all").

Suhrawardi's first point concerns the confusion and belabored justifications that arise when philosophers ignore the modalities of the statements in syllogisms to defend their inferences. Fundamentally, he affirms, there are just three kinds of relations between subjects and predicates. The predicate's relation to the subject either is (1) necessarily true (e.g., "humans are animals"), (2) necessarily false (e.g., "humans are stones"), or (3) neither necessarily true or false (e.g., "people are literate"). Suhrawardi observes that much useless discussion could be avoided if one bore in mind that statements of the third type—that is, those that are possible—prove necessary as soon as the conditions are spelled out for them to hold true (e.g. which people are concerned, when this is the case, etc.). It would be better still not to use such statements in demonstrative reasoning at all. He then specifies two ways to eliminate needless inferences. The first involves understanding modality ("necessary," "possible," etc.) as part of the predicate (rather than a term modifying the statement as a whole)—in effect, it represents an "operator" presupposing an existential quality of the subject. The other step involves treating negation as part of the predicate; this is meant to underscore that all predications (whether affirmative or negative) presuppose or affirm something—an object of some sort—about which the judgment is made.

Suhrawardi's point about reformulating quantified existential statements into universal ones is both insightful and prescient. One must understand universal statements such as "all X's are Y's" properly. Here, the statement concerns each and every individual object described as an X. As we have noted, Suhrawardi maintains that all predications presume positive judgment—that is, they are affirmative judgments about objects. Therefore, we must understand a universal statement as one concerning *any* object whose existence is affirmed ab initio: for *any* such object we might consider, it holds that *this particular* object *is* both X and Y. In order to make this formulation clear, he continues, we should introduce a special marker that *names* the specific objection under consideration. By formulating universal statements in these terms (e.g., "any n that is an X . . . "), Suhrawardi avoids the classical objection to the Aristotelian view that universal statements presuppose an unspecified existential affirmation of *all* objects covered by the subject-term. (To get around this objection, it is common to reformulate the relevant statement as conditional [i.e., to say that if an object a is an X, then it is also a Y].)

By replacing "all" with "any," Suhrawardi reworks the Aristotelian statement into a conditional. In a second step, he extends his reformulation of universal statements (now allowing for objects to be specified *by name*) so that it applies to quantified existential statements. Now, he argues, one may focus on the particular objects covered by the quantifier ("some"); under such conditions, it is a matter of affirming for any of the objects covered by "some"—one by one, and each by its special name— that it is as described. This manner of "reading" existential statements has far-reaching implications.

To explain the interpretation of statements along these lines, Suhrawardi introduces the term *istighraq*. The best translation is perhaps "differential predication," or "instantiation": the predicates X and Y apply to any one of the objects in a class, or make explicit each and every condition or circumstance by virtue of which a contingent statement—including a conditional one—holds true. Applying this interpretation to quantified existential statements, Suhrawardi tries to show how to avoid using them in demonstrative syllogisms. Where they occur, he observes, they can be reworked as universal statements: "some X's are Y's," may be reformulated as a universal statement about all those Xs, *any* of which can be said to be a Y. In other words, the premise in the syllogism, "some X's are Y's," admits interpretation as a universal statement permitting us to pick *any one* of the relevant objects—identified by a marker of particularity, *a*—and affirm that *this one* is an X as well as a Y.

Setting an object apart amounts to *naming it*. Thus, if the quantified existential premise of the syllogism has transformed into a universal statement naming any one of all instances concerned, the conclusion may be drawn that the item at issue—which now has been existentially quantified—has come to be described by the predicate of the second premise. It stands as follows:

1. Some X's are Y's.

2. All Y's are Z's.

1'. (Any named X, a, is a Y.)

3. Therefore, some X's (namely, a) are Z's.

Since a name (a) does not function as predicate, we do not need to include the intermediate step as a premise in the syllogism. (After all, a premise needs to be formed of both subject and predicate.) According to the rules of the day, the instantiation step (1') made by naming an individual instance excludes it from functioning as a premise. Suhrawardi considers this interpretation an implicit and intuitive step allowing one to derive the required conclusion in a straightforward manner.

Suhrawardi reformulated existential statements into universal statements that pick out—and thereby name—a specific object from a universal set covering the item in question; this, in turn, produces an existential statement on the basis of instantiation.[7] The operation was stunningly pre-scient. Two recently developed rules of inference in what is called "first-order logic" concern universal instantiation and existential generalization (which, it has been claimed, mirror each other). Here, the specific infer-ence that a is X can be made when a quantified universal statement is combined with a singular statement; conversely, a quantified existential statement may be inferred from a singular statement.

Needless to say, Suhrawardi did not articulate modern rules of infer-ence. Still, it is clear that he understood the basis for such rules. Today—following the introduction of variables standing in for specific instances (X's and Y's) and with due attention to the order in which these two infer-ential rules are used in the same argument—it has become standard prac-tice to proceed in this fashion when presenting logical proofs.

Suhrawardi extended his critique of philosophical logic to juridical methods of analogical reasoning. These, he argued, do not provide reli-able means for achieving certainty. Suhrawardi considered it impossible to identify, with certainty, what assures that a particular statement holds true, such that it might provide the basis for inferring that another statement is also true. (Let us recall that Ibn Taymiyyah considered proceeding by anal-ogy to be valid *in lieu of* the philosophical method of inference.) Inasmuch as one cannot know *why* a particular prophetic injunction is so, one can-not determine whether a new statement should have the same force as the injunction in question. Suhrawardi devoted a special section to the mat-ter in his discussion of fallacious reasoning. Indeed, his critical mind took him further still: even though he does not mention Avicenna by name, he devotes a section (in the same part of the book) to one of the latter's sig-nature arguments: that nothing can be said about anything when regarded by itself and as itself, except that it is what it is.

Wisdom of Illumination does not mention Avicenna directly. In-stead, Suhrawardi alludes respectfully to "some scholars." When he offers criticism, he adds that it is meant to be constructive and not personally demeaning. One gets the impression of a student speaking deferentially of a professor. However, the substance of such criticism is far-reaching. Suhrawardi affirms the fundamental distinction between "by it" and "with it" as it bears on matters that are causally or conjunctively related. In the first case, one thing is the reason for the other; in the second, they simply happen to occur simultaneously. Avicenna had postulated that each term is independent of the other; this provides the basis for the (logical) transformation of a plenum of possibility into a matter of necessity. In contrast, Suhrawardi posited a world that is an organic whole of light; here, both possibility and being are purely mental notions, instantiated in particular objects insofar as, and through the manner in which, they each partake of that light. On this model, the notion of causality remains a natural relation; the same holds, more generally, for the classical distinction between the essential and accidental properties of objects. This position runs directly counter to that of Avicenna. Suhrawardi points to the argument that "a scholar" *might* make if he advanced the thesis of concurrence while disregarding correlatives: clearly, one cannot postulate one side of a *correlative* relationship by itself and abstracted from everything else (including the other side of the relationship). In such a case, the fallacy would involve inventing a rule applicable to all cases and then calling instances when the rule failed to apply mere exceptions.

Suhrawardi was not "discovered" in the West until the 1950s. Credit goes to the French Orientalist Henry Corbin, whose studies on the role of imagination in the works of the other Sufi master, Ibn ʿArabi, were similarly groundbreaking. As we saw in earlier chapters, some scholars of the period—such as Jabiri, who presented Averroes as the model of Aristotelian rationalism—held that Avicenna had paved the way for such mystical, "Eastern" philosophy. Others, who considered Avicenna to belong to the peripatetic school, thought that Suhrawardi had inaugurated a new, anti-Avicennian tradition. In my opinion, Suhrawardi departed radically from the peripatetic worldview and disagreed with Avicenna on fundamental issues (including the role granted to the imaginative faculty); however, continuity holds insofar as Suhrawardi's approach prized independent "free thinking," which is also a hallmark of Avicenna's philosophy (both in terms of the role played by the faculty of imagination and in terms of his "naturalized" style of philosophic writing).

This imaginative, free-thinking approach may also be understood as a rejection of rigid, Aristotelian rationalism—analogous, in some ways, to what occurred in post-Renaissance Europe, when experimental science paved the way for intellectual progress and invention. If the same did not occur in the Arab world, one should not blame Suhrawardi, Ibn ʿArabi, or Ibn Sabʿin for the fact that intellectual activity slowed down and eventually grew scarce. The reason likely does not involve free-ranging imagination but, on the contrary, the fact that thinking came to be imprisoned by frozen language and concepts. The matter will be addressed in the final chapter. First, however, the "Eastern trajectory" should receive its due as the natural domain where reason in Islam flourished, albeit with its own theosophic flavor.

Fast Forward

If the "Sheikh of Illumination" only saw the light in the West in the last century, his fortunes were different in the East. From the inception, Suhrawardi stood at the forefront of a philosophical trajectory extending all the way to the last major figure in early Islamic philosophy, Sadr al-Din Shirazi—also known as Mulla Sadra (1572–1640). However, Suhrawardi's prominence did not mean that the towering Mulla Sadra—or his forerunner in what has come to be known as "the School of Isfahan," Mir Damad (d. 1631)—adopted his views wholesale. On the contrary, Mulla Sadra rejected Suhrawardi's major thesis, which reduced everything to aspects of light. Indeed, he inverted this position entirely by affirming the primacy of Being (a move that, incidentally, paralleled the emergence in Europe of Descartes' "rationalism," which was also rooted in the consciousness of Being). Nor did Suhrawardi's style shape the new course of philosophy. Ultimately, Mulla Sadra reinvigorated an even more classical sensibility. All the same, he felt compelled to address his forebear's works directly—often in defense of his own "favorite," Avicenna—in elaborating his compendious project. What is more, and perhaps most significantly, Suhrawardi's account of the role of light in the process of emanation became standard theory (albeit not in the way he formulated it)—even in Mulla Sadra's own theory.

More and more, our story of reason in Islam must turn to Persia and a particular brand of philosophical thinking today known as "theosophy," "meta-philosophy," "Gnosticism," "Sufism," and similar titles—though one should be wary of "lumping" these appellations together. Its salient feature is specified by a term we first came across in Avicenna, *'irfan*, which refers to knowledge that encompasses both the so-called rational and trans-rational realms (as described in preceding chapters). If the engine of reason drives the former, the latter may be held to run on the power of imagination. Most representatives of this school held that the two complement each other.[1] Imagination means not just the conceptual ability (or disposition) to postulate a "meta-reality" accounting for what is already accessible by rational means. It also concerns a subjective *experience* of that higher reality, directly *sensing* it in a manner analogous to how one normally perceives and cognizes the external world.

Ibn Tufayl (Averroes's mentor) had likened the matter to a blind man who knows the layout of the town where he lives, then suddenly gains the power to see. In a sense, the object of cognition is the same, yet it is also different. For Avicenna, as we have noted, such cognition extended further: imagination inspires reason—even in elementary, logical calculations—yet it can also reach beyond this realm. The "faint" divine flashes of inspiration that allow us to draw a cognitive map in the first place may be trained to experience a sphere beyond what reason defines.[2] Cultivating the ability to experience such moments of insight eventually permits one to achieve a higher cognitive state. Suhrawardi, as we saw in the last chapter, also invoked experiential *flashes of light* to set insight apart from discursive knowledge: the reality one thereby discerns is far more encompassing than that which one normally sees.

The further story of reason in early Islam involves expanding the way the world is beheld—and one's place within it—beyond what the five basic senses reveal; this broadened scope concerns both discourse and life as it is lived (i.e., daily habits and conduct)—especially in Shiʻa tradition, which flourished in Persia and across the border into Indo-Pakistan. This philosophical trajectory (first associated with the city of Fez and Mir Damad) culminated in what became known as the Isfahan School. Mulla Sadra stands as the "last" representative of the early "giants" associated with this philosophical trajectory.

Given its subjective and experiential nature, it may seem self-evident how this trajectory led to Sufi practices and orders (so-called ways or paths): pious believers immersing themselves in meta-reality and organizing their values and daily conduct accordingly. We should note, however, that these people were not all simple men practicing austere discipline and spiritual exercises. Their number included intellectuals and philosophers as well. Nor did they all hail from the eastern provinces of the Muslim World. Some lived elsewhere. Ibn 'Arabi, for example, came from Andalusian Spain (1165–1240); he led his life as a Sufi but also authored two major works in a discursive class of their own, which offer invaluable mystical insights. No record exists whether he ever met up with Suhrawardi, but surely their paths crossed in Aleppo or somewhere else in Syria, when Ibn 'Arabi made pilgrimage to Jerusalem.[3] Like Suhrawardi, Ibn 'Arabi drew on the example of the mirror to explain the relationship between physical, or "first-order," reality and God: it is merely His reflection, which He beholds as if in a looking glass. From this perspective, physical reality becomes spectral, but loses none of its actuality. What is more, human vision somehow transforms into God's own vision inasmuch as the underlying (meta-)reality is single in nature. (Another major figure from Spain is Ibn Sab'in (1217–1268), who died a sudden death in Mecca under mysterious circumstances; his writings on illuminationist philosophy and the ascetic style of life earned him a major place in the Sufi "hall of fame.")

Admittedly, the meta-philosophies and practices of such exceptional figures strike the average person as incompatible with standing ideas, to say nothing of the practical demands of daily life. We should recall, however—and unlike other excessive forms of religiosity—they were meant to serve as guides and gateways for intellectual and spiritual evolution. The ultimate aim—as Ibn Sab'in, for example, proposed—was a direct vision of the unity of Being that is God. Focusing on personal spirituality, Sufism essentially offers a "humanist" message, emphasizing the values of equality, brotherly companionship, and love among individuals on account of all they share; it has no ideology espousing denominational or ethnic exclusivity or supremacy. Love (e.g., in Ibn 'Arabi's works) stands as the supreme instinct binding God to the world and linking its seemingly disjointed pieces together. Sufism admits no intermediary between God and the individual: there is only a personal journey that each person can take, which will reveal the mystery of this direct connection—and therefore the brotherhood that unites all human beings.

It became commonplace—as we saw in the case of Jabiri—to consider this whole current of thought to have "betrayed" the rationalist school associated with Averroes and the earlier philosophers of the "Baghdad School." In part, this occurred because of the fundamental changes it introduced to received systems, replacing Aristotle's Final Cause with

an Islamic version of a First Cause. As a logical extension of this supposed replacement, religion and reason fused, which rendered political
life (supposedly defined by reason) inseparable from religion. Philosophy's metaphysical system, now arrayed in religious form, was to define
politics—the rules governing individual and communal human behavior.
Consequently, Jabiri likely looked upon Averroes's "double-truth" theory
as an attempt to split religion from politics (or, more precisely, the state),
and to leave them standing as separate domains. Later, this division was
given sociological formalization by an intellectual luminary from North
Africa, Ibn Khaldun (1332–1406), who outlined the growth and decline of
political bodies in strictly material and psychological terms.

In contrast, the Isfahan School adopted a different model, subor-
dinating politics/reason to religion; this theosophical view declared that
human affairs must comply with the latter's ethical message. Hereby, a
virtuous city is not defined by intellectual or material prosperity in the first
instance, but by Islam's ethical message. Let us recall that in the Farabian
model 'true religion' is not a particular religion, and politics therefore is
not about instituting a particular ethic. Politics is defined in epistemic
rather than ethical terms. The Isfahan model replaces Farabi's differentia-
tion between human beings on the basis of intellect—and his allocation
of the nature and degree of happiness on the basis of intellectual achievements—with personal religiosity. The human values defined by the new
metaphysics emphasize love and compassion among individual human beings, each of whom has as much share in God's nature as the next.

The different paths of Sufism represent so many ways of translating this imperative into thought and action. However, a more general
principle—with far-reaching political implications—still held: the old Islamic yearning for an ethical ruler to guide the community and a political order in which the individual human being remains the basic "unit of
worth" (rather than collective interest or ideology setting the tone). "Religiosity"—the paramount purpose of the law—stands above even life itself.
In this view, not only is the unexamined life not worth living—life that,
upon examination, does not prove to be lived ethically is not worth living,
either. The model of the "righteous and wise leader" represents how private
thought and social behavior should be one. Our "story of reason" in the
East, then, tells how philosophy—now in the sense of *'irfan*—and politics
may not be divorced.

Persia brought forth some of the best minds in Muslim science and philosophy. Here, the primal meaning of Islam as an *ethical* political community crystallized over the centuries, ultimately yielding a fusion between *imam* and *khalifa*: the theosophic scholar and the political leader. The significance of this evolution cannot be overemphasized. Although it is standard practice to refer to the various Muslim suzerainties or dynasties as "caliphates" (Umayyad, Abbassid, Fatimid, Ayyubid, Buyid, Safavid, Ottoman, etc.), right at the beginning—with the ascendancy of Mu'awiyah and the Umayyads—the very meaning of *caliph*, or *khalifa*, started to change. The moral and spiritual sense of the term associated with the immediate successors of Muhammad (Abu Bakr, Umar, Uthman, and Ali) ceded to a purely political understanding. Power plays, not righteousness and divine guidance, determined succession and governance of the Muslim community. This, in any case, is how a growing number of Sunnis and Shi'ites came to view the matter. Although formally Muslim, the caliphs ruled in secular fashion, above all—and often ruthlessly. In Sunni Islam, the formal "break" between temporal and religious authority finally occurred when the Ottoman sultan separated civil and religious law in the latter part of the nineteenth century. However, "the moral life" within the Muslim community had long lost definition; for quite some time already, a surface code of conduct had provided a convenient "front" for the machinations of state politics. Many could see that the Islamic *umma* was not being governed by the genuine Islamic code.

Still, the idea of the imam as a spiritual leader persisted, especially among Shi'ites, who held that the divinity conferred upon Muhammad had somehow been transferred to Ali as a *baraka*—a blessing of God to the person He deemed the *right* leader of the Muslim community. Such a leader, guided by divine light (or, at very least, possessing the qualities of moral fortitude and higher wisdom), fuses heavenly and earthly authority. The matter remained theoretical until imams came into political power in recent times: when the Islamic revolution did away with the Persian emperor in the 1950s. This event, together with the dissolution of the Sunni Ottoman caliphate after the First World War—which left the Arab world groping for a cohesive identity—represents a turning point. While the Sunni Arab World sought a political form of rule, Shi'ite Iran looked to rule by religion. In the context of the religious upsurge against secular government, who would perform this role better than those who devoted their lives to studying divinity (both as an objective, rational pursuit and in terms of applied knowledge bearing on the way life is lived)? This is how one should understand why the Imam Khumeini was "retrieved" from France and installed as leader after the Shah was toppled. Imam Khumeini came at the end of a long line of theosophical scholars, extending back to the Isfahan school of Mir Damad and Mulla Sadra (which, in turn, reached back to the Fez School and, further still—however convolutedly—to seminal figures such as Suhrawardi, Ibn ʿArabi, and Ibn Sabʿin).

As dramatic developments in the world today make plain, the fires that fueled the original yearning for a genuine code of Islamic rule—whether in Shiʿite or Sunni regions—are still burning. The "Rosetta Stone" combining religion and politics to ensure an optimal way of life has not been found. For all intents and purposes, the individual human being—the basic unit of worth—remains bereft of what is best in either world; when not reduced to being passive recipients and copiers, believers are left groping for a path to reach the "Promised Land." If many Muslims view the Shiʿite model of the "religious state" as simply pursuing politics through religion—thereby distorting both at the expense of the virtuous and dignified life of the individual—the same holds for Sunni regions of the Arab world where politics is given free rein, but a "false" Islam is upheld as the religion of the state—again, fulfilling neither secular and democratic nor authentically religious life.

Philosophers are said to be idealists; none of the aforementioned thinkers wished for Islamic history to unfold the way it has. The dream was always for an ideal society, in harmony with divine beneficence. Mulla Sadra was no exception. His voluminous *Four Journeys*—which exceed a thousand pages in length—provides both a comprehensive and a critical review of philosophical thought as it filtered into the Islamic world from Greek and other traditions. In addition, it offers an independently structured thesis, according to which Being offers the underlying, generic unity that suffuses the world. The theory incorporates emanation and light; the first explains the organic continuity between God and the rest of the universe, and the second accounts for a hierarchy of "shades," or "degrees of intensity," of Being as it manifests itself physically. What stands out, besides its presentation of a novel, holistic philosophy, is the author's careful critique of his predecessors' claims, both in the tradition of philosophy and in that of speculative discourse. *Four Journeys*, then, represents a valuable depository of intellectual and philosophical history. Its revolutionary view of Being may be read as a synthesis of the Avicennian thesis on the *conceptual* primacy of Being and the Suhrawardian antithesis of denying the *existence* of Being!

As we recall, Avicenna considered concepts such as being, necessity, and unity primary: no epistemological theory can be elaborated without these foundational elements. A corollary of this thesis is that essence— strictly speaking—qualifies as secondary (i.e., as a predicate): it is an *essence* insofar, and only insofar, as it has been joined by another form. It is not an essence *before* it has been completed in this fashion. Suhrawardi, for his part, emphasized that light is the fabric from which the tapestry of the universe is woven; in this view, Being is reduced to instantiated predicates of objects of light. Being is what we use to describe *particular* objects: it is simply a predicate ascribed to light. In turn, Mulla Sadra extracted Being both from the primal conceptual framework to which Avicenna had assigned it and from the secondary position that Suhrawardi gave it. In a further step, he replaced the latter's light tapestry with the former's Being. Being and Light remain immanent, the latter constituting a manifestation of the former.

As we have remarked, Suhrawardi's "light tapestry" implies a certain materiality. His ontology declares that a given entity is either a light for itself or a light for another one. But what is the *thing* that stands at the beginning, which in turn we define as being of such and such a nature? The question is left unanswered. Searching for the primary "stuff" composing the world, Avicenna had postulated entities about which nothing may be said except that they are themselves; objects are modulated by the manner in which they come to exist (in the material, mental, and logical worlds), but it is impossible to explain what they fundamentally are. In a sense, Mulla Sadra overcame this dead end by replacing thingness and indefinite postulates with Being—the thread weaving together the tapestry of the universe. Being is simply immanent. Its distinctness and definition represent functions of its shades of intensity.

On the first pages of this volume we observed that one of the pressing questions facing desert journeyers or dwellers—in moments of absolute quiet and serenity, as they stood spellbound by the majesty of the surrounding universe—concerned the extent to which and the way that (if at all) they were part of what they beheld. A further question followed:

who, or what, governs this spectacle? The answer in Islam (as in many mystical traditions) settles both questions: the unicity of Being. God is Being, and everything is a shade of God.

Yet however one views the matter, it is not easy to determine how the whole is woven together. The question whether existence is a predicate (that is, whether it makes sense to affirm existence as an attribute of something that, in one form or another, we have already identified as admitting predication) is a philosophical concern of timeless relevance. Avicenna and Suhrawardi offered ingenious responses, but one is still left wondering whether the meaning they attach to terms such as *existence* and *being* is not fundamentally different from how we normally understand them. In contrast, Mulla Sadra's formulation seems more forthright: he did not "twist" the meaning of "existence," but simply took it in the sense—somewhat reminiscent of the pre-Socratic philosopher Parmenides—of "the All-That-Is."

Of course, *All-That-Is* cannot be considered a predicate, even remotely. The task remains of understanding the way(s) this higher unity is manifested and offers the basis for formulating and categorizing its aspects or features (whether we call them "forms," "shades," "different intensities of light," "discrete appearances," or something else). Assuming that one could make sense of Being as such primary immanence, one would understand more fully how the *I* to which we refer when speaking were itself a predicate of the All-That-Is: each person's self, then, would simply represent another one of Being's manifestations. Looking at the world "upside-down"—not seeing oneself as a primary substance, but as a reflection or manifestation of Being—would explain why, for example, al-Hallaj claimed that pilgrimage to God may occur through an inward journey (rather than through a voyage to Mecca).

As noted, Mulla Sadra was familiar with the intellectual heritage of ancient Greece and India. Thus, he also knew the line of thinking from Parmenides to Plato, whereby timeless reality is held to lie beyond the changing world of appearances; the first delineates the domain of true knowledge, and the second mere opinions and beliefs. Mulla Sadra also commanded all the conceptual and analytical arguments of the Muslim philosophers who preceded him, which gave him the means to extract—from Parmenides, Plato's system, and Aristotle's "inversion" of it—elements that he combined into a comprehensive account of the primacy of Being.

Accordingly, his work is not a poetic, allegorical, or "mystical" narrative; rather, it proceeds in straightforward, analytical fashion in the best philosophical tradition.

It is one of those strange coincidences that both Mulla Sadra and Descartes—each working in his own milieu and inaugurating a turning point in his respective tradition—focused, at approximately the same time, on Being as the cornerstone of philosophy. This synchronicity seems even stranger given that neither thinker was aware of the other's existence! More generally, Descartes was not alone in no longer feeling the need to refer back to the Islamic heritage for launching his own philosophical meditations: the West's "awakening" from its medieval slumber was influenced more by its own internal developments than by *later* Islamic thought and science (as had occurred to a large extent during the Renaissance). Copernicus, for example, was more interested in the works of Muslim astronomers than in the views of his fellow Europeans. Kepler,[4] in contrast, sought to align his work with that of his contemporary Tycho Brahe (who in turn referred back to Copernicus). And when John Locke, the most famous British philosopher of the Enlightenment, felt he needed to look into that heritage, he turned to its earlier phase (Avicenna) rather than to its later stage (Mulla Sadra).

In other words, interest in Muslim intellectual activity did not subside because it had ceased so much as because scholasticism had already provided Locke and his contemporaries with all that (they thought) they needed. Such a view had not prevailed a few centuries earlier. Copernicus was not the only Renaissance scholar to have displayed interest in Muslim writings (which he reportedly sought out). It was the general rule: these works represented the clearest gateway for scholars seeking knowledge, both for the new perspective they offered and the ancient intellectual wealth they transmitted. After all, Muslim scholars engaged with what they had learned from more ancient civilizations—India, Persia, China, and Greece. It was this intellectual repository that scholars sought when the medieval Christian world awakened to the rich Greek and Hellenistic heritage that reached them through translations, commentaries, and original works in Arabic (often done by Jewish scholars). And while the ferment of ideas occurred directly at first, it continued, indirectly, well into the Age of Enlightenment and later, too—as Descartes, Leibniz, and Spinoza (on the Continent), and Locke and Hume (in England) inaugurated the new age of philosophy.

Whether medicine and pharmacology, optics and ophthalmology, chemistry or astronomy, or mathematics or logic—the wealth of knowledge introduced from the Muslim world provided the foundations on which European universities were built. At first, translators from Italy, Sicily, France, or Spain had worked separately either through private initiative or at the behest of benefactors; they brought Avicenna's *Canon of Medicine* and Rhazes' *Continens*, among other works, to the attention of their contemporaries and church officials. Subsequently, however, the collective, organized work of the School of Toledo—initially associated with the city's archbishop in the eleventh century—admits comparison to the Muslim translation movement in Baghdad. Thanks to scholars' efforts here, Ptolemy's *Almagest* once again saw the light in Latin, as did Aristotle's *Posterior Analytics*, Avicenna's *Healing*, Khawarizmi's *Algebra*, as well as countless other works of science and philosophy. The gates stood open between East and West. If one neglects this fact, it requires a great deal of imagination to picture how it was ever possible for the Medici Academy in Florence, where philosophers and artists gathered to study and discuss the works of Plato and neo-Platonists, to be the forum for the syncretic thinker Pico della Mirandola, whose *Epistle on the Dignity of Man* celebrates Muslim philosophers, or for Leonardo, whom the Ottoman caliph commissioned to design a bridge over the Golden Horn (even though, ultimately, his proposal was turned down as overly bold).

Still, while intellectual and scientific inquiry was on the rise in Europe (and in the far East, too), it was on the decline in the Muslim—and particularly the Muslim *Arab*—world. It seems that reason had decided to move, if slowly. The new era of philosophy epitomized by Descartes announced, in a sense, the break with the Muslim-influenced Aristotelian tradition of medieval scholasticism.

There are two reasons it is instructive to consider Descartes' *Meditations* alongside Mulla Sadra's *Four Journeys*. The first concerns the choice of language in both treatises. Descartes wrote in Latin rather than French, and Mulla Sadra in Arabic instead of Persian. These linguistic choices will receive further attention in the next (and final) chapter. For the moment, it is sufficient to note that even though Latin had come to be considered a "dead" language in Europe at this time, convention holds that Mulla Sadra's Arabic was, in contrast, a *living* language. Indeed, Mulla Sadra might have thought the same. Descartes, on the other hand, knew that the language he used was past its prime, yet he chose it anyway in order to gain the endorsement of the Sorbonne clergy, before making it accessible in the vernacular. The second reason, which bears more directly on the purposes at hand, concerns the habit of viewing reason in discrete and therefore "uni-civilizational," or "linear," terms—as if its history belonged to one race or population to the exclusion of others. This perspective encourages the view of civilizations as entirely separate—if not destined to clash with one another.

By no stretch of the imagination can Descartes' inauguration of a new philosophical age be linked directly to the efforts of his contemporary Mulla Sadra. Still, this should not blind us to the fact that ideas from the ancient and Muslim worlds kept bubbling as late as the Enlightenment. Instead of adopting a narrow focus, one should view the Baghdad of al-Ma'mun and the Toledo of the Archbishop Raymond as "gateways" through which the story of reason entered new terrain; even as the fires of inspiration died down on one side of the portal, their vigor was renewed on the other. Thus, our story has passed from Nusaybin to Baghdad, just as it later traveled from Cordoba and Isfahan to Toledo. As it moved from one era and region to the next, it discarded unnecessary weight and added further discoveries and insights to its wealth.

The prevailing tendency today is to view reason in Europe as falling into two phases: on the one hand, an early "Renaissance" period associated with the schoolmen and luminaries such as Thomas Aquinas, who knew about, and benefited from, Muslim thinking; and, on the other, a later "Enlightenment" period "liberated" from the first phase, exemplified by the science of Newton and rationalist and empiricist philosophies from Descartes to Kant. Likewise, the conventional view sees Islam's Golden Age as running dry early on and being largely over by the time of Averroes (who, in the patronizing words of Leibniz, had at one point been viewed as perhaps the best "Mohammetan commentator on Aristotle"!).

However, the story of reason has neither a linear path nor "cut-off points." The thought of Leibniz himself, whether he knew as much or not, may be understood in relation to the works of Avicenna, which present a complete philosophical landscape of possible worlds—including the "best" of them. His principle of self-sufficiency and the workings of Providence to orchestrate harmony are themes explored at length by his forebear. The same holds for his principle of the identity of indiscernibles; Muslim philosophers had discussed this logical issue at length when seeking to de-termine whether the proof of a Necessary Being leads to the conclusion that more than one such being exists; in the post-Avicennian period, the matter came to be known the "Ibn Kammunah" paradox (after the Jewish philosopher by this name). One might continue the list, though it is im-portant to bear in mind that while there are cases like Lavoisier consulting the works of Jabir Ibn Hayyan (where the former was acquainted with the latter's works), there are also others where discoveries occurred indepen-dently (e.g., William Harvey and Ibn al-Nafis figuring out the pulmonary circulation of blood).

In the Muslim world, as we have seen, our story continued in Persia and further east in the Asian subcontinent. Here, it proceeded more and more along the "rationalist" trajectory defined by seeking holistic, univer-sal models in which the human being remained a basic "unit of worth." The political paradigm it finally came to assume—for better or worse—is the theocracy of present-day Iran. Within the Arab world, the paradigm slowly began to shift to secure a working ideology that would fill in the vac-uum created by the fall of the caliphates. Intellectual efforts now focused on addressing ways to overcome the backward social and economic condi-tions prevailing in the Arab world—pan-Arabism, Islamism, Marxism, na-tionalism—and liberation from colonialist hegemonies. Freedom—of the people and the individual—became the predominant practical and intel-lectual concern.

Meanwhile, in Europe, a new "empiricist" trajectory emerged, as-sociated with figures such as John Locke and David Hume. Attention began to shift toward the external world, leaving "man" the function of being simply an instrument of observation (if not a "unit of utility"). But wherever we look—whether at systems professing spiritualist or material-ist supremacy—we still find human beings excluded or estranged from the purposes for which they pursue understanding. In East and West, some-thing proves missing. As "common sense" would surely tell us, meaningful and integrated human existence is better served by breathing through both "lungs." As natural twins, East and West—Absal and Salaman—need each other; one should not view them as destined to clash. Nor, in the Muslim world, should reason (the pursuit of knowledge and progress) and religion (a virtuous code of ethics) be viewed as mortal enemies.

Language and Reason

The Dilemma

Language and thought are crucially interwoven. Our *Story of Reason in Islam* should have shown as much, as it is also the story of the classical Arabic language. The inspired language of the Qur'an set the wheels of reason in motion; around the seventeenth century, when Ottoman came to replace Arabic, forward movement stopped. Henceforth—and right up to the First World War—Arabic was rendered effectively inoperative. Whether in hermeneutics, *kalam*, *fiqh*, *falsafa*, or the various sciences, including astronomy, the "substance" of reason in Islam had been held within and defined by Arabic.

This point cannot be overemphasized. In contrast, consider the natural ease with which Christian thought extended from Jesus, who spoke Aramaic, to Paul, who wrote in Greek, to Augustine, who used Latin; in turn, it flourished in scholastic Latin and the Romance languages of Europe. In Islam, on the other hand, incomparable importance attached to the fact that the *Word* was Arabic—which was also a living language that continued to be used for intellectual discourse. Arabic therefore determined the style and substance of all theoretical endeavors. But just as it sprouted and bloomed in the desert and went on to flourish across continents and over centuries, a time came when it began to wither and shrink into isolated patches. Indeed, this process proved so severe that, by the nineteenth century, what later came to be called a *renaissance*—now associated with Arab identity—was deemed necessary. This reawakening manifested itself in the activities of famous figures such as Jamal al-Din al-Afghani (1839–1897), Muhammad Abduh (1849–1905), Butrus Bustani (1819–1883), Jurji

Zeidan (1861–1914), Farah Anton (1874–1922), and Taha Hussein (1889–1973). The development warrants a story of its own—but one that is entirely new inasmuch as it is anchored more in contemporary issues than in the thought of the past. Here, the challenge has been how to treat and use a rich language long in "deep freeze" in a modern form to address issues of contemporary concern.

How should one understand the intellectual recession in Islam's story of reason and the subsequent stirrings, in the eighteenth and nineteenth centuries, across the Arab world? Islam itself—as a religious calling and a historical movement—is not bounded by language. Instead, it has been defined by all the circumstances that accompany the ascent of a civilization or of an empire to power. In this civilization, Arabic was indeed—and for a long period—the *language of power*. However, as Islam expanded, Arabic came to be the spoken language of smaller and smaller percentages of the population. Today, the world's Muslim population numbers more then 1.6 billion, but people who speak Arabic constitute less than one fifth of this total. Arabic—both as the medium of the Qur'an and as the bearer of Reason's "story"—no longer functions as the lingua franca of the Muslim world. Whether in China, Bangladesh, India, Persia, Pakistan, or Indonesia, intellectual advancement and progress have been invigorated by indigenous languages and circumstances.

Chinese rocket science, Indonesian political thinking, nuclear advances in Pakistan or Iran, Turkish Nobel-winning literature—all this, and much more, no longer has anything to do with Arabic. Illustrious Muslim writers in India, such as Muhammad Iqbal (1877–1938), already expressed their philosophical and political ideas in Urdu and Persian. Indeed, Islamic intellectual discourse has continued in all these languages, but with hardly the same creative tenor as before. Once the lingua franca of reason and science, Arabic ceased to play this role, shrinking back to becoming the "property" of the Arabs. An Afghani, Malaysian, or Bengali Muslim may now pray in Arabic and read out passages from the Qur'an, but only a tiny minority of those doing so understand the language—to say nothing of being able to work with it as a means for advancing knowledge. In these regions, Arabic has ceased to be the language of power and transformed into a secondary instrument to be used in "bytes" by those *in* power who speak in the tongue of their nations; occasionally, they enlist a religious quotation in Qur'anic Arabic to evoke a legitimacy for their authority.

Meanwhile, what has become of this language (and the wealth it carried) in the Arab world—its natural habitat, so to speak? The short answer is that it underwent a long period of decline, lagging behind scientific and intellectual development elsewhere—even in the Muslim world. Islam's very success meant that Arabs no longer stood at the forefront of the Muslim world, and their language was no longer that of those in power. By the seventeenth century, deleterious effects were evident in the language as a medium of intellectual discourse. In regions belonging to the Ottoman caliphate (1517–1924), Arabic ceased to serve political and governmental administration. Ottoman replaced it. Arabic had become the spoken language of a ruled and secondary population. Although Ottoman (like some other languages in the Muslim world—e.g., Urdu and Persian) retained the Arabic script, it did away with the language itself as the medium of authority and governance. A minority of religious scholars still used classical Arabic in their works; increasingly, however, it represented a historical language belonging to the past. This held until the end of the First World War and the dissolution of the caliphate; Ottoman script became Latinized as an expression of secular national identity. From this point on, Turkish scholars discussing classical figures such as Avicenna would write in Turkish rather than Arabic.

Other parts of the Arab world, notably North African countries, had to contend with the expanding hegemony of Western powers (France and Britain). Under these conditions, an Arab seeking enlightenment would travel to Paris or London to learn about the latest in science or culture. Neither under the Ottomans, nor under Western hegemony, did Arabic as a language—a signature of identity, and the traditional scholarly medium—receive the political sustenance or cultural encouragement needed for continued growth. In the nineteenth century, this language lag—identified with the Arab world's general backwardness—was felt so acutely that new political and intellectual stirrings arose.

To appreciate the significance of this "last page" in our story of reason, one need only consider the striking contrast in the ways that paper and movable type were employed when the Muslim world gained access to them. Both in terms of cause and effect, these revolutionary instruments of literacy shed light on the bigger picture. As we have seen,[1] when contact was established with the Tang Dynasty in China, the Umayyads enthusiastically welcomed the arrival of paper; the Abbasids, in turn, expanded its use even more. Before long, paper had come to serve as the standard medium for recording scholarly and intellectual works, including the text of the Qur'an. In the early centuries, hunger for literacy seemed insatiable, and the results were singularly impressive. Arabic was the "factory" for producing intellectual innovations. In contrast, movable print (which became widely available in Europe in the late-fifteenth century) took *almost two hundred years* to be broadly used for printing in Arabic. Clearly, there was no comparable enthusiasm to utilize the new invention for the propagation of the language. When the Ottomans finally permitted the use of movable type—which occurred slowly at first, in Istanbul—they did so for the purpose of printing Ottoman texts (which were written in the Arabic alphabet at the time), rather than Arabic. Even some Hebrew texts appeared!

Paradoxically, the first up-to-date printing press for Arabic came with Napoleonic conquest at the end of the eighteenth century. Napoleon intended to use it to establish control of the population during his Egyptian campaign (1798–1801). Also—in further, striking contrast—the first printed, Arabic-language texts were made in Europe, not in the Muslim world. This included the Qur'an itself, which was first printed in Italy in 1537, not in Istanbul! (A final, "critical edition" of the Qur'anic text approved by the Al-Azhar Religious Establishment in Cairo was produced only in 1924, after the fall of the Ottoman caliphate; it is now used as the basis for all editions in the Arab world.[2]) Whereas a Catholic printer had seen no reason why the holy text of Islam should not appear alongside the Old and New Testaments, the matter was viewed differently in the caliphate; here, the Qur'an in its transmitted, calligraphic forms was held in such reverence that subjecting it to print seemed a sacrilege.

In sum, then, whether due to a religious hesitation to subject the Qur'an to print or other motives (see following), the enthusiasm with which early Muslims greeted paper technology, found no echo when the Ottomans encountered a new means of promoting literacy; indeed, the Ottoman caliphs actively resisted this technology. In contrast, Arabic print was being promoted both by religious Christian establishments in Europe as well as by invading European forces. Why? Modern scholars[3] tend to hold that these twin facts reflect opposite motivations: on the one hand, Western powers wished (whether for religious or political reasons) to disseminate their own literature among the Arab world's Christian communities (especially in Lebanon and Syria), or among Muslim populations coming under their control;

on the other hand, the Ottomans (justifiably) feared that the dissemination of Arabic literature might rouse nationalist sentiments and prompt the Arab world to rise up against Turkish domination. Indeed, Christian Arab intellectuals and missionary institutions (such as what evolved into the American University of Beirut) played an important role in the so-called *awakening* of the Arab world, when literacy rose and Arabic was used for instruction at schools, poetry and literature experienced a renaissance, and, eventually, nationalist movements emerged. (This included the newssheets and underground political leaflets that called for rebellion against Turkish rule prior to World War I; later, after the end of the Second World War, the same factors played a major role in the formation of the modern pan-Arabist movement). This awakening had begun with Muslim revivalists in the nineteenth century, but it soon expanded to become a nationalist and cultural movement drawing on growing pride in Arabic heritage and a sense of urgency to propagate literacy in the population. In 1924, when Taha Hussein, one of the literary giants representing this trend, was appointed Minister of Education in Egypt, one of his first acts was to institute free education at schools so that all children would learn their national language.

It may be a moot point to argue that if this restriction had not been imposed on Arabic (and if the language had not been demoted from the official means of intellectual and cultural exchange), then continuity with past achievements might have been maintained. Even so, the matter warrants reflection. Its weight is compounded by concurrent developments in the spoken language: increasingly divergent dialects prevailed in the fractured Arab world, and they all differed more and more from Arabic in classical form; at the same time, literacy rates declined (as Taha Hussein and earlier revivalist figures noted with alarm).

At any rate, such circumstances attended Ottoman resistance to printing the Arabic language. In addition to political concerns about keeping revolt at bay, factors included religious and economic considerations. In the eighteenth century, a contemporary observer had estimated that as many as 70,000 people earned their living as scribes in Istanbul; were the new technology introduced, they would face immediate unemployment. But the power of this "constituency"—mostly belonging to the religious establishment—was compounded by the general belief that submitting the holy text to mechanical reproduction amounted to sacrilege! This aura surrounding the Qur'an—and the attendant hesitancy to subject it to printing technology (later, using copying machines to produce calligraphic versions did not occasion the same concern)—still exists today. It is possible that the "army of scribes" in Istanbul included a sizeable number of religious scholars who objected to printing the Qur'an on religious grounds and enjoyed professional and class connections to the religious hierarchy—all the way up to the "Sheikh of Islam" (a position instituted by the caliphate to secure orthodoxy). After all, this same body of religious scholars (*'ulama*) had made the caliph destroy the observatory near Istanbul in 1580, just three years after its completion.[4] Istanbul's clerics were already predisposed to conservatism; therefore, they would naturally have been inclined to lend a sympathetic ear to the city's scribes, whose job included writing Ottoman *firmans* (caliphate orders) in Arabic, in addition to making copies of the Qur'an.

Ottoman reticence to use print for the Qur'an, then, takes us back to early discussions about its nature—how it is understood as the Word of God. Handing the Word over to a machine—not a Muslim scribe trusted to show meticulous care and reverence—constituted (as it still does today) a fundamental conceptual challenge. Is a machine a religiously proper medium? The Qur'an explicitly identifies Arabic as God's chosen language. In other words, it is not just the text that is holy. Through the ages, the Qur'an has been passed down in *handwritten* form. Since it explicitly calls on Muslims to recite its words, it has also led an *oral* life. The Ottomans might easily have considered these two features of the Qur'an—its calligraphic and oral forms—to constitute the true value of Arabic. In contrast, the "lay Arabic" in actual use by the people under their dominion was looked down on as being of secondary intellectual importance.[5] Even so, some Muslim scholars in Istanbul, such as Galanbawi—a jurist, engineer, and logician—continued to distinguish themselves as scientists and philosophers through the classical medium of Arabic as late as the end of the eighteenth century; their works—as well as their tradition of scholarship—reached as far as Egypt, and traces are still to be found in the field of Muslim jurisprudence today. Other patches of Muslim scholarship in the classical Arabic medium also persisted—most prominently, the works of Muhammad Ibn Abd al-Wahhab (1703–1792), in Saudi Arabia.[6]

When print finally took off, the vernaculars that had proliferated were not supported and institutionalized by technology. Instead, classical Arabic—now hardly spoken—was. In other words, print did not capture speaking habits as they had evolved; elites remained literate, but the rapidly growing population still was largely unable to read. Under the political circumstances, there was nothing surprising about this. Nor is it astonishing that the religious sanctity surrounding and effectively cloistering the written text ultimately came to represent the "holy grail" of Arab national revivalism. The classical form of the language emerged as a symbol of national identity; restoring it would bring about emancipation from Ottoman rule. The unicity of Qur'anic language, in contrast to vernacular forms, represented the underlying unity of the Arab nation. Reestablishing it as a living language would lay the foundation for the united effort to secure liberation from foreign domination, a means of becoming fully independent. In other words, the classical written language came to possess a sanctified halo of its own. Now, however, this sanctity had become political.

Even so, supporters of spoken Arabic—those who saw a preeminent modern value in institutionalizing this form of speech as "print-worthy"—persisted. As a thorough and insightful study has recently demonstrated, apropos of Egypt,[7] the "tug of war" between the two schools preoccupied Arab intellectuals for a considerable part of the past century. To what extent should the living, vernacular forms of speech be given expression in print—made readable for all? Alternatively, to what extent should these forms be suppressed in the public sphere in favor of a unified, standard form as close to the classical as possible?

In effect, while the classical form slowly regained its status as the "reference language," a binary reality in the public language sphere evolved, arguably bringing with it fundamental constraints on intellectual development. Two kinds of spoken Arabic—one vernacular and more immediate, and the other formal and imitating the classical form—often proves mentally schismatic. For example, films, plays, and radio interviews employ the vernacular, whereas newspapers or books typically adhere to a modern form of the classical, written style (a "standard Arabic"). Today, a television journalist might read the news in classical (standard Arabic) style, but advertisements during the program or the political discussion that follows will often be in the spoken style.

Such bifurcation between two versions of Arabic potentially constitutes an impediment, starting with children. They must figure out how to understand the same story when a parent reads it to them from a book and tells it to them using ordinary speech; in one case, it will sound formal and distant; in the other, it will seem "closer"—like a real "mother tongue." (Even television cartoons are using the classical spoken style more and more.) Although both forms of language resemble each other, they sound—and often are, in syntactic terms—very different.[8] Consequently, speakers can express their ideas effectively, yet still be illiterate—both in terms of the nonexistent written/printed form of their vernacular, as well as in terms of the classical form. Such speakers have to learn the classical form in order to engage in formal intellectual debates, whether orally or in written form. In view of this circumstance, one of Taha Hussein's main projects, when he became Minister of Education in Egypt, was to make free schooling available to all Egyptians; Arabic literacy was placed at the top of the list in the curriculum.[9]

Why does all this matter? Earlier chapters have discussed the relative ease with which the discipline of speculative discourse was assimilated into the Islamic intellectual milieu—in contrast to philosophy (*falsafa*), which encountered difficulties. Whereas the former successfully employed the common speech of the time—in retrospect, the classical style—the latter sought to develop a new, technical language. Unlike the language of science—for example, geometry or medicine—it dealt with matters that already belonged to the intellectual space of speakers. It was Arabic, but it seemed contrived and cumbersome, critics held. *Falsafa* sought to express meanings associated with a different language; it took time before it became "naturalized" (in admittedly technical settings, such as in treatises on medicine or astronomy—but it did eventually become very much part of Arabic's high culture). In contrast, by keeping close to actual speech practices, *kalam* managed to remain a free-flowing and a "living" means of exchanging ideas, while still providing a suitable medium of debate for scholars. Not only was its language that of the spoken Arabic of the day; more important, it was the language of the Qur'an and the *hadith*—the indigenous repository of truth and knowledge. *Kalam's* inclination to investigate how words are used in speech (as opposed to adopting formal explanations wholesale) followed naturally from the belief that any truths or meanings to be found must be embedded in the language itself. It was therefore assimilated more easily than *falsafa*. By the nineteenth and twentieth centuries, however, the situation had changed completely. Now, while vernaculars (actual *kalam*) had gained ascendancy as the natural means of communication, what was being sought as a unified language was something almost technical—a spoken or written language of the past. Reinstituting it as a standard (now also in print) became almost like introducing a foreign language—almost like *falsafa*—which had to be learnt (not, of course, by the elite, but by an exponentially expanding population).

Such linguistic dissonance has prompted the bold suggestion that the sacred text (and the classical linguistic form it was cast in)—which once sparked a veritable intellectual avalanche—has long been an anachronistic artefact whose rejuvenation involves imposing a restriction on intellectual development as required today. The language of the past, both in form or content, has been argued no longer to hold practical relevance. Indeed, it is said to impede the ability to deal with practical concerns. A new discourse must be developed to deal with modern issues and dilemmas. After all, old concepts and concerns—such as "first cause," "light," "essence," "being," "active intellect," and so on—are obsolete; they have been replaced by pressing matters like "independence," "freedom," "pluralism," "scientific progress," "democracy," "rationalism," and so on. More recently still, a computer language has emerged, used far more by a younger generation not yet properly skilled in classical Arabic. All these matters demand present-day speech practices more than those of the past. The compulsion to resort to the classical language to reflect intelligent exchanges over these issues only serves to impede—or even halt—creative thinking.

How should we understand a criticism viewed by some as a sacrilegious assault both on Qur'anic language and the medium heralding Arab identity? The development of a living language goes hand in hand with the free flow of speech, allowing for spontaneity and direct expression of genuine thoughts and feelings. In contrast, being bounded by an "inert" language—that is, feeling the need to *import* phrases and constructions from past speech practices—restricts relevance and creativity in discourse. A "flow gap" emerges when the language *of* thinking is different from that of *expression*. In concrete terms, it might appear as follows: two young IT-savvy youths are talking; the first speaker expresses herself in classical style, shifting as she does so from one paradigm (the language *of* thinking—how she "talks" to herself) to the other (formal language). The shift already reflects a distance between spontaneous and formal locutions. Listening, her interlocutor performs a similar operation in reverse—translating the language of expression into the language of thought. As he formulates a response, another shift occurs. In this manner, the dialogical exchange plods as it adapts to classical speaking habits, instead of reflecting immediate thoughts.

It must be stressed that the process described here does not concern articulation—where the *same language* (of thinking and speaking) serves expression. Nor does it admit comparison to the distinction between "formal" and "informal" speech that exists in all tongues, where locution and syntax diverge yet remain recognizable and familiar. In Arabic, expressions, pronunciation, and grammar can be entirely different in the vernacular and the classical. The argument, then, is that language which is not immediate or spontaneous—where something like *translation* is constantly at work—is less likely to provide a vehicle for genuine expression and dialogical exchange.[10]

An even deeper and more critical hurdle exists if we take translation as a paradigm—where *learning* is done through what comes to resemble a translation process: in general terms, one might argue that learning a subject at school resembles acquiring a new language. As is always the case, a certain degree of memorization is required. In Arab schools, however, the difficulty of learning this new subject is compounded. Students learn the new subject alongside learning classical Arabic. Thereby, two "languages" are taught simultaneously. In order to instill knowledge of classical Arabic, a great deal of emphasis is placed on rote learning: memorizing whole passages from the Qur'an, classical literature, and poetry. It may be claimed that this method of teaching is optimal, as it combines rules with concrete examples. However, since the subjects the student is learning is being taught as subjects *in* that language, these come to be dealt with in the same manner, such that learning a sentence in chemistry or history becomes like learning a sentence in classical Arabic. Also sentences in these subjects come to be learnt through rote—the rules and applications being drawn upon for doing this being alike to the rules and examples drawn upon for studying classical Arabic structures. Much has been made of the negative effects of the rote learning prevalent in Arab schools, which involves committing structures to memory rather than dealing with ideas and arguments analytically or critically. But what consequences does this problem hold on a deeper level? What happens, in other words, when rote learning is applied to equations in physics or theories in politics?

Students, of course, are already familiar with Arabic, if not in classical form. It already "resonates": words may not be entirely familiar, but they belong to the same family and are therefore accessible. As students

study classical Arabic through memorizing examples from classical poetry or literature or passages from the Qur'an, they know that unfamiliar
elements—"blanks in their minds"—can be filled in later in time, once a
higher level of competency is achieved. A self-assured confidence of having acquired knowledge of them—never mind their meanings—is underwritten by the belief that their full meanings in their linguistic repository
will eventually become clear to them. But in the rest of the subjects, a different process prevails: there is no "backdrop" language—an inherent repository—for suspending knowledge judgments until later. There are no
"blanks" held in place by the relative familiarity of the rest of a given sentence. Consequently, the student does not regard material as unfinished
and open; instead, she or he registers it as an integral unit. In so doing,
the student takes knowing it simply to mean being able to repeat that material when prompted. Although memorization is still key, this particular
aspect of it might be called a "copy-paste" approach, where "to know" is
simply "to repeat." Whether in physics, political theory, or another subject, students who can answer questions correctly have not necessarily
grasped the material at a deep level.[11] Here, arguably, the classical language itself is not the issue, but rather the mindless application of a good
way of learning it to other subjects at schools, which need to be taught in
a different manner. (Indeed, once one is competent in the language one
is using to learn a new subject, or it is the only language that one is learning in—where no "blanks" are left for delayed recognitions—then the
student is less likely to fall into the copy-paste trap. Perhaps this is why
Arabs studying knowledge-material in foreign-speaking schools or expa-
triate scientists such as the Nobel Laureate Ahmad Zweil seem more able
to excel in their fields.[12])

In the Arab world today, the application of critical thinking at
schools and colleges as well as the maturation of a "standard Arabic" propagated through media outlets—is bound to bear fruit. Much progress has
already occurred in literary writing, and a new wave of philosophical and
other forms of discourse is beginning to come to light in Arabic journals
and publications, much of it reflecting contemporary debates in the West
more than continuing with classical concerns. This intellectual development warrants a "story" of its own.

.   .   .

To conclude, the same language that was once the midwife, and then the medium, of Islam's story of reason ceased at one point to be the language of power; with this, the unique and glorious intellectual output it had carried for centuries came to an end. Once Arabic was revived in the nineteenth century, although yet to come of age as a new language, it was settled upon as a common medium combining spoken and written as well as scientific communication: a new story had begun. Arguably, however, for another intellectual avalanche to occur, much more is required than bringing the classical and the vernacular "in sync." Given socioeconomic and political conditions in present-day Arab society, a turn of historical proportions is needed to give free rein to the imagination and permit reason to conceive a new course—as happened, so long ago, right at the beginning.

Notes

CHAPTER 1: THE ARABIAN DESERT

1. See Chapter 14.

2. Until then, Edessa had counted as the major seat of theological learning in the Antioch tradition. In addition to theology, scholars studied the scientific and philosophical corpus that had been the glory of Alexandria from its founding up to the third century; indeed, Edessa welcomed intellectual refugees from this city. Works included medical treatises by Galen (d. 200), the cosmology of Ptolemy (d. ca. 168), and the metaphysics of the neo-Platonist Plotinus (d. 270).

3. Founded by Khosrow I (531–579), the academy combined indigenous, Persian learning with science imported from Greece and India.

4. Alfarabi's account of how philosophy was transmitted from Alexandria was first questioned by Max Meyerhof, "Transmission of Science to the Arabs," *Islamic Culture IX* (1937): 17–29, a classic article drawing on a far wider range of dates and figures. Beginning in the nineteenth century, a rich vein of scholarship started to examine the transmission tradition as a whole, both by way of Syriac and directly from Greek sources.

CHAPTER 2: THE DAUNTING IDEA OF GOD

1. These were tenets later taken up in the Qur'an, which affirms that he was miraculously born through God's spirit and not crucified.

CHAPTER 3: FREE WILL AND DETERMINISM

1. Of course, mystics of different hues had long been a feature of desert culture. But now an Islamic form of mysticism began to develop, which would later occupy a major place in the region's history. Hasan's "appropriation" in this story (and other, similar ones, too) may be read as a way of legitimizing Sufism—reaching back to a well-known scholar of the Qur'an to shore up a new tradition. Indeed, some later writers went so far as to claim that Hasan had been a mystic entirely unique in kind. For example, al-Jahiz (776–868) described him as a man shrouded in melancholy and fear—which may be taken as a sign of a supernatural

bent of mind. But for all that, anything Hasan may have said that seemed a riddle was likely due to the political climate in which he lived, the simple and pious life he led, and the nature of his character. At any rate, it is uncontroversial that he played a founding role in the formation of a rational discourse about divine matters inspired by the Qur'an.

2. Wasil's move represents a major juncture in the history of Muslim thought, following which the doctrines of an entire school came to be articulated. See Chapter 5.

CHAPTER 4: THE QUR'AN

1. Some traditions maintain that Ali kept his own recordings of the verses, but that he was asked to look over the Uthman compendium and approve it before it was then distributed in four "original" copies.

2. In fact, the project is also said to have begun under the two earlier caliphs. As we have already noted, any written version of the different verses later on— when diacritics were introduced—also had to correspond to the different *readings* of those verses. The story of how these variant readings was finally resolved into the version now commonly in use is found in S. H. Nasser, *The Transmission of the Variant Readings of the Qur'an* (Leiden, Netherlands: Brill, 2013). So long as there was no single definitive reading, the written text (*mishaf*) could be considered different from the Word and therefore admitted scholarly interpretation.

3. In a controversial treatise written in the twelfth century, the philosopher Averroes—seeking to strike a balance between faith and reason—presented much the same doctrine, albeit in an elliptical and far less forthright style.

4. In due course, what has come to count as a middle ground was reached; a "science of interpretation" developed, which established very strict rules for what is subject to human interpretation, and under what conditions. One can imagine the chaos that would arise today if scholars suggested that not every verse possesses sanctity in the same way the Qur'an does as a whole.

CHAPTER 5: FROM WASIL TO IBN HANBAL

1. Setting the Qur'an to print has its own story, as we will see in the final chapter. Since the rise of the Internet and digital technology, however, "printed" verses and chapters have come to be as common as commentary exchanged on social media.

2. Needless to say, orthodox, Sunni histories appealing to this declaration include Mu'tazilism among the 71 to 72 movements considered to have strayed from the right path.

CHAPTER 6: EARLY ISLAM

1. Originally composed in Sanskrit sometime in the fourth century CE, the work became known to Muslims in Persia, where it had been translated into Pahlavi; they then translated it into Arabic, and it became one of the more popular fable books. It subsequently found its way into European languages—and, later still, made its way back into Hindustani. Using different animals as its characters, the fables essentially set out to educate three young princes.

2. See Jonathan Bloom, *Paper Before Print: The History and Impact of Paper in the Islamic World* (New Haven: Yale University Press, 2001).

3. The Umayyad caliph Abd al-Malik Ibn Marwan, under whose reign the famous Jerusalem Dome of the Rock was built (609–691 CE), is also said to have been the first under whom official records of the caliphate were written in Arabic. Until then, Christian and Jewish scribes, employed by the Byzantines for the same purpose—and therefore using Greek—had performed the task.

4. India itself proved unconquerable at first; architectural marvels such as Agra's Taj Mahal did not come into existence until the Indo-Islamic Moghul dynasty in the seventeenth century.

5. This may seem unsurprising, given the alleged debauchery of many Umayyad caliphs. Some are said to have had the royal baths filled with wine during all-night orgies frequented by homosexual poets and others of "questionable" character. Yazid, the second-to-last caliph in the Umayyad line, was known for writing verses on the virtues of love and wine. Indeed, he excelled to such an extent that Abu Nuwas, the most famous author of poetry on such themes (who enjoyed the intermittent patronage of Haroun al-Rashid's son and successor, al-Amin), is supposed to have taken him as a model.

6. This is not to discount major figures—such as the astronomer al-Qushji (fifteenth century) or the logician Isma'il Galanbawi (late-eighteenth century)—under the Ottomans. However, our "story" of more or less coherent intellectual discourse on interrelated subjects basically ends here—with only elements continuing, in a specifically "theosophical" form, in Iran (up to the present). For one account of this line of continuity, see the introductory notes by T. Izutsu, *The Metaphysics of Sabzvari*, trans. M. Mohaghegh and T. Izutsu (New York: Caravan, 1977.) Also, see Chapter 24.

CHAPTER 7: SPECULATIVE DISCOURSE

1. In time, orthodox opponents of the Mu'tazilites would describe them in any number of unflattering terms. Mu'tazilites were accused of a range of things from apostasy and lacking true faith to moral debauchery (e.g., "alcohol-consuming homosexuals") and were derided even for nonnative birth (many of them were of Persian—or other—descent). Often, the attitude of Ibn Hanbal and his compan-

ions proved so antagonistic that they would refuse to sit at the same table for the open debates organized by the Abbassid caliph (see Chapter 10).

CHAPTER 8: DISCOURSE

1. The ontological perspective characterized the philosophical tradition influenced by Greek thinking that was emerging at the time.

2. In the discussion that follows, we will see that the Greek notion of *nous* (intellect), which Alfarabi employed to qualify matters that are known (intelligibles), proved of no use to these scholars, who were interested in the person him- or herself. Interestingly, *al-'Aql*, the noun normally translated as "intellect," does not occur once in the Qur'an; instead, the related verbal form is employed, signifying an activity (*to reason*) God enjoins people to practice.

3. In due course, we will see that if one takes time out of the equation, this view is analogous to one that Avicenna (coming from the discipline of *falsafa*) seems to have adhered to.

4. These contemporaries included al-Jahiz, whose work also presents a primitive theory of evolution. Al-Jahiz duly studied Greek texts on the animal and plant worlds before writing his own compendium in which he expressed this view.

5. A summarized version of these compendious volumes was also found among the Geniza records in Egypt, which were uncovered in the nineteenth century; recently, they have been edited and published by the German scholar, Sabine Schmidtke.

6. "Immediate," in this context, means not only logical principles, but also sensory knowledge and moral principles (e.g., knowing that injustice is wrong).

7. Similarly, our sense of confidence that what we buy in a store is what we take it to be explains why we decide to buy it in the first place; if we later determine that the item is not what we thought it was, this does not affect our initial sense of confidence (even though it has become clear that it was misplaced).

8. As we will see in the next chapter, al-Ghazali rejected this last condition.

9. For example, when the question is whether the man before us is a scholar, the "lead" may be any number of circumstances—we have seen him coming out of a library, carrying a book, looking distracted, wearing thick glasses, matching the description of some scholar we have already heard about, the kind of clothes he is wearing, and so on.

10. Similarly, one may picture two entirely different and separate information grids, where the generation of further data in the one does not produce data in the other. In the field of web semantics today, the inferential connection between the two grids is made possible by a search engine, which establishes a new language (Resource Description Framework) allowing the search engine to connect data from different websites and pages that were originally not fed into the system. The new language system, in "third position," simply allows the search engine to make

the inference. Here, the relationship between the joined parts does not involve analytic deduction (concepts that somehow presuppose or imply one another). It is simply an inferential "action" connecting relevant facts located on discrete websites.

11. See Chapters 9 and 17.

12. In another instance of historical irony, Abd al-Jabbar—the man whose works were unearthed in this discovery—had started his discourse career as an Ash'arite, eventually rebelling against the tradition in which he had grown up.

CHAPTER 9: LAW AND MORALITY

1. A recent paper by Adam Sabra, "Ibn Hazm's Literalism: A Critique of Islamic Legal Theory," in *Ibn Hazm of Cordoba: The Life and Works of a Controversial Thinker*, ed. C. Adang et al. (Leiden, Netherlands: Brill, 2013) argues that Ibn Hazm's critique was inspired by a liberalist reaction to what had become a self-appointed class of "clerics" (legal scholars or *'ulama*) who claimed religious authority Islam does not grant them: he wished for the Qur'an to be reclaimed by the people for whom it was revealed, who did not need scholarly mediators to understand it.

2. See Chapter 16.

3. It is worth noting that at a point early in his career he received the instruction of Juwayni (d. 1085); in general, his list follows a *kalam* pattern.

4. Indeed, his works on logic are far more clearly written than those of many of the logicians and philosophers themselves.

5. This example, as we will see when we get to Ibn Taymiyyah in Chapter 17, is not quite as straightforward as he makes it out to be.

6. Its inclusion is surprising, as we will see when discussing the issue of self-consciousness (especially in relation to Avicenna, whom al-Ghazali criticized). However, the other items are standard logical and mathematical principles: that opposites cannot both be true, that two is greater than one, and so on. These matters do not depend on experience or learning to be believed. If we ignore the inclusion of self-consciousness, they represent what has come to be called *a priori* truths: truths that are known prior to, and independent of, experience; one believes them without knowing when or how they came about. Moreover, once their constituent elements are brought together (e.g., "one," "two," "greater than"), one cannot deny the relationship between them.

7. Al-Ghazali's message to the legalists is that what they take to be a different form of argument (by analogy) really boils down to a matter of syllogism. In adopting this viewpoint, he shows preference to logic in its "Aristotelian form"—a point of contention with both Ibn Taymiyyah (later on) and Abd al-Jabbar and the *kalam* tradition; another (non-Aristotelian) figure we will encounter, Suhrawardi, also adopted the viewpoint that legalist arguments by analogy do not stand on a firm foundation.

8. That said, and in contrast to other philosophers—who considered the process essentially passive—he ignored the fact that the Mu'tazilites viewed it as an act performed by an agent. In so doing, he dodged the Mu'tazilite effort to produce what one might understand as synthetic *a priori* or *a posteriori* truths.

9. For instance, the goodness of saving someone about to drown, of expressing gratitude to one who bestows benefits, and of telling the truth—or, in contrast, the disagreeableness of apostasy, hurting the innocent, and pointless lying.

10. Al-Ma'mun's reign was also marred by political turmoil; much against his intentions, it probably marked a critical juncture in the fateful divide between Sunni and Shi'a.

CHAPTER 10: AL-MA'MUN AND THE DEVIL'S BANQUETS

1. Consider the sad contrast between this great achievement and the legalists' revolt, some 700 years later, against the Ottoman observatory, which led to its destruction toward the end of the sixteenth century. This occurred around the same time that Tycho Brahe's observatory was ushering in the new age of astronomical research in Europe, confirming Galileo and the heliocentric model of Copernicus!

2. Available in translation as *The Book of Ingenious Devices (Kitab al-Hiyal)* (Dordrecht: Springer, 1979).

3. See Chapter 8.

4. They, as well as Christians and Jews, were to experience the complete opposite under the reign of a later Abbassid caliph, al-Mutawakkil (who ruled for about fourteen years before dying in 861).

5. In his biography of major Muslim doctors and scientists, Ibn Abi Usaybi'a (d. 1269) relates the story (transmitted orally and going back to Alfarabi himself) of how the discipline of philosophy originated in Greece and later moved to Alexandria and then to Byzantium; the entire corpus of Aristotelian logic, except for *On Demonstration*—which was deemed harmful from a Christian point of view— was commonly taught; one cleric, Youhanna Bin Haylan, agreed to read the entire corpus with him, including *On Demonstration*.

6. See Chapter 9.

7. See Chapter 16 for a discussion of *The Incoherence of the Philosophers*, his attack on metaphysical "frenzy."

8. See Chapter 4. Arabic writing had to develop tools to distinguish between groups of different consonants that have similar shapes, and between vowels and cognate sounds that produce different meanings.

9. Studies about the grammarians (e.g. Sibawayh, al-Mubarrad, etc.) and their schools are widely available. See, for example, Monique Bernards, *Changing Traditions: Al-Mubarrad's refutation of Sibawayh and the Subsequent Reception of the Kitab* (Leiden, Netherlands: Brill, 1997) and "Pioneers of Arabic Linguistic Studies," *In the Shadow of Arabic: The Centrality of Language to Arabic Culture*, ed. Bilal

Orfali (Leiden, Netherlands: Brill, 2012), 197–220; for discussion of al-Zajjaji's theory of grammar, cf. Kees Versteegh, *The Explanation of Linguistic Causes* (Amsterdam: J. Benjamins, 1995).

10. Cf. Chapter 15. The first school, in Basrah, was associated with Sibawayh, while the second school, in Kufa, was associated with Kissa'i. These two "fathers of Arabic grammar" are supposed to have crossed swords in what is known as the "Hornet Debate." Sibawayh took a rules-based approach to discussing the sentence, "I used to think the scorpion's sting was more dangerous than the hornet's, but (it turns out) the former is (the same as) the latter." In Arabic, he observed, both "the former" and "the latter" are filled in by third-person pronouns (masculine and negative, respectively); therefore, he concluded, the second pronoun should be in the nominative case, like the first. Kissa'i replied that it could either be nominative or accusative. To settle the difference, the audience attending the "duel" decided to bring in native speakers, and it was determined that both cases are used indifferently. It is said that Sibawayh's "defeat" prompted him to withdraw to his hometown, where he eventually became a recluse and devoted himself to music and the taxonomy of poetic meter.

CHAPTER 11: THE LANGUAGE-LOGIC DEBATE

1. For more on his intellectual milieu, see Nuha A. Alshaar, *Ethics in Islam: Friendship in the Political Thought of Tawhidi and his Contemporaries* (London: Routledge, 2015).

2. In *Mu'jam al-Udaba'* [Dictionary of writers], by Yaqut al-Hamawi (d. 1229). It might seem that Tawhidi's erudition would have been enough to ensure a good living and a respected status in society. However, the complete opposite proved to be the case; before the end of his life, reportedly as an act of vengeance for the "repudiation" he had experienced, he deprived society of his literary contributions by burning all his works. It is only by chance that any of them survived. (One of them, *Al-Imta' wa-l Mu'anasa*, provides a source for the debate mentioned in this chapter.)

3. The identification he provides is the only historical evidence we have of who they were. Also see Richard Netton, *Muslim Neoplatonists: An Introduction to the Thought of the Brethren of Purity (Ikhwan al-Safa)* (London: Routledge, 2002).

4. For more on al-Sijistani and his students, see Joel L. Kraemer, *Philosophy in the Renaissance of Islam: Abu Sulayman al-Sijistani and His Circle* (Leiden, Netherlands: Brill, 1986).

5. It is only fair that Matta's student, Yahya bin Adi, be mentioned here. Matta himself is not really given a chance to defend himself in the debate, but Yahya elsewhere offers an articulate defense of his teacher's positions—specifically, the question of how logic and grammar can be distinguished from one another.

6. See following; as we noted in Chapter 8, early Mu'tazilite scholars were not keen on giving abstract nouns (e.g., *justice* or *whiteness*) a special status as denot-

ing abstract entities in the world. By refusing to reify such entities—preferring, instead, to reduce such references to down-to-earth, contextual practices—they anticipated the interpretation, later used by logicians, that confers some kind of existence on these entities and therefore the relationship between them and the objects they are associated with.

7. The idea here is that a pronoun, unlike a general term, has a clear existential reference to a particular object.

8. For a detailed and incisive treatment of Alfarabi on the subject, see Shukri B. Abed, *Aristotelian Logic and the Arabic Language in Alfarabi* (Albany: SUNY Press, 1991).

9. See next chapter.

CHAPTER 12: BACK TO THE HUMAN WILL AND LANGUAGE

1. See Sari Nusseibeh, "Al-'Aql Al-Qudsi: Avicenna's Subjective Theory of Knowledge," *Studia Islamica* (1989): 39–54. This article discusses Avicenna's approach to what knowledge (as articulated by language or by logic) consists of, as well as to his philosophy more generally. Not only are linguistic and logical "meanings" constructs: strictly speaking, even *primary substances* are not directly cognized. While the article mainly draws on Avicenna's more "classical" works, direct support for this interpretation can be found in his other writings, such as *Al-Ta'liqat*. It is worth observing that this interpretation does not fit with most classical views of Avicenna, which tend to minimize the significance of such "deviations" from Alfarabi's position—or, at any rate, not to view them as elements of an entirely new system that effectively renders the distinction between essence and existence meaningless.

2. Even so, it warrants mention that Abd al-Jabbar uses the term "heart" as a location on one or two occasions; however, the sense is most likely figurative, serving to highlight the psychological state of the person experiencing the feeling of knowledge—as opposed to a putative location of cognition in the intellect or brain.

3. This raises the issue, which clearly received no attention at the time, whether parrots, robots, or computers may be viewed as "agents of utterance," that is, as enunciating sentences that convey information. Avicenna, who lived at about the same time as Abd al-Jabbar, maintained that the true-false quality of sentences implied the listener as much as the speaker: that is, the former must either believe or deny what is said. This double requirement ties the sentence directly to actual speech contexts. Since parrots, robots, or computers can hardly be said to *assert* a fact (let alone to *issue* orders or to *ask* questions) through speech, it would be mistaken to ascribe truth or falsehood to their sentence forms "containing" information.

4. Interestingly, in the introduction to the first and only Arabic version of J. L. Austin's *How to Do Things with Words* (Ifriqya/al-Sharq, Tunisia, 1991), the translator, Abdul Qader Qainini, notes the striking similarity between Austin's

ground-breaking work in the philosophy of language, and that of early language and *kalam* scholars—including the writings of Abd al-Jabbar.

CHAPTER 13: EXPANDING THE VIEW

1. Abd al-Jabbar is said to have sold hundreds of his silk garments as part of his effort to raise the money demanded of him during his incarceration.

2. After it fell to the Tajik Sunni Dynasty, he lived under the Buyids—until the Seljuks assumed power.

3. A far more important encounter with India later occurred when he met al-Biruni—see p. 118.

4. Cf. G.S. Reynolds, *A Muslim Theologian in a Sectarian Milieu: ʿAbd al-Jabbar and the Critique of Christian Origins* (Leiden, Netherlands: Brill, 2004). For a comprehensive study on Abd al-Jabbar, see J. R. T. M. Peters, *God's Created Speech* (Leiden, Netherlands: Brill, 1976).

5. See Chapter 16.

6. The same holds for the tendency to see Alfarabi as a "closet-Imamite."

7. See Sari Nusseibeh "The Possible Worlds of Avicenna and Leibniz," in *The Misty Land of Ideas and the Light of Dialogue: An Anthology of Comparative Philosophy*, ed. Ali Paya (London: ICAS Press, 2013), 239–278.

8. Mindful of this limitation imposed on philosophers, let us recall that even Descartes—the father of modern European philosophy—prefaced his *Meditations* with a letter to the church deans at the Sorbonne, seeking their endorsement of his views; otherwise, he said, his work would not find sympathetic ears. What is more, he initially wrote in Latin to restrict the book's circulation.

CHAPTER 15: PHILOSOPHY AND POLITICS

1. Placing these *acts* of speech at the bottom of the "language ladder" already lends them less epistemic weight than what he (and Aristotle) would eventually give to propositions used in syllogisms. As we have seen in the previous chapters, the "traditional disciplines" already tended to view all parts of speech as acts (and therefore speaker-related); accordingly, what they signified remained bound to context—instead of representing "windows" opening onto a world of abstract ideas.

2. Alfarabi, who was Turkic by birth, learned Arabic under a famous grammarian who belonged to the Basra School of Sibawayh; his approach defined grammar as the rules inferred from the core of spoken Arabic; in contrast, the competing Kufa school of Kissa'i based grammar on usage.

3. Alfarabi was clearly well aware of Plato's argument in *Phaedrus* that attaining and "teaching" knowledge is best achieved through *discourse* rather than *writing* (where words are "sown" in minds rather than on blank paper). Significantly, however, when he refers to this (in his *The Philosophy of Plato and Its Parts*), he presents Plato's position as one concerning a *temporal* sequence: oral teaching pre-

cedes teaching by means of writing. He thereby minimizes the status Plato gives to oratory and dialectics, in line with his general argument in favor of deductive reasoning. He therefore completely ignores Plato's interesting point (as voiced by Socrates) that *the written word* is more of a dead image than a live means of "creating" knowledge. In *Phaedrus* Socrates sets out to show, after hearing Lysias's account of love recounted almost verbatim by Phaedrus, that *reading* or simply *hearing* an account is not at all the same as coming to know it. Knowledge requires living engagement between speakers, where critical thinking through dialogue attends each word being processed. See A. R. Badawi, ed., *Aflāṭūn fī l-Islām* [Plato in Islam], 2nd ed. (Beirut: Dar al-Andalus, 1980), 19–20.

4. That is, where a *milla*, instituted in an *umma*, receives an already-perfected governance system comprising both theoretical knowledge and prescriptions.

5. Some scholars claim that what he assumed to be the *Enneads* of the Alexandrian philosopher Plotinus (d. 270) was an Aristotelian work circulating under the name of *The Theology*. While this may have been a common misperception at the time, it had changed by the time of Avicenna, who explicitly expresses doubt about this attribution.

6. See next chapter.

7. His compendium of medicine *al-Hawi*—translated into Latin in the thirteenth century by Faraj ben Salim (a physician of Jewish-Sicilian origin)—was widely acclaimed throughout Europe.

8. Arguably, his own account of the "material" needed to explain existence—Creator (*al-Bari*), soul, matter, time, and space—could easily have been understood as a "heretical" theory, influenced as much by Zoroastrian as by Greek sources.

9. Needless to say, the paradigm for this philosophical dilemma (of which both Alfarabi and al-Razi were fully aware) is the life—and death—of Socrates.

CHAPTER 16: THE PHILOSOPHERS' "FRENZY"

1. Arguably, the (supposedly rational) Farabian system, which understands the philosopher to be someone able to achieve perfect knowledge through union with the "Active Intellect," is not all that different.

2. When al-Ghazali identifies a class of "imitators" as the reason for his concern, one suspects that his campaign to "crush" their idols does not involve the theories themselves so much as the (perceived) need to prevent them from reaching people who would misuse them to disfigure Islam's fundamental articles of faith. It may be worth mentioning here that the "imitators" al-Ghazali had in mind were his own contemporaries—not their "misguided" Muslim idols.

3. As we have seen, Alfarabi possibly foresaw how his theories would be viewed and treated by legal scholars.

4. It is not clear when the notion of the earth's spherical shape became common belief among Muslims, but al-Ghazali was certainly aware of the Ptolemaic

astronomy Muslim philosophers and mathematicians worked on; according to one account, he is said to have been explained Ptolemy's system—including the "retrograde motion" of the planets, which he also mentions in his account. See Chapter 21 (The Cosmos).

5. When addressing and explaining Avicenna's theory of prophesy, al-Ghazali refrains from direct criticism. The matter is different when it comes to Avicenna's theory of God's knowledge of particulars. Perhaps he held that this theory posed a greater danger to religious doctrine inasmuch as it seemed to provide a sensible answer reconciling God's universal and timeless nature (as in the model), with the claim that He can know particular objects and events in the world (as the Qur'an affirms). For all that, it is doubtful whether he really understood Avicenna's theory (a "knowledge-by-description" as opposed to a "knowledge-by-ostension" approach); if he did, he may have deliberately chosen to criticize a simplified version of the doctrine. See Sari Nusseibeh, "Avicenna: Providence and God's Knowledge of Particulars," in *Avicenna and his Legacy: A Golden Age of Science and Philosophy*, ed. Y. T. Langermann (Turnhout, Belgium: Brepols, 2009), 275–288.

6. That is, that existence has two "natures," possible and necessary, and therefore the nature of possible existence is existence just as the nature of necessary existence is existence. Here, al-Ghazali is touching on a fundamental metaphysical argument used by philosophers right up to the Enlightenment: that God's existence (unlike the existence of all other things) is guaranteed by the "fact" that His nature is, precisely, to exist.

7. For example, arguments about time and space: whether the concepts of "before" and "after," like those of "above" and "below," would allow us to conceive of something beyond the space and (movement-based) time that the model outlines.

8. Arguably, it was a version of already existing theories either in *kalam* or Avicenna's works.

9. It was echoed later in the works of philosophers such as Spinoza to prove the existence of a First Cause.

10. Farid al-Din 'Attar claimed Hassan and Rabi'ah as two of Islam's earliest Sufis.

CHAPTER 17: BACK TO WINE AND LOGIC

1. See Chapter 10.

2. Today, regular visitors to the Umayyad Palace in Jericho are not even made aware of the wine pool it houses.

3. Arguably, Ibn Taymiyyah's proposal here raises the same difficulty—determining what he calls the "reason"—that, he claims, philosophers encounter when they seek to determine what essences are. Suhrawardi (see Chapter 22) points this out as a weakness of the analogical method employed by jurists.

4. Here, the distinction between "any" and "all" is crucial, and we will encounter it again when dealing with Suhrawardi (Chapter 22): whereas "all" in a typical general statement ("All *X*'s are *Y*'s") seems to require one-by-one investigation of all the objects that are *X* for verification, "any" anchors the predication to a single object, one at a time. Today, this is formulated by a conditional—that, for any object at all, if it is an *X* then it is a *Y*.

5. Al-Ghazali, who borrows ideas from Avicenna, never acknowledges as much—see the next chapter.

6. This is a very important, and little appreciated feature of Avicenna's philosophy: it tells us that essences (*mahiyyat*) are in effect meaningless! But if so, then essences as "essences *of*" cannot be regarded as having a *prior* status (however conceived) of existence. Contemporary scholars of Avicenna have generally assumed that he must have thought them to have an ontological status different from that of being in existence *as essences of* something. However, at *that* presumed ontological level, as Ibn Taymiyyah rightly observes, Avicenna denies that such essential configurations exist. Indeed, considering them as pure ideas or forms, they are—as he states clearly—in themselves *just themselves*! When Ibn Taymiyyah remarks that we do not *know* that *rational* is more of an essence for *man* than *biped*, he is simply elaborating the Avicennian thesis that, *in themselves, rational, biped,* and *man* are totally unrelated to one another! Their ultimate coalescence (on the level of forms) is contingent if considered in essentialist terms. The common perception that Avicenna took essences to be prior to existences of objects—such that one object cannot come to exist except after having an essence conferred on it (and that must therefore be prior to it)—does not hold in a context where the so-called object and the so-called essence have the same status, that is, in the world of ideas. Indeed, this is precisely the significance of Avicenna's causality thesis: that the coalescence of ideas (as in the material world) is a causal rather than an essential relationship. At the level of pure ideas, or forms, then, there is no order of priority. For him, what comes to be viewed as an essence is so *only insofar* as it comes to *exist*. Existential simultaneity is key. This leads to the controversial conclusion—counter to the standard view among scholars of Avicenna—that essence is *logically* secondary to existence and not prior to it.

7. Assuming, of course, that this is not an analytic statement (i.e., one that is true by virtue of the meanings of the words).

8. Interestingly, this falls in line with the Mu'tazilite view.

9. See Chapter 9.

10. Tobacco is forbidden during a fast; wine, of course, is forbidden in general.

11. See Chapter 8.

12. They contested the underlying causal theory by which a *daleel* could be viewed as a natural or intrinsic cause for the truth of whatever is said to be an object of knowledge.

13. Wahhabism, as a puritanical religious movement that arose in the 18th century in the Arabian Peninsula to vie with Ottoman rule, is commonly looked

upon as the breeding ground for the radicalism that eventually produced al-Qaeda and present-day ISIL.

14. See Chapter 24.

15. Unlike al-Ghazali, he lists them among objects of knowledge that are certain.

16. At one point, he points out the latter's disagreement with Avicenna's view of the world in terms of necessity and possibility; see the next chapter.

17. As later expressed in the philosophies of Suhrawardi et al. Compare to his comment that philosophers influenced by Avicenna were "non-Muslim."

CHAPTER 18: MOTION AND LIGHT

1. See Chapter 16.

2. That said, the foundations of logic contained in his major works do in fact deviate from the standard treatment that Baghdad Aristotelians gave them.

3. In Averroes's eyes, this distinction was not tenable.

4. Avicenna's implicit rule here is part of a more general modal logic that also incorporates the truth-value equivalence of the two statements "it is possible that such-and-such is the case" and "such-and-such case is possible." The latter formula, recently introduced to scholarly literature, is mentioned by Timothy Williamson in *Modal Logic as Metaphysics* (Oxford: Oxford University Press, 2013), 45, as the one Avicenna observes in his major work (cf. Zia Mohaved, "*De Re* and *De dicto* in Islamic Traditional Logic," *Sophia Perennis* 2.2 (Spring 2010): 5–14).

5. Gad Freudenthal, "Samuel Ibn Tibbon's Avicennian Theory of an Eternal World," *Aleph 8* (2008): 41–129.

6. Averroes's "double-truth" theory finds its fullest articulation in his *Decisive Treatise*. See Averroes's *Decisive Treatise and Epistle Dedicatory*, translated by Charles Butterworth (Provo, Utah: BYU Press, 2002). This treatise is also translated by George Fadio Hourani as listed in the Primary Source section of the Further Readings.. Here, he argues that the truths of religion and philosophy do not stand in conflict, and when this seems to be the case, they can be reconciled. Although some scholars claim the treatise offers proof that Averroes thought religion and philosophy to be equal, the fact that he explains reconciliation in terms of religious statements' conformity to philosophical ones clearly grants the latter a more solid status. The overall purpose of the work was to allay pious concerns by affirming that religion and philosophy both lead to the truth—there is no reason, then, to ban the study of philosophy.

7. An earlier critic of Avicenna's theory of necessity/possibility, the Aristotelian Jewish convert Abu'l Barakat al-Baghdadi, had also tried to account for creation in time by proposing to separate time from motion: because motion and time are explicable in terms of each other, it makes sense to conclude that the world can only be viewed as being eternal and infinite (as Aristotle saw it). Avicenna accepted this

logic but then proposed a non-Aristotelian theory to explain it; in contrast, Baghdadi and Averroes held to Aristotle but then tried to "integrate"—whether for show or in a sincere effort—the idea of creation into their theories.

CHAPTER 19: THE NATURE OF TRUTH

1. See Chapter 8.
2. See the previous chapter.
3. Cf., in this context, how the notion of the idea in itself—the "I don't know what" of the empiricist philosopher John Locke—rests upon a substrate in nature.
4. This line of reasoning, which declares essence posterior to existence, conflicts with a long-held view about Avicenna. However, if we take his causality model seriously—about which general consensus prevails among scholars—as well as his explanation of "pure forms," we can only conclude that none of them are other forms in essence. It follows that the world is a "construct" put together by God. Logically, it is one possible construct of many. Analogously, our mental and logical worlds are constructs, put together by us. This is obvious given what we are told about ideas being modulated by mental or logical categories. Thus, if we claim that one realm reflects another, we must be careful to add that we are talking about one (possible) construct reflecting another—and not about an intellectual *sighting* of reality (as Aristotle's logical apparatus is supposed to yield).
5. Strictly speaking, relationships between "pure ideas" in the metaphysical plenum also come to be connected causally in the mind through the inspiration provided by the Active Intellect. As such, connections between ideas are thoroughly causal rather than essential—brought about either by higher intellects (when the metaphysical plenum stands at issue) or by us (where our own edifice of knowledge is concerned).
6. As we have seen, al-Ghazali adopts this view when he places self-knowledge at the top of his list of certainties.
7. In another context, Avicenna does suggest *a posteriori* proof for the existence of God; however, one has the impression, especially in view of the preceding, that he offered it for those who insist on using reason to see what is, in fact, self-evident and intuitive. See Toby Mayer, "Ibn Sina's *Burhan al-Siddiqin*," *Journal of Islamic Studies* 12(2001): 18–39.
8. See Chapter 3.
9. Including its backward parts—and maybe even Hell.

CHAPTER 20: FARDAJAN AND BEYOND

1. See, for example, the two volumes edited by Jules L. Janssens, *An Annotated Bibliography on Ibn Sina* (Leuven, Belgium: University of Leuven, 1991 and 1999). Supplements are expected to follow, given abiding interest in his work. A good collection of essays edited by Peter Adamson, *Interpreting Avicenna: Critical Essays*

(Cambridge: Cambridge University Press, 2013), contains treatments of different aspects of Avicenna's philosophy by prominent scholars—including one by Robert Wisnovsky, whose work on Avicenna is cited in the short bibliography at the end of this volume. Another contribution, by Deborah Black, addresses the issue of meaning—for instance, what horse-ness as horse-ness is—which the previous chapter explored. The collection also includes an essay by Dimitri Gutas surveying contemporary scholarship on Islamic philosophy. Gutas distinguishes between three approaches that have typified the field: *Orientalist* (e.g., H. Corbin and R. Walzer), *Illuminationist* (S. H. Nasr) and *political* (M. Mahdi); of course, areas of overlap exist. He also outlines his own taxonomy of Islamic philosophy, presenting the "Baghdad School" (exemplified by Alfarabi) as a high point; by this account, the Greek-inspired philosophical tradition and Avicenna (and his school) represent a disassembled form of that tradition. A more elaborate presentation of his theory can be found in Dimitri Gutas, *Avicenna and the Aristotelian Tradition* (Leiden, Netherlands: Brill, 2014). As one may gather, I take a wider view of the philosophical thought of that period, where the "high points" are more widely spread, and where the "Aristotelian phase" is simply considered introductory to one trajectory, leading up to Avicenna. Gutas himself ponderously remarks that Avicenna may yet prove to be of far more philosophical importance than any of his peers.

2. The reference to Leibniz, incidentally, is not arbitrary, as one can find many features of Avicenna's philosophy reflected in his work.

3. It may have influenced, among others, John Locke—specifically, his notion of *tabula rasa*. Cf. Gül A. Russell, *The "Arabick" Interest of the Natural Philosophers in Seventeenth-Century England* (Leiden, Netherlands: Brill, 1994).

CHAPTER 21: THE COSMOS

1. See George Saliba, "Arabic Versus Greek Astronomy: A Debate over the Foundations of Science," *Perspectives on Science* 8.4 (2000): 328–341, who notes (p. 329) that Qusta b. Luqa was the first in the Islamic tradition to use this term apropos of Ptolemy's *Almagest*. The article addresses the wider issue of whether Muslim astronomers mainly pursued an earlier tradition of investigating phenomena empirically or had consciously begun to treat astronomy as a new *science*. Saliba emphasizes Muslim astronomers' methodological departure from Ptolemy and early Greek practices. In a sense, the chapter at hand seeks to steer a middle course, where both the physical and the mathematical aspects of the discipline are viewed as a single effort. A more general account can be found in Saliba's *Islamic Science and the Making of the European Renaissance* (Cambridge, Mass.: MIT Press, 2007).

2. See F. Jamil Rageb, "Ali al-Qushji and Regiomontanus: Eccentric Transformations and Copernican Revolutions," *Journal for the History of Astronomy* 36 (2005): 359–371.

3. F. Jamil Rageb, "Freeing Astronomy from Philosophy: An Aspect of Islamic Influence on Science," *Osiris* 16 (2001): 49–70.

4. While it is clear that Qushji's move to Istanbul meant that impressive science was still being pursued there at this late age, we should recall that religious scholars in the Ottoman caliphate had already achieved such power that they were able to prevail upon their ruler to destroy the impressive observatory he had commissioned just outside the city (which had just been completed).

CHAPTER 22: COSMIC LIGHTS

1. Contra the main exponent of the later Isfahan school, Mulla Sadra: see the next chapter.

2. See Chapter 13.

3. Indeed, scientists now speak of multiple neurons firing rather than a camera-like, inverted image subsequently "righted" by the brain.

4. In this context, he draws an unfortunate analogy to the sun. It is worth recalling, however, the theory of relativity: a body with a mass cannot exceed the speed of light; light, therefore, is not held to be a body.

5. Needless to say, one might object that Suhrawardi has predicated his edifice of light on the even more basic notion of *thingness*, which he does not account for; the next chapter will address this matter.

6. He was likely quite familiar with Avicenna's "flying-man" thought experiment (describing a process for arriving at the realization that one is but a thinking being—a mental exercise that has achieved some fame in the recent literature).

7. An analogous argument can be made to explicate the move from the statement, *It is possible I am imagining something*, to the statement, *There is something I am imagining*. In Suhrawardi's account, one can see how such logical shifts work. What I imagine could be understood, first, as a universal statement picking any number of things out of a set, then as an instantiated matter receiving a particular name: *what* I imagine.

CHAPTER 23: FAST FORWARD

1. Although, as we have seen, Suhrawardi was critical of the role Avicenna ascribed to the imaginative faculty, one might still argue that—in an important and positive sense—his own philosophy was singularly imaginative.

2. Let us recall the role of the middle term in a syllogism, whose role is to bridge between two other concepts, thereby producing a new statement of fact. Avicenna argued that the mind apprehends it through inspiration—in a flash of light, as it were; he argued that the disposition to receive such insight should be trained so that one may discern, more quickly and more thoroughly, all the causal connections in the world. What he called the "Holy Mind" is so suffused with light that it can "see" the entire world at once.

3. As al-Ghazali had done before him—and as Rabi'ah al-'Adawiyyah seems to have done earlier still.

4. See Chapter 21.

CHAPTER 24: LANGUAGE AND REASON

1. Chapter 6.

2. In the nineteenth century, two other versions were produced—the first in Russia, and the second in Germany (Leipzig).

3. For example, see George Antonius, *The Arab Awakening* (Allegro Editions, 2015).

4. This happened around the same time that Tycho Brahe's observatory and calculations made their mark on scientific history by disproving the Aristotelian notion of a fixed outer sphere; around the same time, using the Copernican geometric model, Kepler developed his three planetary laws. See Chapter 21.

5. Today, following the introduction of copy machines deemed acceptable for making handwritten copies of the Qur'an, and then the proliferation of media technology that encourage digital typing and communicating, submitting the Word of God to mechanical reproduction has become much less of a taboo, even though "originals" in handwritten form are still preferable.

6. Trained in traditional Hanbali jurisprudence, Abd al-Wahhab managed, through a pact with the House of Saud, to promote what he saw as a genuine code of Islamic rule (in contrast to that of the Ottomans). His "philosophy" embraced "purification": putting back together and restoring to health what he saw had become a degenerate practice of Islam. In a sense, Wahhabian Sunnism reflects the Shi'ite religious revolution against the rule of the Shah in the fifties. With different starting points, both sought to reinstate Islam's uncontaminated message. One may understand recent phenomena such as al-Qaeda and the "Islamic State" in light of the fact that twentieth-century pan-Arabist projects (and offshoot Marxist ones) have "failed to deliver," and in light of the perceived dilution of the Wahhabi doctrine by the House of Saud. These movements advocate the use of terrorism and violence to dismantle existing political and religious structures, which they seek to replace with a new regime supposedly purified of all innovations introduced to Islam since the times of the Prophet.

7. Niloofar Haeri, *Sacred Language, Ordinary People* (London: Palgrave, 2003).

8. A recent study in Israel to determine why Arab children seem to lag behind their Jewish counterparts in school examinations concluded that one of the major causes was precisely this dissonance between speaking and writing (which requires different efforts than when two different languages stand at issue).

9. In a recent UN Human Development Report, low literacy was still cited as a major impediment to progress in the Arab world, where the population has been expanding at enormous rates. The population in Taha Hussein's Egypt has dou-

bled, by one hundred million, since he launched his literacy campaign through free schooling.

10. In this context, it may be worth mentioning the immense popularity of the television show run by the late Egyptian exegete Sheikh Mutwalli al-Sha'rawi. His captivating use of the Egyptian vernacular in his exegesis of the Qur'an was not just an act of *interpreting* verses, but more significantly a highly successful act of *translating* from the classical to the vernacular.

11. Of course, they are enabled to grasp it in due course, as familiarity develops. Even so, a difficulty remains: since many of the expressions used in the relevant literature (e.g. sociology or political thought) are themselves translated from a foreign language, it is uncertain just how far comprehension goes in terms of *deep* meaning (which depends on conceptual interrelation with other expressions belonging to the same linguistic family).

12. See Faouzia Charfi, *La science voilée* (Paris: Odile Jacob, 2013), who notes that religious conservatism—and even fundamentalism—occurs most often among science students at Tunisian universities. The same holds across the Arab world.

Further Readings

By necessity, the following list is wide-ranging. It omits references made in footnotes. (A) includes general works, some more focused than others; (B) features studies of main figures mentioned in the text; and (C) provides translated sources. Tamim Ansary's book is recommended as a "light read" for anyone totally unfamiliar with Islam, past and present. The Qur'an, well translated by Tarif Khalidi, may be used for reference.

(A) GENERAL REFERENCE

Ansary, Tamim. *Destiny Disrupted: A History of the World Through Islamic Eyes.* New York: Public Affairs, 2010.

Antonius, George. *The Arab Awakening.* London: Hamish Hamilton, 1938.

Arberry, A. J. *Revelation and Reason in Islam.* London: George Allen & Unwin, 1965.

———. *Sufism.* London: George Allen & Unwin, 1969.

Armstrong, Karen. *Muhammad: A Prophet for Our Time.* New York: HarperCollins, 2006.

Boullata, Issa J. *Trends and Issues in Contemporary Arab Thought.* Albany: State University of New York Press, 1990.

Bowersock, G. W. *Roman Arabia.* Cambridge, Mass.: Harvard University Press, 1994.

Butterworth, Charles E., ed. *The Political Aspects of Islamic Philosophy: Essays in Honor of Muhsin H. Mahdi.* Cambridge, Mass.: Harvard University Press, 1992.

Diner, Dan. *Lost in the Sacred: Why the Muslim World Stood Still.* Translated by Steven Rendall. Princeton: Princeton University Press, 2009.

Duri, Abd al-Aziz. *Early Islamic Institutions: Administration and Taxation from the Caliphate to the Umayyads and Abbasids.* London: I. B. Tauris, 2011.

Ernst, Carl W. *Sufism: An Introduction to the Mystical Tradition of Islam.* Boston: Shambhala, 2011.

Fakhry, Majid. *A History of Islamic Philosophy.* New York: Columbia University Press, 2004.

Freely, John. *Aladdin's Lamp: How Greek Science Came to Europe Through the Islamic World.* New York: Knopf, 2009.

Gabrieli, Francesco. *Muhammad and the Conquests of Islam*. Translated by Virginia Luling and Rosamund Linell. New York: McGraw-Hill, 1968.

Goldziher, Ignaz. *Introduction to Islamic Theology and Law*. Translated by Andras Hamori. Princeton: Princeton University Press, 1981.

———. *On the History of Grammar among the Arabs*. Translated by Kinga Dévényi and Tamás Iványi. Amsterdam: Benjamins, 1994.

Hazeleton, Lesley. *The First Muslim: The Story of Muhammad*. New York: Riverhead, 2013.

Heck, Paul L. *Skepticism in Classical Islam: Moments of Confusion*. London: Routledge, 2014.

Holt, P. M., Ann K. S. Lambton, and Bernard Lewis. *The Cambridge History of Islam*. 2 vols. Cambridge: Cambridge University Press, 1970.

Hourani, Albert. *Arabic Thought in the Liberal Age*. Cambridge: Cambridge University Press, 1983.

Hourani, George, ed. *Islamic Philosophy and Science*. Albany: State University Press of New York, 1975.

Jabiri, Mohammad Abed. *The Formation of Arab Reason*. London: I. B. Tauris, 2011.

Kaukua, Jari. *Self-Awareness in Islamic Philosophy: Avicenna and Beyond*. Cambridge: Cambridge University Press, 2015.

Leaman, Oliver. *An Introduction to Medieval Islamic Philosophy*. Cambridge: Cambridge University Press, 1985.

Luxenberg, Christof (pseudonym). *Christmas in the Qur'an*. Edited by Ibn Warraq. New York: Prometheus, 2014.

Masters, Bruce Alan. *The Arabs of the Ottoman Empire (1516–1918)*. Cambridge: Cambridge University Press, 2013.

Menocal, Maria Rosa. *The Ornament of the World*. Boston: Back Bay Books, 2002.

Mousawi, Jasim Muhsin. *The Medieval Islamic Republic of Letters*. Notre Dame: University of Notre Dame Press, 2015.

Netton, Ian Richard. *Islamic Philosophy and Theology: Critical Concepts in Islamic Thought*. 2 vols. London: Routledge, 2007.

———, ed. *Muslim Neoplatonists: An Introduction to the Thought of the Brethren of Purity*. London: Routledge, 2002.

Nicholson, Reynold A. *A Literary History of the Arabs*. New York: Scribner, 1907.

O'Leary, Delacy. *How Greek Science Passed to the Arabs*. London: Routledge and Kegan Paul, 1951.

Sabra, A. I. and Jan P. Hogendijk, eds. *The Enterprise of Science in Islam: New Perspectives*. Cambridge, Mass.: MIT Press, 2003.

Saliba, George. *A History of Arabic Astronomy*. Albany: State University of New York Press, 1994.

Schoeler, Gregor. *The Oral and the Written in Early Islam*. Translated by Uwe Vagelpohl. New York: Routledge, 2006.

Starr, S. Frederick. *Lost in Enlightenment: Central Asia's Golden Age*. Princeton University Press, 2013.

Stroumsa, S. *Freethinkers of Medieval Islam*. Leiden, Netherlands: Brill, 1999.

Von Grunebaum, Gustave E. *Logic in Classical Islamic Culture*. Wiesbaden: Harrasowitz, 1970.

———, ed. *Medieval Islam*. Chicago: University of Chicago Press, 1953.

Watt, W. Montgomery. *Islamic Philosophy and Theology*. Edinburgh: Edinburg University Press, 1988.

Wood, Philip. *"We have no king but Christ": Christian Political Thought in Greater Syria on the Eve of the Arab Conquest*. Oxford: Oxford University Press, 2010.

Young, M. J. L., J. D. Latham, and R. B. Serjeant, eds. *Religion, Learning and Science in the Abbasid Period*. Cambridge: Cambridge University Press, 1990.

(B) ABOUT AUTHORS

Adamson, Peter. *Al-Kindi*. Oxford: Oxford University Press, 2007.

Alshaar, Nuha A. *Ethics in Islam: Friendship in the Political Thought of Tawhidi and his Contemporaries*. London: Routledge, 2007.

Corbin, Henry. *Creative Imagination in the Sufism of Ibn Arabi*. London: Routledge and Kegan Paul, 1969.

———. *Avicenna and the Visionary Recital*. Translated by Willard R. Trask. Princeton: Princeton University Press, 1988.

Griffel, F. *Al-Ghazali's Philosophical Theology*. Oxford: Oxford University Press, 2009.

Kalin, L. *Knowledge in Late Islamic Philosophy: Mulla Sadra on Existence, Intellect and Intuition*. Oxford: Oxford University Press, 2010.

Kennedy, Edward S. and Imad Ghanem, eds. *The Life and Work of Ibn al-Shatir*. Aleppo: Institute for the History of Arabic, 1976.

Mahdi, Muhsin. *Alfarabi and the Foundations of Islamic Political Philosophy*. Chicago: University of Chicago Press, 2010.

———. *Ibn Khaldun's Philosophy of History*. Chicago: University of Chicago Press, 1971.

Morris, J. W. *The Wisdom of the Throne: An Introduction to the Philosophy of Mulla Sadra*. Princeton: Princeton University Press, 1981.

Omar, Saleh Beshara. *Ibn al-Haytham's Optics*. Minneapolis: Bibliotheca Islamica, 1977.

Peters, J. R. T. M. *God's Created Speech: A Study in the Speculative Theology of the Mu'tazilite Qadi l-Qudat 'Abd al-Jabar*. Leiden, Netherlands: Brill, 1976.

Wisnovsky, Robert. *Avicenna's Metaphysics in Context*. Ithaca: Cornell University Press, 2003.

(C) PRIMARY SOURCES

Alfarabi. *Philosophy of Plato and Aristotle.* Translated by Muhsin Mahdi. Ithaca, New York: Cornell University Press, 1969.

———. *The Political Writings: "Selected Aphorisms" and Other Texts.* Translated by Charles E, Butterworth. Ithaca, New York: Cornell University Press, 2001.

Al-Ghazali. *Deliverance from Error and Mystical Union with the Almighty.* Translated by Muhammad Abulaylah. Washington D.C.: Council for Research in Values and Philosophy, 2002.

———. *The Incoherence of the Philosophers.* Translated by Michael E. Marmura. Provo, Utah: Brigham Young University Press, 2002.

Attar, Farid. *The Conference of the Birds.* Translated by Afkham Darbandi. New York: Penguin, 2011.

Averroes. *On the Harmony of Religions and Philosophy.* Translated by George Fadio Hourani. Cambridge: Luzac, 1961.

———. *Tahafut al-Tahafut (The Incoherence of Incoherence).* Translated by Simon van der Bergh. Cambridge: Luzac, 1978.

Avicenna. *Kitab Al-najat.* Translated by Fazlur Rahman. Oxford: Oxford University Press, 1952.

———. *The Metaphysics of Avicenna (Ibn Sina).* Translated by Parviz Morewedge. New York: Columbia University Press, 1973.

———. *The Physics of the Healing.* Translated by Jon McGinnis. Provo, Utah: Brigham Young University, 2010.

———. *Remarks and Admonitions: Part Four.* Translated by Shams C. Inati. New York: Kegan Paul International, 1996.

———. *Remarks and Admonitions. Part One: Logic.* Translated by Shams C. Inati. Toronto: Pontifical Institute for Medieval Studies, 1984.

———. *Remarks and Admonitions: Physics and Metaphysics.* Translated by Shams C. Inati. New York: Columbia University Press, 2014.

El-Bizri, Nader. *Epistles of the Brethren of Purity.* Oxford: Oxford University Press, 2008.

Khalidi, Tarif, trans. *The Qur'an.* New York: Penguin, 2009.

McGinnis, Jon and David C. Reisman. *Classical Arabic Philosophy: An Anthology of Sources.* Indianapolis: Hackett, 2007.

Suhrawardi. *The Philosophy of Illumination.* Translated by John Walbridge and Hossein Ziai. Provo, Utah: Brigham Young University Press, 1999.

Name Index

If a note number appears more than once on the same page of the endnotes, an identifying chapter number has been placed in parentheses as part of the endnote locator.

Cultural Memory | *in the Present*

Richard Rorty and Eduardo Mendieta, *Take Care of Freedom and Truth Will Take Care of Itself: Interviews with Richard Rorty*

Jacques Derrida, *Paper Machine*

Renaud Barbaras, *Desire and Distance: Introduction to a Phenomenology of Perception*

Jill Bennett, *Empathic Vision: Affect, Trauma, and Contemporary Art*

Ban Wang, *Illuminations from the Past: Trauma, Memory, and History in Modern China*

James Phillips, *Heidegger's* Volk*: Between National Socialism and Poetry*

Frank Ankersmit, *Sublime Historical Experience*

István Rév, *Retroactive Justice: Prehistory of Post-Communism*

Paola Marrati, *Genesis and Trace: Derrida Reading Husserl and Heidegger*

Krzysztof Ziarek, *The Force of Art*

Marie-José Mondzain, *Image, Icon, Economy: The Byzantine Origins of the Contemporary Imaginary*

Cecilia Sjöholm, *The Antigone Complex: Ethics and the Invention of Feminine Desire*

Jacques Derrida and Elisabeth Roudinesco, *For What Tomorrow . . . : A Dialogue*

Elisabeth Weber, *Questioning Judaism: Interviews by Elisabeth Weber*

Jacques Derrida and Catherine Malabou, *Counterpath: Traveling with Jacques Derrida*

Martin Seel, *Aesthetics of Appearing*

Nanette Salomon, *Shifting Priorities: Gender and Genre in Seventeenth-Century Dutch Painting*

Jacob Taubes, *The Political Theology of Paul*

Jean-Luc Marion, *The Crossing of the Visible*

Eric Michaud, *The Cult of Art in Nazi Germany*

Anne Freadman, *The Machinery of Talk: Charles Peirce and the Sign Hypothesis*

Stanley Cavell, *Emerson's Transcendental Etudes*

Stuart McLean, *The Event and Its Terrors: Ireland, Famine, Modernity*

Beate Rössler, ed., *Privacies: Philosophical Evaluations*

Bernard Faure, *Double Exposure: Cutting Across Buddhist and Western Discourses*

Alessia Ricciardi, *The Ends of Mourning: Psychoanalysis, Literature, Film*

Alain Badiou, *Saint Paul: The Foundation of Universalism*

Gil Anidjar, *The Jew, the Arab: A History of the Enemy*